MONEY, CREDIT AND THE ECONOMY

By the same author
The Theory of Money and Finance (Macmillan, 1980)

Money, Credit and the Economy

RICHARD COGHLAN

London
GEORGE ALLEN & UNWIN
Boston   Sydney

First published in 1981

GEORGE ALLEN & UNWIN LTD
40 Museum Street, London WC1A 1LU

© Richard Coghlan, 1981

British Library Cataloguing in Publication Data

Coghlan, Richard
    Money, credit and the economy.
    1. Money supply – Great Britain – Mathematical
        models
    I. Title
    332.4'941   HG939.5   80-41788

        ISBN 0-04-332079-1

Set in 10 on 11 point Press Roman by Alden Press
Oxford, London and Northampton
and printed in Great Britain
by Biddles Ltd., Guildford, Surrey

for

Josephine and Christopher

The Theory of Money and Finance by the same author, published in 1980, provided an introduction to the basic theory and concluded by introducing the idea of monetary disequilibrium, with the money supply process operating through bank credit creation. This book develops that theme and provides empirical evidence in support of such an approach. In particular Chapter 3 extends the argument given in Chapter 10 of *The Theory of Money and Finance* and I would like to thank The Macmillan Press for permission to use parts of that chapter.

Contents

1

Introduction

The period covered by this study presents an interesting cross section of monetary policy operations. It encompasses a quite significant change in emphasis from the attempt to stabilise interest rates to trying to stabilise the quantity of money. This change has not been abrupt but has developed over time. It was encouraged by the targets for domestic credit expansion (DCE) set by the International Monetary Fund (IMF) at the end of the 1960s, but has been particularly associated with the rapid acceleration of inflation in the mid-1970s. For the majority of the period money has, in fact, been considered not to be important.

Events rather than theories have dictated the change in policy orientation, as is evident from the variety of justifications that have been put forward to explain it. However, if such policies are to be consistently applied a firm intellectual base is required. It is not suggested that this study provides all the answers but it does address itself to the question, and attempts to develop a consistent framework.

In embarking upon this book the objective was to analyse monetary policy in the United Kingdom since 1945. It became clear, however, that it was necessary first to adopt a consistent theoretical framework within which to place the analysis. The standard models available of an exogenous money supply, or an endogenous but unimportant money supply, seemed unacceptable. What was required was somehow to tie together the two sides of banks' balance sheets, and take account of both the demand for money and the demand for credit, allowing the money supply to be endogenously determined and yet still be an important determinant of aggregate demand.

Clearly this approach — relating credit flows to money supply and the rest of the economy — is concerned with a broad definition of the money supply, and for the United Kingdom this is sterling M3 (£M3), but excluding public sector bank deposits. There has so far been little agreement on how money should be defined, which reflects the uncertainty about exactly why money is important. Such indecision naturally weakens the argument that money is important. In this case the theory leaves little room for ambiguity (see Chapter 3 below). It is also argued that narrow definitions of money will generally reflect

demand pressures, and therefore do not provide independent information on the future movements of other economic variables.

The problems connected with the underlying approach to be
adopted came to dominate the study, so that an important aspect of
the work became associated with developing this analytical framework.
Moreover, given the present emphasis on empirical estimates and
computer models, it seemed necessary to provide some broad test of
the main elements of the theory. Because of constraints of time and
space the resultant model is small by conventional standards. Although
I am somewhat sceptical of the gains to be had from a high degree of
disaggregation the size has not been determined by methodological
considerations, and the empirical model presented here (Chapter 5)
could easily be extended. Indeed, a number of further developments
would be necessary before such a model could provide an adequate
means of *forecasting* movements in the economy. Also, because any
model must be judged against the alternatives available, a survey of
monetary models of the United Kingdom is included (Chapter 2), and
emphasis is placed on how these differ from the present approach.

Before the model estimates are given a summary of monetary policy
in the United Kingdom since 1945 is included (Chapter 4), paying
particular attention to the main institutional and policy changes over
the period. This gives some indication of the problems facing the
authorities and the responses they have made. The estimated model
tries to incorporate as much of the institutional detail as possible in
addition to the main policy variables, within the constraints imposed by
its size.

Having estimated the model over the full data period (1954–1976)
the next step was to determine whether the main characteristics were
preserved if the period of rapid monetary expansion, and the floating
of sterling, in the 1970s was excluded. The model was therefore also
estimated up to 1971. The introduction of Competition and Credit
Control (CCC) in that year provides a convenient break point; it was
followed by rapid monetary expansion, accelerating inflation and the
floating of sterling. However, contrary to the more popular view the
introduction of CCC is not held responsible for these changes.

Certain simulations have been conducted with the model in order to
see how well it performs over the period, and also in order to get some
impression of the stability and size of the dynamic multipliers resulting
from exogenous shocks (Chapter 6). These results give some indication
of the alternative policy measures the authorities might have taken had
the theoretical approach suggested here been adopted.

Although in this study the model has been applied to the United
Kingdom the approach should have wider application to other countries.
Moreover, the specific empirical formulation of the general theory
could probably be improved upon, and there are certainly alternative

ways of giving practical expression to the ideas put forward here. For these reasons the remainder of this chapter introduces the theoretical approach adopted, which is developed in Chapter 3.

Over the period since 1945 there has been considerable debate regarding the role of money in the economy. Much of this debate has been conducted at the extremes of possibility. On the one hand, if money was to have an effect on the economy it generally had to be exogenously determined by the authorities via a high-powered money multiplier. Alternatively, if the authorities did not control the monetary base – the reserves of the banking system – the conclusion reached was that money did not matter and simply accommodated the demands for money within the economy.

Although these extreme views have continued to dominate the popular debate, encouraged by the wide use of the static *IS/LM* framework for macroeconomic teaching and analysis, there has been increasing discussion of the importance of money as a disequilibrium 'buffer' stock (for example, Jonson, 1976a). This development allows the supply of money to be endogenously determined and yet still have important effects on the dynamics of the economy. The theoretical model presented here goes further and argues for a direct relationship between the financial demands and supplies which create money, and observed expenditures. The approach develops from the arguments presented in Coghlan (1978c, 1979a, 1980a, 1980c).

The model emphasises the importance of bank credit in the process of the creation of money. The majority of monetary analysis has tended to stress only one side of banks' balance sheets. The Radcliffe Committee, for example, emphasised the importance of bank credit, but did recognise (Radcliffe Report, 1959, para 528) that it was necessary to control credit to both the private *and* public sector. This latter point is mentioned because of the tendency in the 1960s to implement 'Radcliffian' policies by restricting only private sector credit expansion. As soon as bank lending to the public sector is included we have something similar to the current definition of £M3.

The monetarists, on the other hand, have stressed the quantity of bank deposits and have generally given little attention to the associated changes in bank credit. The work of Brunner and Meltzer has been a notable exception in this respect, although they have continued to stress a multiplier relationship based on an exogenous monetary base, and more importantly have not related credit creation to expenditure decisions; see Chapters 3 and 5. There is still a marked tendency to divide the economy into two halves, defined as 'real' and 'monetary', and to build separate models to explain each half, only combining them later on (see Chapter 2). This approach tends to emphasise the role of money in a wealth portfolio rather than as a medium of exchange and means of payment, and therefore abstracts from what is the crucial characteristic of money.

The same criticism can also be made of most presentations of the monetary approach to the balance of payments (MABP), for example, the collection of papers edited by Frenkel and Johnson (1976a). Although these identify the two sides of the banks' balance sheet by emphasising the importance of DCE, this latter variable is generally taken to be determined exogenously. Overseas flows into the money supply, therefore, respond passively to movements in the demand for money given the fixed constraint on domestic credit. But there is every reason to believe that credit demands and supplies exist independently[1] of the demand for money. Not only are the components of domestic credit likely to shift in response to behavioural factors that will make control difficult, particularly if this is to be achieved through market forces via the manipulation of a restricted set of financial rates of return, but also there must surely exist direct substitution possibilities between borrowing from a domestic bank and borrowing from abroad, certainly if the borrower happens to be a multinational company.

The model developed in the following chapters brings together both sides of the banks' balance sheets. It is important to recognise that there is a difference between the demand for money, that is, the liabilities of the banks, and the demand for bank credit, that is, the assets of the banks. The latter demand is, in fact, important for explaining the *supply* of money. Credit demands are in turn related to expenditure decisions which produce a relationship between the supply of money and the behaviour of the so-called 'real' economy. This relationship I have termed the 'primary effect' of monetary creation; see, in particular, Chapter 4 below.

I have argued elsewhere (Coghlan, 1980b, Ch. 2) that it is easier to make sense of the standard *IS/LM* diagram if the *IS* curve is interpreted as the 'demand for finance' schedule, and the *LM* curve as the 'supply of finance schedule'. In the real world it is also necessary to take account of imperfections in financial markets and such things as quantitative restrictions on the availability of finance. Such an approach at least implies that it is unrealistic to separate out 'real' and financial markets.

The 'real' outcome, in terms of, say, an increase in real investment is a combination of the increase in the incentive to invest, the availability of finance to make those desires effective and the factors determining the supply of capital goods. To propose a single equation with real investment as the dependent variable on a number of influences affecting the desire to invest, possibly including a single interest rate, seems an inadequate way of capturing these underlying relationships. When explaining the level of demand in nominal terms it is necessary to take account of the extent to which finance is available. Finance is an important element in explaining effective demand; it is not part of a separate market. The extent to which these nominal demands result in an increase in real expenditures will, in turn, depend on the real forces determining the potential supply of goods and services within the economy.

In addition to these direct 'credit' effects there will also be continuing reactions to any disequilibrium between the demand for and supply of money. Although money will be accepted it may only be as an intermediary in the process of exchange and need not necessarily represent a position of long-run equilibrium. These reactions, which are discussed in Chapter 3, help to determine the lags of adjustment in response to any exogenous shocks to the system. This effect reflects the 'buffer' stock argument referred to above, and is what I have called the 'secondary effect' of money on the economy.

The primary and secondary effects between them provide a direct relationship between expenditures and the supply of money. Although the emphasis on the stock of money clearly distinguishes the approach from traditional Keynesian models, the explanation does not fit easily into standard monetarist theory in the sense that the money supply, and bank reserves, are endogenous to the system, and perfect markets are not assumed. In fact, as is explained in Chapter 3, it does not make much sense to think in terms of the effect of money on the economy. Because the supply of money is endogenously determined it operates as the channel through which the separate influences on the money supply work their way through the economy. Attention should, therefore, be directed at these underlying forces, from which it follows that monetary control should also be concerned with the particular causes of monetary growth, and not only with a single figure for the money supply (see also Coghlan and Sykes, 1980). It might be more accurate to think of this as a financial, or credit, approach to modelling the economy.

Accepting this approach has important implications for the interpretation of the results of previous studies. To see this it is worth considering the relationship between the present approach and the attempts to estimate the demand for money directly, and to establish unidirectional causality extending from money to the rest of the economy.

To take the demand for money studies first, it suggests that attempts to estimate demand for money equations for the broad definitions of money, employing non-simultaneous estimation techniques, should not be expected to produce stable results. Such equations would represent a misspecification of the relationship and we should not be surprised that such relationships have broken down in the United Kingdom following the rapid upsurge in the supply of money during the first half of the 1970s. Similar estimation procedures should, however, be reasonably successful in identifying demand functions for narrow definitions of money (see Coghlan, 1978b, and 1980b, Ch. 5). The difficulty in that case is in identifying the correct explanatory variables, particularly if competitive incentives are changed by an attempt by the authorities to control the quantity of money so defined. In general, however, the stock of money narrowly defined should remain demand determined.

Accepting this approach also suggests that attempts to identify unidirectional causality between money and nominal expenditures (see Coghlan, 1980b, Ch. 3, for a summary), under the assumption that money is exogenously determined, are unrealistic. Most studies of the United Kingdom have concluded that causality seems to run both ways, and that is indeed the conclusion suggested by the model presented here. Such studies may meet with some success, because of the suggested long-run (but not necessarily constant) relationship between the stock of money and nominal expenditure. The approach is, however, too simple, and money is itself assumed to be endogenously determined. It is more likely to respond with reasonable results if the main economic variables have been following a fairly stable growth path. If the economy has experienced more erratic movements it will be important to provide a coherent explanation of the way the system is supposed to work, and precisely how the supply of money affects the rest of the economy.

Finally, in concluding this introduction, it is worth re-emphasising the change in orientation of monetary policy and analysis that occured in the 1970s. It is only since 1971 (approximately) that the money supply has really been thought to be important, and consequently critics have attacked this rediscovery of money as due to spurious correlation (see Chapter 2). It will therefore be interesting to see whether the approach adopted here succeeds in explaining the earlier period. This is an extremely difficult test given the scepticism in the 1950s and 1960s regarding the importance of money. Most econometric models have changed substantially from those estimated during the 1960s, and it would be encouraging if some continuity could be identified. Furthermore, it would suggest that the events of the 1970s, in particular the rapid growth of the money supply and inflation, need not have taken the authorities so much by surprise.

Note

1 This independence refers to the existence of separate behavioural relationships, not that behaviour in each market is independent of behaviour in other markets.

2
Money in Macroeconomic Models

The objective of this chapter is to describe the main characteristics of existing econometric models of the monetary sector at a macroeconomic level, in order to provide a background against which to contrast the approach adopted here. Attention is concentrated on models of the UK economy, but even so, it is difficult to summarise adequately the great variety and complexity of the different approaches adopted. As Peston (1978) has pointed out, only the model builders themselves (and perhaps not even they) are likely to understand the full implications of their models. Moreover, models and model building are adapting rapidly to changing circumstances so that any comment is likely to become obsolete even as it is written. It is, however, hoped to indicate the paths along which the monetary/financial side of econometric model building has developed, and is developing.

By way of introduction it might be useful to trace, very briefly, the historical development of these models, and the main forces that have influenced thinking about the modelling of the monetary side of the macroeconomy. The first section, therefore, begins with the early development of model building in the United Kingdom. That takes in the period up to, and including, the early 1970s, before economic events changed dramatically and the existing models ceased to perform well at all. This is followed by a discussion of the monetarist attack that built up in the 1960s, together with the less ideological call for the full recognition, and inclusion, of balance sheet constraints within the model framework. The third section examines how money and the financial side of the economy have been treated in recent years. This is done by considering recent developments in the monetary side of existing econometric models and the construction of independent monetary models. Finally, the summary and conclusions emphasise the main points to emerge from the preceding discussion.

Early Developments

The pioneer studies
The earliest attempts to construct macroeconometric models were by Tinbergen. He began by estimating a model for the Dutch economy

7

(Tinbergen, 1937), and quickly followed this by estimating a model for the United States (Tinbergen, 1939). At about the same time he also constructed an empirical model of the UK economy, but because results were not as good, it was not published until 1951 (Tinbergen, 1951). These early models form the basis of modern econometric model building,[1] despite the attack Keynes levelled at the 'alchemy' of multiple regression (Keynes, 1939); see, in particular, Patinkin (1976).

The linkages from the financial side of the economy to the 'real' side were through returns on a variety of financial assets, but these effects were not found to be particularly important in general; see, for example, Tinbergen (1939, pp. 183–5) for the United States, and Tinbergen (1951, pp. 37 and 133) for the United Kingdom. There were also highly developed financial sectors which included

(i)   The joint supply of bonds, shares, and short claims by other firms and, with regard to the last items, speculating individuals;
(ii)   The supply of money by the banks;
(iii) The joint demand for short claims and bonds by the banks;
(iv)   The demand for money by other firms and individuals;
(v)   The joint demand for bonds and shares by individuals. (Tinbergen, 1939, pp. 74–5)

It can be seen that both the demand for, and supply of, money were estimated, the supply of money determining the short rate of interest. This short rate is, however, not an own rate on bank deposits, but is treated as the opportunity cost of holding money in the demand function.

The next stage in the development of macroeconometric models of the economy was entered with the development of the Klein–Goldberger model of the US economy (Klein and Goldberger, 1955; see also Klein, 1968). This model represents the starting point of modern interest in econometric model building. The financial sector was more rudimentary than in the Tinbergen models with only the demand for, and supply of, liquid assets explained, the definition of liquid assets being somewhat wider than conventional definitions of money – including holdings of US Government securities and a percentage of the private share capital of Savings and Loan Associations, in addition to bank deposits and notes and coins. As with Tinbergen the supply of liquid assets determined the short rate of interest, and lagged values of this rate explained movements in the long rate. Again there was no own rate on liquid assets included in the demand function. This is difficult to understand given the broad definition of liquid assets employed, and the supply and demand justification for determining a price within the market.

A significant development with this model was the inclusion of lagged liquid assets in the expenditure functions. This provides an important additional linkage between financial markets and so called 'real' markets. It should be noted, however, that this liquidity definition included a wide definition of financial assets, and left little scope for a separate monetary influence, or policy. In this respect it had more in common with the Radcliffe Committee (Radcliffe Report, 1959) view of the world, or even with the Cambridge New School (see below, pp. 13, 16).

A few years later Klein extended his model building activities to the United Kingdom (Klein *et al.*, 1961). In this case measures of liquidity were not included in the expenditure equations, the explanation being that the data were not available. Moreover, the supply of, and demand for, liquidity equations had disappeared, to be replaced by a single equation to explain the long-term rate of interest. This rate was taken to be a function of bank rate (which was exogenous to the system), the income velocity of circulation of money (notes and coins plus clearing bank deposits) and, in the quarterly model, the change in the general price level.

Early UK forecasting models
The main forecasting models in existence at the beginning of the 1970s were those at the London Business School (LBS), the National Institute of Economic and Social Research (National Institute) and the Treasury. Fortunately it is possible to get a very clear idea of the way in which those models operated at the time from the report on an SSRC conference on model building held in 1972 (Renton, 1975). The Southampton model (Heathfield and Pearce, 1975) is not included as the details of its development have not been discussed as widely as the others, and it is not clear what are the exact channels of monetary influence.

In 1972 all the models were notably Keynesian − in the sense in which that word has come to be used in relation to macroeconomic models. The Treasury model, for example, was

> ... built round, the income and expenditure flows [that is flows in real markets not financial markets] leading up to an estimate of aggregate demand and output. In particular, the approach adopted reflects such initial presumptions as a "full cost" approach to pricing, the absence of sharply defined constraints on the supply side and demand relationships in which the dominant role is played by income-expenditure rather than portfolio considerations.
>
> (Shepherd *et al.*, 1975)

The position of UK macroeconomic models at that time could be well summarised by a statement Klein had made some years before,

... my theoretical predilections are very much in favour of a theory of the 'real' economy. The monetary economy, if in good house-keeping order, will not have a dominant influence on real affairs. Nevertheless, I have tried hard over the years, in several models, to give the benefit of every doubt to money and interest rates when making statistical estimates. My empirical verdict, thus far, is that little evidence can be found for the actual influence of money or interest rates on real activity.

(Klein, 1964, p. 56)

Fisher and Sheppard (1972, p. 50) note that by the early 1970s, Klein's view had 'changed substantially' on this point. However, in the United Kingdom the financial side of the economy remained 'little more than a vestigial appendix to the main "real" forecasts' (Goodhart, 1978b, p. 10).

Of the three main models in regular use in the United Kingdom in the early 1970s the largest was that at the LBS, which contained sixty-eight behavioural equations representing 'a fivefold increase in size since 1969' (Ball *et al.*, 1975). Next came the Treasury model with approximately fifty behavioural equations (Shepherd *et al.*, 1975) and finally the National Insitute model which contained only eleven behavioural equations (Bispham, 1975).

In all of these models the money supply was taken to be exogenous, although there was a declared intention to try and improve on this situation as far as the first two models were concerned. And, of course, the Treasury did, and still do, undertake a full flow-of-funds consistency check, but with little, if any, feedback into the 'real' side.

In effect the model builders were starting from an income–expenditure accounting identity of the form:

$$Y \equiv C + I + G + X - Z$$

where

Y = national income/expenditure
C = private sector consumption expenditure
I = private sector investment expenditure
G = public sector expenditure
X = exports of goods and services
Z = imports of goods and services

all measured at constant prices.

The various behavioural components of this expression were then explained, and the disaggregation was in order to look at individual categories of 'real' expenditure, and to explain the wage/price/un-employment nexus. Apart from this there was no real attempt to dig deeper and look more closely at the behavioural interrelationships existing between demands for and supplies of goods and the demands for and supplies of finance. In all cases, not only was the financial side of the economy inadequately explained, or left unexplained altogether, but the linkages between the financial and 'real' sides of the economy were practically non-existent.

It was, however, recognised that under certain circumstances exogenous financial restraints might be important, and both the Treasury and the LBS included an effect of hire purchase (HP) controls on private sector expenditure. This was not extended to include general credit availability, nor did there seem to be any investigation of offsetting effects within financial markets; see Chapter 4.

One or two interest rates provided the only potential linkage from financial market conditions to the real economy, and the whole of the financial side of the economy was summarised within a demand for money function (the National Institute model did not even have that). This last equation was generally included only for the sake of completeness, since the main rate of interest was taken to be exogenous. It was possible, however, to reverse an estimated demand for money function in order to endogenise the rate of interest − as is still done as part of the MIT–Penn–SSRC (MPS)[2] model in the United States (Ando, 1978). It is hard to understand why, if the money supply is taken as given, and the money market determines the rate of interest, this latter variable is not estimated directly as the dependent variable of the equation. Estimating it the other way round is likely to produce inconsistent results as the error term will be correlated with one of the included explanatory variables, which in this case is the rate of interest.

The only earlier model in the United Kingdom to follow this procedure was that built by the Treasury, but in this case it was the demand function for money by the company sector that was reversed (Shepherd *et al.*, 1975). Here, in addition to the problem of justifying the overall approach, there is the question as to why the short rate of interest was determined solely by the company sector demand for money, and how this market was isolated from the behaviour of the other sectors.

In summary, it is possible to argue that the model builders had concentrated on the investment-saving (*IS*) side of the *IS−LM* model[3] paying little attention to the interrelatedness between the 'real' and financial sectors, or to the financial sector itself. In fact, as will be argued later (in Chapters 3 and 5), it is the absence of financial linkages, rather than the neglect of a detailed financial sub-sector, that is absolutely crucial. Dicks-Mireaux (1975), when discussing the models presented at the 1972 SSRC Conferences, commented on the lack of monetary influences, noting that, 'Possibly it is the very Keynesian framework itself which is tending to inhibit the search for monetary effects', adding that 'the greatest need now is for a better understanding of the role of monetary factors and their impact on the economy'.

Challenging the Keynesian Macro-Model

There are three main challenges to the type of model structure discussed above which can be categorised as the monetarist attack, the introduction of balance sheet constraints and the real balance effect.

The monetarist attack

The main thrust of this attack came from Milton Friedman and the Chicago based economists. They set out in various works (for example, Friedman, 1956, 1969) to undermine the Keynesian position which relegated money to a subsidiary role. In the early 1960s Friedman and Meiselman (1963) and Friedman and Schwartz (1963) provided strong evidence in support of the monetarist position. These studies, particularly the former, generated a great deal of controversy and subsequent empirical work.

There very quickly developed a considerable literature on the reduced form debate, with additional evidence in favour of a strong, substantial effect of money on the economy provided by the economists at the Federal Reserve Bank of St. Louis (for example, Andersen and Jordan, 1968; Andersen and Carlson, 1970). Moreover, these studies found little support for a strong effect of autonomous expenditures or fiscal policy on the rest of the economy. This debate is summarised elsewhere (Coghlan, 1980b, Ch. 3) and need not be repeated here.

It is, however, interesting to note that this debate had a much greater influence on macroeconomic model building in the United States than in the United Kingdom, as witnessed by Modigliani's (1975) contribution to the SSRC Conference in 1972. The main reason for this was probably the strength of the monetarist results obtained for the United States which, if nothing else, at least established a case that required an answer. In the United Kingdom, on the other hand, the results seemed much less favourable to the monetarist cause (see, for example, Artis and Nobay, 1969; Goodhart and Crockett, 1970; Williams, Goodhart and Gowland, 1976). Even so, in both countries a lively debate has continued as to the correct specification of macroeconomic behaviour and the importance of money in the economy.

Balance sheet constraints

The argument for including all balance sheet and accounting identities is that it introduces possible feedbacks to the rest of the economy which might otherwise be neglected. Brainard and Tobin (1968) demonstrated the importance of consistency for the financial sector, and Parkin *et al.* (1975) and Purvis (1975) have since extended the argument to a much wider portfolio choice, along the lines originally suggested by Hicks (1935).

The introduction of accounting identities for the government has generated a great deal of debate concerning the effects of different means of financing public sector deficits (for example, Ott and Ott, 1965; Christ, 1967, 1968; Silber, 1970; Blinder and Solow, 1974). This has created most attention in the debate surrounding the question of possible public sector 'crowding out' of private sector expenditures (Culbertson, 1968; Spencer and Yohe, 1970; see Coghlan, 1980b, Ch. 2, for a brief summary of this debate, and Currie, 1978, for a more detailed analysis).

This introduction of accounting identities was further extended to include the external balance sheet accounts, and the way these fed back on to domestic portfolios (for example, Oates, 1966; Helliwell, 1969; McKinnon, 1969). This work established equilibrium portfolio conditions incorporating standard behavioural relationships which possessed the long-run properties of the monetarist approach to the balance of payments, or the Cambridge New School (Godley and Cripps, 1974; Cripps *et al.*, 1974). This latter view posited a direct relationship between the size of the current account and the size of the public sector borrowing requirement. Oates (1966) developed a model having exactly this property:

> Whatever financial assets are being injected into the system by the budget deficit are simultaneously drained out by the deficit in the trade balance. Conversely, if the government is running a budgetary surplus, equilibrium requires a balance-of-trade surplus to offset the government drain of financial assets from the system. (p. 493)

Many of the models mentioned above were not based on money as such, but concentrated on total *financial* wealth. Implicitly they require a potentially infinite circulation of money in order to be able to guarantee a solution while ignoring the relationship between expanding wealth and expansion of the money supply.

The monetary approach to the balance of payments (MABP), on the other hand, has employed the balance sheet relationships, together with the assumption of a stable demand for money, in order to demonstrate the importance of money (for example, Polak, 1957; Johnson, 1958; Mundel 1968; see Whitman, 1975, and Frenkel and Johnson, 1976b, for surveys of the arguments involved, and Hahn, 1977, for a more critical appraisal). Aspects of the MABP will be discussed in greater detail in Chapter 3. However, it is worth noting, at this point, that the method of financing a public sector budget deficit is generally considered within the MABP to be a crucial determinant of domestic credit expansion (DCE), and therefore of international reserve flows; in other words, the balance of payments. Thus, controlling the size of the public sector borrowing requirement (PSBR) is frequently identified as a major means of achieving balance of payments stability. However, the relationship is even more direct in the Oates/Cambridge New School model in which the financing of the deficit is unimportant and is incapable of reducing the impact. Coghlan (1978a) draws out the comparisons that exist between the MABP position and the Cambridge New School.

Helliwell (1969) presents a structural model of an open economy in which money has an important role to play, and which incorporates the feedbacks from the balance of payments on to the financial side of the economy. Given certain assumptions, for example, that DCE is given, this model is capable of producing MABP conclusions. Such a model is important for incorporating the stock adjustment feedbacks[4] stressed by the MABP, but within a more conventional structural model. More recently Beenstock (1978) has demonstrated explicitly the compatibility of monetary stock adjustment and a structural model of the economy.

The real balance effect

The final development I would like to draw attention to here is the disequilibrium real balance effect (Patinkin, 1965; Archibald and Lipsey 1958). The importance of this development is not that it provides a solution to short-run unemployment, and Patinkin (1948) has emphasised the long-run nature of any such mechanism. What is important is the role played by real money balances in smoothing out the adjustment process of real expenditures. It is worth briefly summarising the Archibald and Lipsey (1958) argument in order to demonstrate the process involved.

The basic model consists of a two-dimensional diagram (Figure 2.1). In this example real money balances held at the start of the period, OM (income plus money balances retained from the previous period), are measured along the vertical axis, and real expenditures made during the period OE are measured along the horizontal axis. Given a single uniform price level these real balances could be exchanged for real goods of equivalent value (that is, $OM = OE$), and the line ME gives the budget line relating real balances and real goods. The line OV represents the expansion path generated by the tangency of the individual's indifference curves and the possible budget lines.

The point of the model is to demonstrate that only when there is no tendency for real balances to change will the system settle down to equilibrium. But in the process it is the real balances that will bear the burden of adjustment.

Assume, for example, that the individual starts off with real income OY and real balances YE. His budget will be given by EM and his preferred position will be at point a, where the indifference curve is tangential. However, with income of OY, he can only achieve that position by running down his real balances by YZ. In the next period

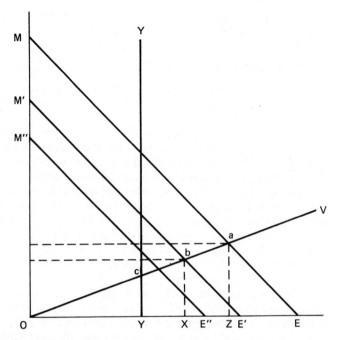

Figure 2.1   *Adjustment through real balances*

the individual's real balances will have been reduced by $YZ \, (= E'E)$, and he will have a new budget line like that given by $M'E'$. In this case the preferred position will be achieved by running down real balances by YX. Consequently, the budget line is further reduced to $M''E''$ $(E''E' = YX)$, and the process is continued as the individual approaches equilibrium at c. In the opposite case the individual would gradually build up his stock of real money balances, at each point justifying an increased flow of expenditure, the process continuing until a new stock-flow equilibrium was achieved.

Any shift in income from one position to another, for example, from OZ, with equilibrium at c, results in a multiplier process of the type just described. The point that needs to be emphasised is the importance of disequilibrium money balances in the process of adjustment.

The weakness of the real balance argument as developed is that it does not describe the process through which money comes into existence. When Archibald and Lipsey (1958, p. 7) consider an increase in the money supply they assume that 'each individual simply wakes up on Monday morning to find his nominal money balances doubled'; it is, in effect, 'helicopter' money. In failing to deal with the process of money creation they are telling only half the story, and it is this question that is dealt with in Chapter 3.

Recent Developments in Model Building

The criticisms, discussed above, of the way in which money enters into macroeconomic models had existed for some time prior to the 1972 SSRC Model-Building Conference from which the examples of UK models were taken, without, it is clear, having any great impact on the structure of these models. Certainly, in the United States financial variables played a substantial role in the MPS model, and even in the early 1970s this model possessed many of the long-run properties of the monetarist approach (see, for example, Fisher and Sheppard, 1972). In this country, as in most countries, money came to be thought increasingly important as inflation accelerated and the main forecasting models failed to provide reasonable predictions or explanations. It would seem, as Friedman (1978) has claimed, that events rather than theory have convinced practitioners – the importance of theory has been to provide a convenient 'respectable' alternative.

In considering this question of the development of the monetary aspect of macroeconomic model building it is convenient to distinguish between the larger forecasting models, which are in a continual state of development, and the smaller, more specific, monetary models or sub-models that have been built. The number of forecasting models has increased in the 1970s, and attention is concentrated on those discussed at two recent conferences on macroeconomic model building: see Posner (1978) and the LBS Conference on Macroeconomic Model Building, 3–5 July 1978 (hereafter referred to as the LBS conference).

The monetary side of forecasting models
The easiest example to deal with is the model developed by the Cambridge Economic Policy Group. This model has been designed specifically to take a longer term view of economic prospects and policy (see Cripps *et al.*, 1974; Cripps and Godley, 1976). Those equations which have been estimated econometrically have employed annual data for 1962–74 (Cripps and Fetherston, 1978).

In this case money plays no role, 'the model contains no mechanism whereby money and/or fiscal restraint directly moderates inflation. Tight monetary control and restriction of real incomes might well generate more, not less, inflationary pressure' (Cripps and Fetherston, 1978).

The other main forecasting models – those of the LBS, the National Institute, the Treasury and Bank of England – have, to different degrees, remained faithful to their Keynesian origins. Some attempts have been made to identify additional wealth, or liquidity, effects (see, for example, Latter, 1978; Shepherd, 1978) on private sector expenditure, though the National Institute has expressed reservations about the importance of these effects (Ormerod, 1978; see also Coghlan, 1977a; Coghlan and Jackson, 1979). In the main, however, the linkages between the 'real' and financial sector continue to be through one or two rates of interest (see, for example, Savage, 1978a).

All of these model builders have been involved in trying to develop the financial side of their models but, in each case, as a separate sector of the model. For example, although the monetary sector of the National Institute was 'conceived as a part of the overall National Institute model with the primary role of explaining financial variables which have an impact on the real economy', it was also argued that 'the task of explaining the causal linkages between the monetary and real sectors is not regarded here as part of the monetary model' (Savage, 1978b, p. 1).

The separation of 'real' and financial markets in this way has been fundamental in the Keynesian macroeconomic models that have been estimated and follows Hicks' (1937) classical *IS* and *LM* dichotomy. However, one way of interpreting the criticisms of the Keynesian model outlined above is in terms of breaking down this sharp dichotomy. It may be that this argument should be taken much further, and such an extension represents an important element in the theoretical developments in Chapters 3 and 5.

The Bank of England, in conjunction with the Treasury, has a long tradition of forecasting flows of funds through the economy (Hewitt, 1977). It comes as no surprise, therefore, that it identifies a matrix of financial flows (Latter, 1978). At present these largely involve imposed relationships derived from long experience providing judgemental forecasts. This is, however, changing as more of the financial flows are estimated empirically. The stock of money can 'be derived by aggregation of the appropriate elements in the matrix' (Latter, 1978, p. 6). This essentially results in a supply of money, but as no separate demand function is identified the supply must also be demanded. The demand function must, therefore, be residually defined and this is also a property of the National Institute and Treasury models.

The National Institute has built a preliminary model of the monetary sector (Savage, 1978b) which has much in common with the Treasury model. It is not, however, clear whether this model has been, or will be, incorporated into the main body of the macroeconomic model. In the National Institute model as of July 1978 (Ormerod, 1978) the monetary sector was represented by a single demand for money relationship which was estimated directly. Interest rates were either taken to be given exogenously, or the demand for money function was reversed to determine the rate of interest, taking the stock of money as exogenous. It has already been noted above that this procedure is not necessarily valid; in this particular case it results in a very strange equation, as noted by Goodhart (1978a, p. 186), in which the consol rate depends on the real money stock, and rate of inflation, six months in the future.

The Treasury financial sector (Spencer and Mowl, 1978) took over four years to develop and represents a major achievement. As with the National Institute monetary sector the linkages with the 'real' side were taken as given. Although the Treasury has spent considerable effort examining potential linkages (for example Shepherd, 1978), the builders of the financial sub-model were required to take that side of the relationship as given. This necessarily restricted the form the model could take. The aggregate financial surpluses and deficits are taken as given in the financial sector which then concentrates on the allocation of these funds. In addition, equilibrium in the money market is achieved by making the demand for money a residual. This is similar to the National Institute monetary sector in which time deposits perform the role of residual, even though it is recognised that this is an unreasonable assumption to make (Savage, 1978b, p. 10).

Both the Treasury and the National Institute financial models derive the stock of money by disaggregating, and then explaining, the asset side of bank balance sheets (or flows of funds), though the breakdown emphasised is not the same in both cases. Having thereby obtained an explanation of the *supply* of money it is disappointing that equilibrium is automatically achieved by defining a residual behavioural equation. One implication of splitting the economy up in this way is that the velocity of circulation of money is not restricted and can vary quite widely. In particular, movements in prices and the stock of money can be in different directions (see Middleton *et al.*, 1979). It will be argued below, particularly in Chapter 3, that the unique characteristics of money mean that monetary disequilibrium is reflected in all markets throughout the economy.

In estimating the financial flows these models have made fairly extensive use of dummy variables representing bank lending restrictions and the introduction of Competition and Credit Control (CCC) in 1971. While quantitative controls almost certainly had an important influence on bank lending it is difficult to understand why CCC should have had a substantial effect. These, and related, questions are discussed in greater detail in Chapter 4, where an alternative explanation of the results is also provided.

The LBS has been acutely aware of the sharp division between the 'real' side of its earlier models and the monetary/financial side, as is made clear in the following statement (Ball *et al.*, 1978, p. 4):

There was no full articulated account of the role of government at the level of the macro economy, particularly on the revenue side, and more generally no incorporation into the system of the behaviour and significance of the flow of funds for government and for the corporate and personal sectors. The model was in a rather traditional sense a real Keynesian model with no attention being paid to the financial implications of real flows. Moreover, by the same token, the monetary side of the model was rudimentary, with an exogenous money supply and the major monetary influences being translated through interest rates and specific credit variables such as the flow of new credit for consumer durable spending.

In more recent versions of the LBS model DCE has been made endogenous, and there has been a major attempt to relate the stock of money to inflation through changes in the exchange rate. This work is not complete and the money supply is still not explained endogenously.

Moreover, they have ended up with a dichotomous model of inflation in which an increase in the money supply is fully passed on in changes in the price level if the exchange rate is floating, but does not have this effect if the exchange rate is fixed (Ball *et al.*, 1978, p. 28). The degree of capital mobility required in order to justify this approach is unlikely to exist, and anyway does not seem to be an assumption of the model. In particular, this mechanism is contradictory to their own statement that 'if the exchange rate is pegged by the authorities' willingness to support the rate out of the accumulated reserves, fiscal and monetary expansion will induce adjustments largely through the current account of the balance of payments' (Ball *et al.*, 1978, pp. 12–13). It is difficult to see how this adjustment will come about if real changes in aggregate income and expenditure are limited (allowing also for distributional effects) and prices do not respond. It therefore seems appropriate to support Goodhart's (1978a, p. 174) conclusion that the recent work by the LBS 'though the most interesting, lacks internal consistency'.

Specific monetary models
In turning to the subject of the smaller specific monetary models that have been built, it is interesting to note the variety of different assumptions that have been made. A great advantage of small models is that it is easier to see the particular assumptions that have been made, and to understand the process involved. It is convenient to begin with those models which have taken the money supply, monetary base, or DCE as given exogenously.

Smith (1977) takes the broad money supply as given and constructs a model along the lines of the St. Louis models (Andersen and Jordan, 1968; Andersen and Carlson, 1970), employing annual data for 1880–1975. For the United Kingdom, however, it is necessary to explain the balance of payments, which is included in Smith's model, but this seriously undermines the assumption of an exogenous money supply; for a full explanation of this inconsistency see Chapter 3.

Minford *et al.* (1978), on the other hand, employ a narrow definition of money, but which is also assumed to be determined exogenously. An important feature of this model concerns the portfolio of assets that represents money. Money is seen as a substitute for all assets real and financial, within the context of an open economy, and incorporating wealth effects. This model lays great stress on the formation of expectations using a form of the rational expectations hypothesis. A strong argument is put forward to justify a different expectations formation mechanism, and therefore a different model, depending on whether the exchange rate is fixed or floating. Moreover, it is argued that the UK exchange rate has been floating since 1972. The main difference, it is argued, between these two regimes is that under fixed exchange rates domestic prices are expected to follow world prices, whereas with floating rates the expectation is formed on the basis of movements in the money supply. Even so, the model is estimated using annual data for 1945/48–1973/74. There are certain problems with this treatment of expectations. In the first place, as noted by Goodhart (1978b, p. 21), the United Kingdom has not allowed the exchange rate to float freely, 'far from it, there has remained substantial intervention in exchange markets', the justification provided for this intervention being the potentially destabilising effect of a free market in foreign currency (see, for example, Allen and Enoch, 1978). Secondly, the long-run nature of these price mechanisms under consideration would suggest that a simple division of the world into two separate states of nature is not appropriate. For example, domestic prices may rise more rapidly than world prices for some considerable time even with fixed exchange rates, as noted by Laidler (1978, p. 52).

It is also very difficult to justify the assumption that the money supply is exogenously determined in the United Kingdom, particularly the narrow definition, M1. There are very good reasons for believing that the stock of M1 should respond reasonably quickly to the demand for it, a hypothesis for which there is reasonable empirical support (see, for example, Coghlan, 1978b). The assumption of exogeneity is, therefore, likely to bias the model estimates obtained, as well as give a misleading impression of the operation of monetary policy.

All of the remaining models considered here have concentrated on a broad definition of money, and have attempted to separate the domestic components from the external components. In addition they have incorporated some form of disequilibrium between the supply of and demand for money, and in each case the estimation procedure has been based on a full information, maximum likelihood method employing a discrete approximation to a system of differential equations, that is, a model specified in continuous time. The programmes were developed by Wymer (1968, 1972) building on work by Bergstrom (1966), Bergstrom and Wymer (1976) and Knight and Wymer (1976).

Only one of these models has taken DCE to be exogenous and that is the model built by Laidler and O'Shea (1978); see also Laidler (1978). The model was kept simple for pedagogic reasons, and estimated with annual data for the period 1954—70. An endogenous demand for money function (£M3) is estimated with the difference between domestic supply and demand determining the external component of the money supply — defined as the balance for official financing (BOF).[5]

The estimated income elasticity of the demand for money was 0.4 which Laidler and O'Shea considered too low. They suggested that this finding resulted from the fact that they did not include any interest rate effects from the demand function. This value of 0.4 does not, however, seem particularly low. There are reasons to suspect that saving may be a luxury good (see Coghlan and Jackson, 1979), as also may be the net acquisition of financial assets, but this seems harder to justify in the case of broad money. The size and characteristic of transactions costs, and certain institutional constraints such as a minimum acceptable size of transactions for the purchase of non-money financial assets, suggest that money holdings will not increase as rapidly as income or wealth.

Unfortunately, 'a dynamic simulation of the model beyond 1970, using actual values of the exogenous variables produces results that are best described as nonsense' (Laidler, 1978, p. 57). In order to explain this Laidler assumes a sharp change in income trend for the period 1970—76, arguing strongly, and at length, that the structure of the economy changed in the 1970s: 'Whether the structure of the economy would have changed under alternative policies from 1970 onwards may be a moot question, but there is no doubt that in fact it did change, and in a way that has not yet proved completely amenable to formal modelling along the lines set out above' (Laidler, 1978, p. 62).

A major criticism of Laidler's approach is the assumption that DCE can reasonably be considered as exogenous. This assumption has come under strong attack from Goodhart (1978a, p. 188), who has pointed out that it will bias the results. An additional problem concerns the actual definitions of DCE and the external counterpart of the domestic money supply. The way in which these terms have been defined has introduced an exact *statistical* relationship between the two series quite independent of any behavioural relationship. Therefore, any test for a behavioural relationship between these series will be seriously biased. Although the remaining models discussed in this section have made DCE endogenous they have all still employed misleading definitions of these crucial series.

A similar, but rather more detailed, model to Laidler's has been built by Jonson (1976b), also employing annual data, in this case for the period 1888–1970. As in the previous model, external capital flows are determined by the difference between the demand for money and DCE, though in this case DCE has also been endogenously determined. Both of these models include a disequilibrium real money balance effect in the expenditure equation which is justified, at least by Jonson, in terms of the Archibald and Lipsey model (see above).

These models make use of fairly strong restrictions. For example, in Jonson's model the income elasticity on expenditure, exports, money and bonds are all constrained to be the same, and the model has the steady state solution that output, imports, exports, expenditure and real government expenditure all grow at the same rate. Domestic prices are related directly to world prices on the assumption of purchasing power parity, and are not a function of the stock of money. This approach is somewhat misleading. Purchasing power parity is actually a model property, depending on the interaction of all equations in the model, rather than being a direct constraint in the price equation.

The other two UK models which have adopted this model-building approach have concentrated more directly on the operation of the financial system, and have taken the linkages with income/expenditure markets as given. These models are also distinguishable by the fact that they have employed quarterly data in their estimation. Moreover, because they have been estimated into the 1970s, it is of interest to consider how financial policy instruments, and changes in the system, have been dealt with.

In the model built by Melitz and Sterdyniak (1979) equations were estimated (with quarterly data from 1963 to 1974) to explain domestic credit and the demand for money. The option was left open as to whether the system was closed by changes in the domestic price level (the assumption with a floating exchange rate), with adjustment completed in the current quarter in both cases. When concentrating on the financial sector at the expense of 'real' markets there is a potential problem when it comes to closing the model. It was argued above, when discussing the financial sub-models of the larger forecasting models, that it was unsatisfactory to take the financial linkages as given, and this model suffers from the same problem. The sophisticated estimation techniques for modelling disequilibrium systems have not resolved this dilemma. It is unsatisfactory to assume instantaneous adjustment of prices, or of the total balance of payments, so that there is no feedback on to the rest of the economy.

Melitz and Sterdyniak employ two definitions of money, both of which are broader than the conventional definitions: M4 which is equal to M3 plus national savings deposits and claims on local authorities, and M5 which is equal to M4 plus building society shares and deposits and the deposits of finance companies. The M4 definition is found to provide the most consistent results.

In estimating this model considerable use was made of a 0–1–2 dummy explaining direct controls on bank lending, including both qualitative and quantitative restrictions, and a dummy variable to explain the introduction of competition and credit control (CCC) in 1971. Both of these variables enter all the asset and liability demand functions. It is, however, hard to justify the wide inclusion of these variables. For example, bank lending restrictions should reduce bank lending, and, thereby, the supply of money,[6] but it is not clear whether they should reduce the demand for money. This is a subject we shall return to later.

The inclusion of these variables is justified as representing part of the service yield on deposits. CCC, for example, is expected to have a positive effect on the service yield 'since the reform increased the competitive pressure on the commercial banks'. However, one might, in fact, expect exactly the opposite argument to hold. If direct price competition was previously constrained by the restricted competitive position of the clearing banks, it is only natural to expect them to compete through non-price operations. In fact, the inefficiency of such activities was often cited as a major justification for a return to a more market orientated system (for example, the National Board for Prices and Incomes Report No. 34, 1967, and Johnson, 1967). It would therefore be more reasonable on *a priori* grounds to expect CCC to have had a negative effect on the service yield. The appearance of a CCC dummy in the demand for money function is consequently rather hard to justify on behavioural grounds (see, also, Artis and Lewis 1976). This is a topic that will be discussed in greater detail in later chapters.

The model in which the disequilibrium approach employed in this last group of models has been developed most extensively is that of the Australian economy, built at the Federal Reserve Bank of Australia (Jonson *et al.*, 1976). This is a particularly sophisticated model which incorporates disequilibrium money effects in equations explaining household expenditure, wages and prices. However, as pointed out by Davis and Lewis (1977), the logic of the disequilibrium buffer stock argument is that these effects should be observed in many more, if not all, markets.

The justification for including the effect of disequilibrium money balances is firmly based on the real balance effects of Archibald and Lipsey (1958), and the information content of money (Laidler, 1974); this linkage is set out clearly in Jonson (1976a). While the incorporation of such an effect in macroeconomic models represents a significant improvement it still says nothing about the money supply process, and how this might be reflected in other markets. Although the money supply is completely endogenous within the system it is viewed as a residual (Jonson *et al.*, 1976, p. 10) and the supply process itself is not assumed to be directly related to any other form of private sector behaviour in 'real' markets.

Summary and Conclusions

The brief overview presented in this chapter has illustrated the increasing emphasis placed on money in macroeconomic model building. Also, although this review has necessarily been rather cursory, it should be clear that attention has turned away from the almost exclusive search for a stable demand for money function to attempts to identify a dis-aggregated supply of money. An interesting feature of most of this work has been the rejection of an exogenous money supply or DCE, or of naive forms of high powered money multipliers in favour of a port-folio approach to the determination of banking sector assets in which reserves are passively provided by the authorities — at a price.

This money supply process is common to many of the models regardless of whether they are part of a larger forecasting model, or a separate, specific model. All of the larger forecasting models have retained fairly traditional linkages between money and expenditure markets, and most of the smaller models, by not discussing this question, are implicitly assuming a similar connection. Some of the smaller models, however, have developed a linkage through the disequilibrium between the supply of and demand for money. These models have tended to be estimated in a very specific way, that is, using FIML and a discrete approximation to a true model specified in continuous time. It is regrettable that more work has not been done along these lines employing different estimation techniques in order to judge the con-tribution of the particularl econometric methodology, although Minford *et al.*, (1978) do find an important role for money using single equation estimation techniques, and Davidson (1978) is planning to estimate a discrete disequilibrium model using FIML. The authors of the leading model of this type (Jonson *et al.*, 1976, p. 2) admit that 'it is yet to be determined if the benefits of this procedure exceed the costs', and Bacon and Johnson (1977) produced alternative estimates employing different techniques and have questioned the wisdom of this econo-metric approach (see also Fisher, 1976).

The inclusion of disequilibrium money balances in certain expen-diture equations is based on the argument that money serves as a buffer between transactions in other markets. As already noted, the logic of this argument suggests that this disequilibrium effect should be observed in all, or at least most, markets, including those for financial claims. A weakness of this approach is that it still assumes that the credit markets through which money is created bear no direct relationship to expen-diture markets. This is a subject of fundamental importance and is discussed in greater detail in Chapters 3 and 5.

Most of the models have been concerned with the influence of the balance of payments on the money supply and the relationship between DCE and the balance of payments. In all cases inadequate attention has been paid to the definitions employed and this has introduced a direct statistical relationship between the external and domestic components of the money supply unrelated to any behavioural influences. Making sense of statistical definitions can prove tiresome work but, as this example proves, can be extremely valuable. The problem and its solution are discussed further in Chapter 3.

It was also noted that bank lending restrictions and the introduction of CCC were not treated in a consistent manner. In some models dummy variables representing these events have played a major role in explaining movements in a variety of financial aggregates. The exact definitions of these variables, and the justification for their inclusion, has not always been clear. These, and other policies, are discussed in Chapter 4, and are incorporated in a somewhat different form in the model presented in Chapter 5.

One reason for the inclusion of these dummy variables is that they do at least split the period of the 1970s from the 1960s. As we have seen, obtaining a satisfactory econometric explanation of both of these periods has proved rather difficult, and poses an extreme test of any model. For a monetary model, in the sense that money determines prices, this test is of even greater significance. It has been argued (for example, by Tarling and Wilkinson, 1977) that any evidence of a relationship between prices and money depends solely on the inclusion of data for 1973—75, and even then is simply a reflection of the missing influence of rising import prices. It will therefore be interesting to see whether the model estimated in Chapter 5, for the period 1952 to 1976, can also explain the period up to 1971.

Notes

1 It should be noted that an early, if rather rudimentary, model of the UK economy had been published by Radice (1939).
2 Previously known as the Federal Reserve–MIT–Penn (FMP) model.
3 For a description of such a model see Coghlan (1980b, Ch. 2).
4 It is this stock adjustment aspect of the MABP that Hahn (1977) has claimed represents the major contribution of the approach.
5 Previously called the total currency flow.
6 Assuming no offsets elsewhere in private sector portfolios.

3

A Dynamic Model of the
Supply of Money

Monetary influences of one form or another have been incorporated into most existing macro-economic models. In general, incomes and expenditures have continued to be demand determined, with the addition of a separate monetary/financial sector. Aggregated financial surpluses feed into the financial sector from the so-called 'real' sector and one or two rates of return on financial variables have some, though usually very small, effect in the other direction. This separation of markets follows the Keynesian tradition as it has developed; see chapter 2 above.

The approach adopted here is different in that money is assumed to be held as intermediary to all transactions and therefore reflects behaviour in all markets. It is therefore not possible to make such a clear distinction between money/finance and income/expenditure markets. In this view of the world, it is not enough just to include money in a model; the context within which it is introduced is also crucially important. The distinguishing feature of the present model is the money supply process which is a central feature in this study.

An important aspect of any attempt to explain monetary development, history or policy involves the process of money creation, and the means through which money market equilibrium is achieved. One possibility is that equilibrium is achieved as the result of a perfectly flexible supply so that the stock of money simply responds to the demand for it. In this case, however, it becomes difficult to make a convincing argument in favour of monetary targets, and an emphasis on monetary aggregates (see, for example, Benjamin Friedman, 1977).

The argument that the stock of money has an independent role to play is generally presented in such a way that supply is in the main exogenously determined (e.g. Milton Friedman, 1968). This exogenous element is provided by the assumption that the monetary base is exogenously determined, with the money supply related to this base by a stable, predictable, but not necessarily constant, multiplier (see, for example, Friedman and Schwartz, 1963). Alternatively, if the monetary base is not restricted by the monetary authorities, it might appear that the stock of money simply responds to the demand for it.

This has indeed been the argument that has usually been put forward: it is, however, incorrect. It is a view which depends crucially on the existence of continuous equilibrium in money markets. It is argued in this chapter that the demand for and supply of money are determined independently of each other, even when the monetary base is endogenous, and that we need to take account of the existence of disequilibrium. The idea that there can be disequilibrium in money markets is not a new one, and Friedman and Meiselman's description of money as a residual store of purchasing power can be interpreted in this light (Friedman and Meiselman, 1963, esp. pp. 217–22). Macroeconomics has, however, been dominated by static equilibrium models, in particular the *IS/LM* model. This chapter provides the description of an alternative money supply process which has direct implications for modelling the rest of the economy. The supply mechanism is therefore described within the broad outline of a dynamic model of the economy.

The Importance of Bank Credit

The banks stand at the centre of the financial system performing the role of residual providers of finance to the private and public sectors and the non-bank financial institutions (NBFI). Although it is necessary to take account of the rest of the financial system the operation of the payments mechanism does make the banks importantly different from the NBFI (see Coghlan 1977 and 1980b, chapter 9). The banks are, however, still subject to economic forces of supply and demand. This means that an expansion of the monetary base need not result in any simple multiple expansion of the money supply; it is still necessary for a demand for bank credit to exist. The banks play a crucial role in the provision of finance to facilitate an increase in total investment, and this was a fundamental part of Keynes' own theory (in particular, Keynes 1937a and b, see also Coghlan 1980b chapters 2 and 9). This is perhaps worth emphasising, since it provides justification for the model outlined here. For example, as Keynes (1978, p. 666) argued:

> In a simplified schematism, designed to elucidate the essence of what is happening, but one which is, in fact, substantially representative of real life, one would assume that finance is wholly supplied during the interregnum [between planning and execution] by the banks; and this is the explanation of why their policy is so important in determining the pace at which new investment can proceed.

Many discussions of the role of money concentrate on its function as an asset within a financial portfolio, ignoring the all important point that money is employed as the means of payment in the process of exchange — of real and financial assets. This latter function of money is crucial to the role money has to play in the economy. It is quite evident in the quote from Keynes above that the process of money creation through bank credit markets is associated with purchases in other markets. Chick (1979) has emphasised the point that money circulates, and has criticised standard portfolio theory for neglecting this simple fact. Money is used in exchange for all assets, including financial assets. That does not mean the desired substitution is necessarily between money and the financial asset in question. Money is the medium through which payment is made, and will generally reflect an initial portfolio response which will have further repercussions. It is easy to ignore the process of adjustment, and the flexibility of this process, made possible through the existence of an efficient monetary infrastructure.

The approach adopted here has something in common with the money supply models developed by Brunner and Meltzer (1968, 1976), for example, who have included a bank credit market in their money supply relationships. The equilibrium portfolio properties are very similar, but the actual dynamic process of money creation is rather different. The main determinant of changes in the money supply in the Brunner and Meltzer model is the high-powered money — the reserve assets of the banking system. In the model developed here the reserve base is endogenous, responding to the needs and desires of the banking system. Moreover, the connection between credit and expenditure is considered to be crucially important; attention is directed to the motive forces changing economic variables, and the dynamics of adjustment. It is no more realistic to analyse money supply determination, abstracting from the 'real' side of the economy, than it is to study income/expenditure markets without including money.

The approach adopted here also incorporates more market pessimism than Brunner and Meltzer's, who assume perfect market adjustment and the absence of market segmentation. In this case it is assumed that interest rate elasticities may not be all that great, and credit rationing may dominate market behaviour.

Support for the idea that credit may be rationed other than by price is implicitly given by Keynes, see above, and explicitly by Tobin more recently:

Many businesses, like many households, are liquidity-constrained. The pace of their real investment, whether in working capital or fixed capital, is limited by their cash flow and the credit they can obtain. Their own estimate of the marginal efficiency of such capital exceeds the interest rate on such loans. Perhaps they are unobjectively optimistic; perhaps they are risk-lovers instead of risk averters. In any case their borrowing is limited by collateral and margin requirements rather than by rates. Credit rationing is not necessarily a market imperfection. It is intrinsic to the difference of perspective between lender and borrower. As the lender cannot really control the borrower's use of the funds, there is no way the lender can make an actuarially sound loan simply by setting interest rates and letting the borrower decide how much to take. The implication is that there is almost always an 'unsatisfied fringe of borrowers' at existing rates, and these borrowers are sure spenders. When easy money conditions diminish the cost of funds to banks and other lenders, extra lending to venturesome entrepreneurs is a powerful effect. (Tobin, 1978, p. 428).

This quote illustrates the direct relationship between expenditure and credit. In this respect the approach has something in common with the attempts by Cohen (1968, 1972), for example, to re-establish the importance of external finance in explaining expenditures. Moreover, if availability rather than price is the main restriction on quantity then it should be possible to observe an increase in demand associated with an increase in the rate charged on credit, if this improves the margins and profitability on the loan.

The Money Supply and Credit Demand

It has often been argued that the money stock, regardless of definition, has become demand determined because the monetary authorities have endogenised the reserve supply process. Although there has been considerable movement towards controlling the money stock, the control mechanism has still operated through interest rates rather than variations in the quantity of reserve assets. In 1975 Goodhart was able to write

Whereas this [reserve asset control] is often presented in theoretical papers and textbooks as representing reality, or as a desideratum, it is extremely hard to find any attested examples in which central banks — even in countries where most attention is paid to the monetary aggregates, e.g. Germany — actually do behave in this way. (Goodhart, 1975a, p. 8)

Furthermore, even in the United States in the period since monetary targets have been formally adopted, the emphasis has still been on controlling the money supply through changes in the rate of interest. The President of the Federal Reserve Bank of New York has stated that the central monetary authority 'typically attempts to influence monetary growth by instructing the Manager of the Open Market Account to supply or withdraw reserves as needed to hold the Federal funds rate at levels projected to be consistent with the desired monetary growth rate' (Volker, 1978, p. 336). He then goes on to discuss, and to reject, the suggestion that the authorities should 'attempt to control aggregate monetary growth rates by the use of reserve operating targets, such as the reserve base or some measure of aggregate reserves' (p. 336). This possibility has since been discussed within the Bank of England (Foot *et al.,* 1979) with very similar conclusions.

If, in fact, reserves are freely available and/or reserve ratios are infinitely variable, it might be supposed that the money stock becomes demand determined. That has been the argument usually put forward, at least for the United Kingdom, by both Keynesians and monetarists (for example, Kaldor, 1970; Griffiths, 1973). If money is supplied upon demand, as suggested, we then find ourselves in an extreme Keynesian world in which money appears to have no effect on anything. This does not mean that there are no causal links running from money to the rest of the economy, only that the authorities have acted so as to neutralise these effects. Even within this (equilibrium) context it is important to distinguish between an infinitely interest-elastic demand for money and an infinitely elastic supply.

Accepting that the monetary authorities in general have in the past not followed a policy of controlling the monetary base, however defined, but have controlled interest rates, does that in fact mean that the stock was necessarily demand determined? The answer is no; to make such an assumption is to confuse the demand for money with the demand for credit. The distinction is absolutely crucial for, as will be argued below, the true implication is that the supply of money in fact becomes a function of lending by the banking sector. This process would be constrained if reserve assets were controlled, and the economic implications have been ignored because of a failure to consider the way the authorities actually operate monetary policy.

It is perhaps worth considering the distinction between the demand for money and the demand for bank credit more closely. In each case we are concentrating on different sides of the banks' balance sheets. Behaviourally the demands must be very different and to confuse them is misleading and potentially dangerous. Monetary economics has been dominated by one side of the balance sheet, with bank liabilities generally being explained in terms of some automatic multiplier relationship. Extensions of this approach have introduced credit markets, but these have tended to concentrate on long-run equilibrium properties, and have seriously neglected the implied links with expenditure markets. The approach adopted here suggests that real and financial markets are closely integrated and should not be separated in this way.

Given the great scope for substitution between current and deposit accounts at little or no cost in the United Kingdom, it should be clear that any supply instability is nowhere near as likely to show up in a narrow aggregate such as M1, which should therefore be demand determined. For further justification of this position see Coghlan (1978b; 1980b, ch. 5). The exact definition of money is somewhat arbitrary, but something like sterling M3 (£M3), preferably excluding public sector balances, is probably the most suitable.

In defining money it is important to take account of the existing institutional structure. Banks have always been important because of the liquidity of their liabilities. This liquidity has enabled them to behave as 'liability managers' and play a crucial role in the expansion of the economy, a view, which we have seen above, clearly shared by Keynes (1937a, b). An important requirement for the smooth operation of such a system is that a bank can attract back sufficient deposits to cover the credit it has extended. At the time of the industrial revolution this was achieved through the operations of the discount houses in London acting as intermediary between the local banks, and later through the development of branch networks, which recycled funds from the country (the farming surpluses) to the towns (the industrial deficits) (see Dacey, 1967, Ch. VI). In this case the imbalances were geographical, although it was still the ultimate liquidity of bank deposits which ensured a high redeposit ratio.

These imbalances still exist, but there is now an additional imbalance associated with the size of loans and deposits as money circulates between individuals and companies. The recent growth in the importance of wholesale markets can be seen as a further development in banking structure designed to smooth out these imbalances. It could be argued that it would be wrong to consider the retail market in isolation from the wholesale market in the same way that it would be misleading to consider a single branch of a bank. It might still be supposed that only those banks providing current account facilities, essentially the clearing banks, should be included in the definition of the money supply. However, it is at this point that the importance of the institutional structure needs to be recognised. The other banks provide a range of banking services similar in many respects to the clearing banks, compete directly with the clearing banks in wholesale markets and are an important potential source of liquidity to the clearing banks (and vice versa) through the operation of the interbank market.

According to the approach adopted here the importance of banks resides not only in the liquidity of their deposits, though that is a fundamental characteristic, but more in the behavioural relationship between the asset and liability side of the balance sheet. It is this latter relationship, running from assets to liabilities, which is missing in the behaviour of other institutions, and justifies the exclusion of their deposits from the definition of the money supply. In any case, the deposits of, say, building societies do not serve as a means of payment in the same way that some bank deposits do. It is necessary to encash a building society deposit before it can be spent: it is money that serves as the means of payment not building society deposits. The significance of the growth of financial institutions providing portfolio substitutes for bank deposits is not necessarily that the definition of money should be extended, but rather that the banks will face increased competition and that, as a consequence, interest rates may become more volatile.

The importance of money depends on the liquidity of bank deposits, and is related to the role of banks in the creation of credit. This is the crucial importance of banks, and reflects a *relative* advantage rather than an absolute advantage. Of course, banks have to compete for deposits with other institutions, but that must always be true. Even if it were possible (and it is not) to define 'money' so widely that it had no substitutes it would be quite meaningless and totally uninteresting.

If reserves are freely available, then assuming fixed portfolio preferences, the money supply will change as a result of changes in the supply of bank advances; that is, interpreting advances broadly to include money lent to both private and public sectors, or as a result of net external flows to the private sector. Moreover, if we accept that advances can be largely exogenous, for example, because of such things as business confidence or restrictions on bank lending, then the possibility must exist that bank deposits can grow faster (or slower) than money holdings can be adjusted to their equilibrium values.

If the supply of money is determined independently of demand, then the components of demand must adjust in order to bring demand into line with supply. This adjustment is likely to take some time, depending upon a variety of factors which are discussed below, and in the interim there may exist an excess supply of money. The first question to be answered is in what sense the extra money that comes into existence can be thought of as being excessive. The explanation depends critically on the unique characteristics possessed by money. Friedman and Meiselman (1963) viewed money as a residual store of generalised purchasing power (see Coghlan, 1980b, Ch. 3), and Keynes also argued that money cannot be viewed in the same way as any other commodity; it is different in kind. Keynes put the argument in terms of government borrowing, but, given the financial system in existence, it could easily be extended to include all bank lending:

> There is no difficulty whatever in paying for the cost of the war [or any fiscal deficit] out of voluntary savings – provided that we put up with the consequences [by which Keynes meant inflationary price rises]. That is where the danger lies. A Government, which has control of the banking and currency system, can always find the cash to pay for its purchases of home produced goods. After allowing

for the yield of taxation and for the excess of imports over exports, the balance of the Government's expenditure necessarily remains in the hands of the public in the shape of voluntary savings. That is an arithmetical certainty; for the Government having taken the goods, out of which a proportion of the income of the public has been earned, there is nothing on which this proportion of income can be spent. If prices go up, the extra receipts swell someone's income, so that there is just as much left over as before. This argument is of such importance and is so little understood that it is worth our while to follow it out in detail. (Keynes, 1940, p. 61)

In a world in which reserves are freely available, the role of money as a means of payment means that this argument can be translated to the case of borrowing by the private sector. If an individual borrows money from a bank in order to purchase a commodity from within the private sector, then the payment when received is deposited with the banking system to be registered as an increase in the money supply. The money is accepted but it does not necessarily represent an equilibrium demand. While dynamic adjustment is possible, or, rather, inevitable, in the market for any commodity, and while these adjustments will necessarily have implications for other markets, the pervasive influence of money gives it an importance that results in a difference in kind rather than degree. The role of money as a means of payment means that it enters as intermediary in *all* market transactions. For this reason it is the perfect buffer to soak up any disequilibrium in an uncertain, imperfect world. Therefore, any disequilibrium in other markets is likely to be reflected in a disequilibrium in the money market. People will accept money but it would be wrong to suppose that they necessarily wish to retain ownership of it. Money is a means to an end, and only to a relatively minor degree (compared with the transactions it facilitates) is it an end in itself. Money is held but this does not mean that it represents an equilibrium demand for money. Any increase in the supply of money above the equilibrium demand must be followed by an adjustment in the determinants of demand in order to move towards equilibrium. These adjustments can take the form of output, price or interest rate changes and the actual response is obviously very important.

The argument that the supply of and demand for money are not in *equilibrium* should not be interpreted as suggesting that individuals and institutions are not behaving rationally. Equilibrium is a long-run concept, and has been defined as 'any condition in which all acting influences are cancelled by others resulting in a stable, balanced, or unchanging system' (Morris, 1973, p. 442). Because of transactions costs, limits to information, and the essential characteristic of money enabling the separation of the two sides of income and expenditure decisions, both temporally and spatially, money will be held without it necessarily being desired for its own sake. So although economic units can be thought of as optimising their money holdings in relation to their overall portfolio, incorporating all income/expenditure decisions, it need not be an equilibrium position in the sense that the existing relationship will not result in any further changes within the system.

The Process of Adjustment

The process of adjustment in response to an increase in the supply of money is likely to depend critically on, first, the uses for which the original advances were made, and second, the responses of the banking sector.

Money can come into existence as a result of bank lending to the public sector or the private sector and as a consequence of net external flows to the private sector. These are not mutually exclusive categories, since changes in any one of these may well be accompanied by off-setting movements in the others. In particular, the contribution of the public sector to the money supply can usefully be thought of as the difference between the size of the public sector borrowing requirement (PSBR) and the take up of public sector debt by the private sector. In order to simplify the discussion we shall begin by abstracting from the external account and consider only the uses to which domestically generated bank lending to the public and private sectors are put. This establishes the framework within which the external side is introduced subsequently.

It seems probable that the actual type of disequilibrium is likely to affect the length of time taken to correct it. A distinction can be drawn between credit extended for the purchase of existing assets and credit for direct use in income/expenditure markets. If there is an increase in credit which is used to purchase existing assets, in particular financial assets or dwellings, this will be only the beginning of a process of portfolio adjustment, which we might expect to some extent to be concentrated within asset markets. An individual may sell an existing asset because of a change in circumstances, including but not confined to a change in the price of the asset, in order to purchase an alternative asset. If this represents the general case, so that there is some form of market segmentation, the process of adjustment might take a long time. Obviously there will be income effects associated with those transactions, first in terms of payments to intermediaries (brokers of one type of another) and, secondly, as the asset stock changes in response to any shift in relative prices.

A more general use of borrowed funds, by the private or public sector, would be the purchase of goods and services, either for final use or as inputs to the productive process. This may result in a change in price in a particular market, but it is also possible that, in an economy characterised by imperfect markets, lags in adjustment, fixed contracts, stocks and unemployed resources, these extra demands will, at least initially, be accommodated through non-price adjustments. Money can therefore come into existence which is accepted only as a temporary intermediary between transactions, but which is in excess of the quantity desired for retention within existing portfolios. Even if there is some initial price/interest rate change as a result of a credit expansion, the relevant comparison is not with the return on money particularly but rather with the return on other physical and financial assets. Money is being held only in the process of adjustment, and in this case adjustment might be quite rapid and be concentrated in income/expenditure markets. To take one simple example, if a firm borrows money in order to expand the work force, there will be an immediate and equivalent rise in income accompanied by an increase in the demand for money. Adjustment will be quick, and there may not be any significant disequilibrium between supply and demand. For other examples income may respond more slowly and an excess supply of money may persist for some time.

We have arrived at an argument that suggests a direct relationship between money and income, which does not work through the simple mechanism of a restricted set of nominal yields on financial assets. It does not, however, depend upon the existence of perfectly competitive markets, and derives directly from Keynes' view of the financial system, incorporating a reasonable approximation of monetary policy as operated by the authorities.

In a market situation where the banks are free to bid for deposits, as exists at present in the United Kingdom, the process of adjustment can be affected markedly by changes in the interest rate paid on deposits relative to the return available on competing assets. By increasing this differential the banks can induce an increase in the demand for money which may at least partially eliminate any potential excess supply. Such a situation may come about if the demand for private sector advances is growing strongly, and is expected to continue, and the banks are faced with competition for funds from each other or from the public sector. If the non-bank financial intermediaries (NBFI) compete for funds, the effects of any excess supply may be amplified, since the *ceteris paribus* effect of such competition is to increase the velocity of circulation of existing money balances.

To the extent that the banks are effectively competing with the public sector the supply of money will also be greater, since less will be borrowed by the public sector from the non-bank private sector and consequently more will be borrowed from the banks. Thus changes in bank interest rates can influence both the demand for and the supply of money, and the relative effects will obviously be important. Strong competition from the banking sector can significantly affect the pattern of adjustment in response to an initial increase in the supply of money. In particular, if an increase in bank deposit rates increases the demand for bank deposits at the expense of public sector debt, the consequent rise in the money supply might be expected to have different implications for prices and expenditure than if the government simply increased their borrowing from the banking sector at previous interest rate relativities.

On the other hand, if the bank deposit/public sector debt interest differential goes the other way, the money supply can fall, but without fully closing the gap between the demand for and supply of money. It is, therefore, important to try to identify the effect of changes in interest rates on the demand for money, and to take these influences into account when discussing the effect of the stock of money on the economy.

The Primary and Secondary Effects of Money

It is possible to think of the total effect of a change in the money stock on the economy working through two separate channels, which might be called the *primary effect* and the *secondary effect*. The primary effect is directly related to the credit creation associated with the increase in the money supply, and the relationship between this new credit creation and increases in aggregate expenditure. In this view it is not sufficient for individuals in aggregate to *desire* to increase their investment — or more correctly their financial indebtedness — it is also necessary for the additional finance to be made available. For this purpose the banks play a crucial role in the provision of *new* finance. This was a point on which Keynes (1937a, b) placed great emphasis *after* he had written *The General Theory* (see pp. 27–8 above).

A raising of 'animal spirits' has different implications for investment, and the economy, depending upon whether new finance is readily available or not. And indeed, the expectations themselves may be strongly influenced by the availability of credit. The actual outcome of this primary effect is likely to depend on the way in which the new money comes into existence, and the uses to which the credit is put. The process of money creation — through credit markets — reintroduces many influences more generally thought of as Keynesian which can drive the economy, even though the channels of influence are through the money supply.

The secondary effect refers to the continuing influence of money on the economy in the process of bringing demand and supply into equilibrium. It is unlikely that the primary effect will complete this process, and there are anyway likely to be lags in adjustment that will change, and even perhaps reverse, the initial response. The exact speed and pattern of adjustment will depend on the interaction of the various agents, including the banks, in the economy, and their reactions to the disequilibrium. These secondary effects will probably take some time to be completed.

The secondary effect refers to the disequilibrium reactions associated with an excess supply of money, and is closely related to the disequilibrium real balance effect (see, for example, Archibald and Lipsey, 1958, and Chapter 2 above). To this extent the way money comes into existence is not relevant. Previous models which have incorporated disequilibrium monetary effects (see Chapter 2) have restricted the influence of money to this 'secondary effect' and have neglected any effect resulting from the actual creation of money. Such an approach is useful for analysing the process of adjustment to exogenous real shocks, but attaches no importance to the process of money creation. Such models are, therefore, seriously incomplete.

These two effects combine to provide a direct relationship between money and the economy. The approach cannot really be termed monetarist since the money stock is not regarded as an exogenous variable *directly* under the control of the authorities, although they do have control over instruments that will influence the money supply. It, in fact, makes no sense even to talk about the effect of money on the economy — only the individual influences on the money supply. Money is simply the channel through which such changes work their way through the economy.

It is sometimes suggested that the demand for bonds can be thought of as the inverse of the demand for money. Even in a Keynesian world containing a variety of financial assets of differing type and maturity, this is difficult to justify; within this model such a presumption would be completely incorrect. The demand for bonds is likely to have a substantial effect on the *supply* of money, and may also have an effect on the demand for money — depending on relative interest elasticities. Money is envisaged to be a substitute for all goods, financial and real, in the economy, not simply for long-dated public sector debt.

Once we look more closely at the determinants of credit flows, it is clear that we should expect there to be some direct substitution between private sector borrowing from the banking sector and borrowing from abroad. An external capital inflow need not necessarily, therefore, be associated with an excess demand for money, but could result from an excess demand for credit. Inflows can occur because of credit demands without any prior change in the determinants of the demand for money. This is one reason (though others can be adduced) why the expansion of domestic credit (DCE) is unlikely to be exogenously determined by the authorities. It is necessary now to consider these external relations in more detail.

Monetary Disequilibrium and the Balance of Payments

The argument so far has been developed within the context of a closed economy, and this is further complicated when the analysis is extended to an open economy. Extending the model in this way reveals the same problems for the international monetary approach that the closed economy model exposed in the high-powered money multiplier supply mechanism. These centre on the failure to take account of the distinction between the demand for money and the demand for credit. If anything, this distinction is even more crucial for the international monetary argument. There is no disagreement with the definition of the balance of payments as a monetary phenomenon, and the equilibrium conditions remain the same, but it is not possible to describe disequilibrium situations, and the process of adjustment, simply in terms of the gap between the demand for and supply of money.

The monetary approach to the balance of payments (MABP) emphasises the relationship between the balance of payments,[1] and/or the exchange rate, and divergences between the supply of, and demand for, money. If the exchange rate is fixed, the authorities can only control domestic credit, and the quantity of foreign reserves and the supply of money become endogenous. In the case of floating exchange rates reserves are given, the money supply becomes a potential control variable, and the exchange rate changes in order to restore equilibrium. The argument that follows is conducted in terms of fixed exchange rates, as is normally the case, but it can easily be turned around to apply to a situation where exchange rates are allowed to find their own level. It should also be pointed out, and it will become clear below, that although the disequilibrium mechanism mentioned above is rejected as a general description of the process involved, the conclusions regarding potential control remain unaltered.

Main attention is centred on the suggestion that balance of payments disequilibrium is associated with disequilibrium between the demand for and supply of money. This contention is found embedded in the very foundations of the monetary approach. There are many references to this effect in an essay written by Frenkel and Johnson (1976b) introducing some of the major papers that have been written in this area. For example, 'a surplus in the money account reflects an excess domestic flow demand for money', so that naturally 'the monetary approach focuses on the determinants of the excess domestic flow demand for, or supply of, money' (Frenkel and Johnson, 1976b, p. 21). The following description of the adjustment process comes from one of Harry Johnson's contributions to that volume (Johnson, 1976, p. 273):

> Disequilibrium between the demand for money and the initial stock will be corrected through a divergence of expenditure from income

and a balance of payments surplus continuing until its cumulative effect has been to make the stock of money held by domestic residents equal to the quantity demanded, as determined by real income and the price level... Balance of payments policies will not produce an inflow of international reserves unless they increase the quantity of money demanded, and unless domestic credit policy forces the resident population to acquire the extra money wanted through the balance of payments via an excess of receipts over out-payments; the balance of payments surplus will continue only until its cumulative effect in increasing domestic money holdings satisfies the domestic demand for money.

There would therefore seem to be no room for ambiguity about the suggested process; disequilibrium in the balance of payments will be related to inequality between the demand for and supply of money. This argument can be easily summarised as

$$\Delta R = f(M^d - M^s) \tag{3.1}$$

The change in foreign reserves, ΔR, is related to the gap between the demand for, and supply of, money $(M^d - M^s)$. (The exact definition of foreign reserves is important to the argument and this is considered further below.)

Moreover, 'the essential foundation of the monetary approach is the assumption that the demand for money is a stable function of a few macroeconomic variables' (Frenkel and Johnson, 1976b, p. 25). Thus, for example, given real income, Y, prices, P, and interest rates, r, the demand for money can be written as

$$M^d = g(Y, P, r) \tag{3.2}$$

Therefore, real disturbances which change any of these behavioural determinants will also create a monetary disequilibrium. In addition, of course, any monetary disequilibrium originating in the rest of the world (ROW) will feed back to the domestic economy. This implies that we may observe a balance of payments disequilibrium without there being any apparent imbalance between the demand for and supply of money. For example, if the result of excess money balances (that is, excess to equilibrium) in ROW is to increase the exports of the domestic economy then domestic incomes will rise along with the money supply, and the *demand* for money may also rise by an equiv-alent amount. However, even if the supply of and demand for money increase simultaneously, this does not rule out subsequent adjustment to restore equilibrium on the balance of payments Tsiang (1977) has pointed out the inconsistency of the monetary argument in apparently ignoring the income elasticity of the demand for money, thereby requiring the demand for money not to vary with income during the process of adjustment.

One area in which the MABP is deficient is in its neglect of the process through which the money supply actually comes into existence. Once this is taken into account, the analysis needs to be further qualified. This does not deny that the balance of payments is a monetary phenomenon, nor that the equilibrium conclusions of the international monetarists still hold; what it does do is substantially qualify the adjustment mechanism that has been widely referred to in the literature. This is important because if the monetary approach is to have practical value, it must be capable of describing disequilibrium situations, and the path and timing of any return towards equilibrium.

Given the present organisation of the monetary system in the United Kingdom, and in most other countries, the money supply is not controlled directly by restricting the availability of bank reserve assets, but through changing the price at which bank reserves will be supplied. This approach, combined with the political sensitivity of interest-rate movements, means that the domestic contribution to the supply of money will be determined by the quantity of credit (to all customers) provided by the banks. This process was described above for a closed economy. It was emphasised that there is no necessary requirement for the equilibrium demand for money to change by the same amount as the demand for bank credit, and therefore the supply of money, though the motives for demanding bank credit should also result in expenditures (on goods and securities) that will have the effect of raising the demand for money. The speed with which equilibrium is achieved depends critically on the form the expenditures take. This model now needs to be extended to allow for external currency flows influencing the money supply, and adjustment through the balance of payments.

The idea that there can be disequilibrium between the demand for and supply of money is not new, and, of course, underlies the monetary approach to the balance of payments. However, there are important implications for this model once we recognise the significance of the demand for credit in determining the money supply, and that there is no need for this to be matched, in the short term, by an equilibrium demand for money, or if it is, only because of the expenditures facilitated by the credit creation. It should be helpful to consider one or two examples. In all cases we start from a position of universal equilibrium, and assume there are no exogenous shifts in real variables (apart from an increase in credit demand).

First, suppose that there is an increase in the demand for bank credit but that it cannot be provided domestically, perhaps because of quantitative restrictions on bank credit expansion to the private sector. There is no reason why the additional credit cannot be provided from overseas. In this case there will be an increase in reserves and the money stock, not caused by any prior excess demand for money, which will result in an excess supply. The MABP would suggest that a surplus on the balance of payments should be associated with an excess of money demand over money supply. Given a stable demand for money as a function of a few variables (for example, equation 3.2) the MABP requires one of these behavioural determinants of the demand for money to change, with a fixed money supply, in order to create a balance of payments disequilibrium. We now find, however, that the determinants of credit demand are also capable of creating such a situation. Moreover the MABP provides support for this process, once the money-supply mechanism is recognised, for if the behavioural determinants of the demand for bank credit and the demand for money were the same, there could be no disequilibrium between the supply of and demand for money. The process and speed of adjustment will depend on the uses to which the credit is put, and this is considered below. It is, however, unlikely to depend on disequilibrium between the demand for and supply of money.

One obvious example where an inflow from abroad in response to a demand for credit will not result in automatic monetary disequilibrium, or compensating outflows, is when the borrowing is undertaken by the public sector. If the balance of payment is defined as the 'balance for official financing', or confined to the current account and long-term capital account (the so-called 'basic balance'), then the purchase of public sector debt from abroad will lead to a balance of payments surplus, but will have no direct effect on the money supply. An indirect effect is possible if the inflows stimulate confidence in the economy. However, in this case the effect is likely to be a *reduction* in the money supply, as sales of public sector debt to the non-bank private sector will be encouraged. The process is explained in detail below, where it is also suggested that the correct application of the monetary approach requires a redefinition of the external component of the money supply.

Even if we restrict our attention to the private sector, it is still possible for there to be a direct substitution of borrowing from abroad for domestic credit. In this case there will be inflows across exchanges but no necessary monetary disequilibrium. The possibility of such substitution is made more likely by the existence of large multinational companies operating in the United Kingdom. It should therefore be clear that one implication of this suggested approach to money supply determination is that there are likely to be substitutions between the various sources of credit, and in particular that DCE is unlikely to be exogenously determined by the authorities. Or even if it is directly controlled, inflows can occur because of credit demands without any prior change in the determinants of the demand for money.

It may well be that control of DCE is a suitable objective for the authorities to follow, but this does not mean that they have done so, and, even more importantly, such an assumption ignores the process through which control is achieved. After all, DCE has not been *directly* determined by the authorities, but has resulted from behavioural interrelationships between all sectors of the economy – including the overseas sector if, as argued above, there is substitution between domestic and external finance. To take DCE as exogenous ignores the channels through which control may be exercised, and the problems involved. If these questions are ignored, not only does the analysis become rather sterile, in the sense that it does injustice to the institutional structure, but it abstracts from important political–economic decisions, and is incapable of analysing the real policy choices facing the authorities.

We turn now to consider increases in the money supply resulting from an expansion of domestic credit. One possible use of new credit is the purchase of existing assets. In that case disequilibrium between the demand for and supply of money could persist for some time, but without resulting in substantial external flows. For example, if the new credit is demanded because of an increase in the demand for housing, relative returns and income/expenditure may be slow to change. Because of uncertainty and imperfect information and markets, an excess supply of money may exist under such circumstances without causing a balance of payments outflow. In fact the balance of payments may only respond as the disequilibrium is transmitted to other markets.

Suppose, on the other hand, that new money is spent in such a way that it leads to an increase in the demand for money. It is even possible that if the money, the new credit, is spent on increasing wage payments, for example, then demand might actually increase to the same extent as supply. But that does not mean there will be no repercussions on the balance of payments. As the increase in income is spent some will flow abroad, thereby reducing the supply of money, income and consequently the demand for money. All will be moving together; the fact that balance of payments equilibrium requires money market equilibrium is irrelevant to the process of adjustment. (We are back with Tsiang's observation of simultaneous adjustment.) It should be clear from these examples that there is no necessary connection between balance of payments disequilibrium and inequality between the demand for and supply of money.

Before proceeding to consider how we are to define the various components of the money supply in practice, it is of interest to consider the attempts that have been made to verify empirically the validity of the monetary approach. Two criteria are generally thought to be fundamental: first, domestic credit expansion must be exogenous (see below), and second, the demand for money must be a stable function of a few variables. The first is usually taken as datum (explicitly or implicitly), and empirical testing has concentrated on the latter. These studies have in general been successful, within their own terms of reference, in that they have been able to conclude that a stable demand for money can be identified (see, for example, the evidence and references contained in the volume edited by Frenkel and Johnson, 1976a).

It is obviously true that the MABP, or any monetary approach, depends crucially on the existence of a stable demand for money function. However, it is quite another thing to be able to measure it directly employing nonsimultaneous equation techniques. Within the monetarist framework the supply of money is always adjusting towards demand (in other words, demand and supply are not equal), with, it would seem, quite long lags which are reflected in balance of payments disequilibrium. In consequence, single equation techniques should be incapable of identifying a stable demand for money schedule – even though such a stable relationship may actually exist. Thus the claims that stable demand functions have been estimated, far from providing strong support for the monetarist cause, are more suggestive that that particular approach is invalid. The introduction of the further complications discussed above only serves to make it even more unlikely that a stable demand relationship can be identified in this way.

Defining Foreign Reserves

Adherents of the monetary approach of the balance of payments write the supply of money as

$$M \equiv D + R \qquad (3.3)$$

where

M = the stock of money
D = the stock of domestic credit
R = the stock of foreign reserves, the external counterpart of the money supply

and ΔR reflects any balance of payments disequilibrium.

The monetarist description of the endogeneity of foreign reserves (and money) obviously requires reserves and domestic credit to be statistically independent. It would not be much use if a change in foreign reserves automatically implied an identical change in domestic credit in the opposite direction. The normal assumption, in fact, is that domestic credit is exogenous, determined by the authorities, and therefore totally independent of any change in reserves. Of course, there is always the possibility of a behavioural relationship existing, at least in the short run, through the 'reactions' of the authorities to sterilise reserve changes. This is, however, very different from the existence of a direct statistical dependence between the two series.

Any use of this approach for the analysis of the UK economy naturally requires an empirical interpretation of identity (3.3). It was pointed out in Chapter 2 that changes in foreign reserves have nearly always been assumed to be the 'balance-for official financing' (BOF). This is, however, invalid, and such an assumption is misleading. Because of the importance now given to money-supply statistics, and to the balance of payments, it is essential that the interrelationships existing between these two aggregates are fully understood. The best way of ensuring this is to identify as closely as possible those flows having an independent influence on the domestic money supply.

To begin with we need to establish three basic identities: for money, the public sector borrowing requirements (PSBR) and BOF.

The central definition of the money supply employed in the United Kingdom is sterling M3 (£M3) and it is on this we shall concentrate our attention.

$$\Delta \pounds M3 \equiv \Delta NC + \Delta \pounds Lg + \Delta \pounds L - (\Delta Df - \Delta Lf) - (\Delta \$D - \Delta \$L)$$

$$- (\Delta \$Dg - \Delta \$Lg) - \Delta NDL \tag{3.4}$$

The change in £M3 is equal to the changes in notes and coins, ΔNC, bank lending in sterling to the private and public sectors, $\Delta \pounds L$ and $\Delta \pounds Lg$, the net overseas indebtedness of the banking sector. $(\Delta Df - \Delta Lf)$, the net foreign currency position of the private and public sectors with the banks, $(\Delta \$D - \Delta \$L)$ and $(\Delta \$Dg - \Delta \$Lg)$, and the change in the non-deposit liabilities of the banking sector, ΔNDL.

$$PSBR \equiv \Delta NC + \Delta B + \Delta Bf + \Delta \pounds Lg + \Delta \$Lg - BOF \tag{3.5}$$

The PSBR plus BOF is financed by issues of notes and coins, and net lending by the private, overseas[2] and banking sectors to the public sector, ΔB, ΔBf, $\Delta \pounds Lg$ and $\Delta \$Lg$.

$$BOF \equiv CA + \Delta Nf + \Delta Bf + (\Delta Df - \Delta Lf) \tag{3.6}$$

BOF is equal to the current account plus the change in net overseas lending from abroad to the private and public sectors, ΔNf and ΔBf, plus the banking sector's net overseas indebtedness.

In order to obtain BOF on the right-hand side of the money supply identity we need to substitute for $\Delta \pounds Lg$ in (3.4) from (3.5).

$$\Delta \pounds M3 \equiv PSBR - \Delta B + \Delta \pounds L + BOF - \Delta Bf - (\Delta Df - \Delta Lf)$$

$$- (\Delta \$D - \Delta \$L) - \Delta \$Dg - \Delta NDL \tag{3.7}$$

Comparing this expression with identity (3.3) we can see that if BOF is equal to the change in the external counterparts of the money supply the remaining terms on the right-hand side must be equal to the change in domestic credit. This, however, is a most unsatisfactory set of definitions, as should be clear from an inspection of the components making up BOF, identity (3.6). To take just one example, an increase in public sector borrowing from abroad will increase BOF *and* Bf, in identity (3.7), by an exactly equal, and offsetting amount. To the extent that BOF can be interpreted as a change in the external counterpart to the money supply this means that there is an exactly equal and opposite change in domestic credit and foreign reserves. A change in BOF tells us absolutely nothing about the money supply, past, present or future. This is hardly consistent with the monetary approach, which at a very minimum requires the definition of domestic credit to be independent of the definition of the external counterparts. Moreover, it should be clear that any attempt to employ these definitions to determine empirically the causal relationship between DCE and foreign reserves will be biased by the inclusion of common elements in both variables.

In order to concentrate attention on those elements of the external account that have an independent effect on the money supply, it is necessary to substitute for BOF from identity (3.6). This gives

$$\Delta \text{£M3} \equiv [(\text{PSBR} - \Delta \$ \text{Dg}) - \Delta B + \Delta \text{£L}] + CA + \Delta NF$$

$$- (\Delta \$ D - \Delta \$ L) - \Delta \text{NDL} \tag{3.8}$$

However, even this fails to identify separate components of the money supply that are statistically independent of one another. This is because there are components of the current account of the balance of payments which represent flows to, or from, the public sector. These in turn represent income or expenditure items which enter into the PSBR. For example, Government purchases of aircraft from abroad would represent an outflow on the current account and an equal, offsetting, increase in the PSBR (expenditure minus income). It is therefore possible conceptually, though not in practice, to split the PSBR into that part which results from domestic expenditure exceeding domestic income, the domestic PSBR (DPSBR), and that part resulting from foreign expenditure exceeding foreign income, the foreign PSBR (FPSBR); in other words,

$$\text{PSBR} \equiv \text{DPSBR} + \text{FPSBR} \tag{3.9}$$

In order to eliminate the common elements from the analysis, it is necessary to subtract FPSBR from both the PSBR and the current account. That leaves the domestic borrowing requirement and the current account transactions of the private sector, CAPR. The new identity we end up with is

$$\Delta\text{£M3} \equiv [(\text{DPSBR} - \Delta\text{\$Dg}) - \Delta\text{B} + \Delta\text{£L}] + \text{CAPR}$$

$$+ \Delta\text{Nf} - (\Delta\text{\$D} - \Delta\text{\$L}) - \Delta\text{NDL} \tag{3.10}$$

where each of the components is statistically (although not necessarily behaviourally) independent of the others. By defining those flows contained within the square brackets as domestic credit expansion we can see that the external influences are restricted to the current account transactions of the private sector, net foreign lending to the UK non-bank private sector, and the change in the private sector's net foreign currency position with the banks. A more convenient categorisation, however, is to aggregate these flows together and define those external transactions affecting £M3 as the current account of, and net overseas capital flows to, the private sector *as long as they are converted to sterling*. The change in public sector foreign currency deposits, $\Delta\text{\$Dg}$, has been substracted from the DPSBR in order to eliminate any statistical dependence between DCE and external flows. Otherwise, if these flows were included among the external counterparts, the PSBR would increase by the same extent, $\Delta\text{\$Dg}$, that external flows fell, and there would be no net effect on the money supply. This procedure is anyway more consistent with the idea of taking the public sector's borrowing needs as predetermined.

It may help to clarify the position if we compare this exposition with the official definitions as contained in table 11.3 of the *Bank of England Quarterly Bulletin*. The first thing to notice is that officially domestic credit expansion is defined to include sterling lending to overseas, as well as the FPSBR and foreign currency deposits of the public sector. If we are to follow suit and add these items to domestic credit expansion, we must necessarily subtract them from the external counterpart, giving

$$\Delta\text{£M3} \equiv [\text{PSBR} - \Delta\text{B} + \Delta\text{£L} + \Delta\text{£Lf}] + \text{CA} + \Delta\text{Nf}$$

$$- (\Delta\text{\$D} - \Delta\text{\$L}) - \Delta\text{\$Dg} - \Delta\text{£Lf} - \Delta\text{NDL} \tag{3.11}$$

Domestic credit is now as officially defined, so it remains only to see if the external influences defined here are reconcilable with 'external and foreign currency finance' (EFCF) as defined in table 11.3 of the *Bulletin*. EFCF is broken down in terms of flows to:

$$\text{Public sector} = \text{BOF} - \Delta\text{Bf} - \Delta\text{\$Lg}$$

that is, official financing of the balance of payments, BOF, less market related flows to the public sector from abroad, ΔBf, and foreign currency lending by the banks to the public sector, $\Delta\$$Lg,

$$\text{overseas sterling deposits} = -\Delta\text{£Df}$$

and

$$\text{foreign currency deposits (net)} = -(\Delta\$D - \Delta\$L)$$

$$-(\Delta\$Dg - \Delta\$Lg)$$

$$-(\Delta\$Df - \Delta\$Lf)$$

This is quite straightforward and defines the banks' switched position.

Combining these three expressions gives

$$\text{EFCF} \equiv \text{BOF} - \Delta\text{Bf} - \Delta\$\text{Lg} - \Delta\text{£Df} - (\Delta\$D - \Delta\$L)$$

$$- (\Delta\$Dg - \Delta\$Lg) - (\Delta\$Df - \Delta\$Lf) \qquad (3.12)$$

This certainly reinforces our previous argument that BOF is a totally inadequate measure of the external influence on the money supply (and, of course, changes in the level of official reserves would be even less useful in this role). However, it remains necessary to reconcile this definition with that previously obtained in identity (3.11). At first sight this may seem a difficult task since they appear to be very different and totally unrelated. If they are indeed equal, being different definitions of the same total, then the result of setting them equal to each other would be the definition of BOF given in identity (3.6). And that, in fact, is what happens. In other words,

$$\text{BOF} - \Delta\text{Bf} - \Delta\$\text{Lg} - \Delta\text{£Df} - (\Delta\$D - \Delta\$L)$$

$$- (\Delta\$Dg - \Delta\$Lg) - (\Delta\$Df - \Delta\$Lf)$$

$$\equiv \text{CA} + \Delta\text{Nf} - (\Delta\$D - \Delta\$L) - \Delta\$Dg - \Delta\text{£Lf}$$

reduces to

$$\text{BOF} \equiv \text{CA} + \Delta\text{Nf} + \Delta\text{Bf} + (\Delta\text{Df} - \Delta\text{Lf}) \qquad (3.6)$$

It is interesting to note that the way DCE and external influences have been officially defined introduces a direct statistical relationship between the two supposedly independent influences. EFCF as defined in identity (3.12) may on the face of it appear to be independent of DCE in that it contains no items automatically identifiable with the components of DCE. However, since EFCF is also equal to the external counterparts identified in (3.11) we can easily see that the public sector's current account transactions, banks' sterling lending overseas and any change in the public sector's foreign currency bank deposits are all included in DCE *and*, with an opposite sign, in the external counterpart. The inclusion of these common elements would obviously bias the results of any statistical attempts to verify the monetarist hypothesis. Such a test would first require the cancellation of these offsetting items, and this would return us to identity (3.10), which would therefore seem the most logical starting point for any empirical test. There is a problem, however, in that it is not possible to identify separately many, if not most, of the public sector's current account transactions. In practice there will always remain certain common elements that will bias any statistical test in favour of confirming the monetarist's hypothesis, which is not to deny that such a behavioural relationship may actually exist.

This example provides a good illustration of the problems to be faced in trying to obtain reliable evidence and to identify in the real world the practical counterparts of the abstract theory. Great care must therefore be taken in defining the concepts implied by the abstract theory of the monetary approach. As is so often the case, the correspondence between theory and reality is not as close as might be superficially supposed. It is, in fact, quite easy for us all to give different meanings to the same word. In addition, the obvious importance of credit flows in the supply function we have ended up with illustrates the danger of ignoring the demands for credit in any analysis of monetary adjustment mechanisms.

Sterlisation of External Currency Flows

Reference was made above to the possibility that the authorities may adopt a policy of deliberately offsetting any external currency flows. It is quite easy to see from identity (3.10) that if, for example, the current account of the private sector were in deficit, thereby tending to reduce the money supply, this could be offset by deliberate action by the authorities either to reduces sales of debt to the non-bank private sector, or to increase the DPSBR. Alternatively, the private sector could offset this tendency by borrowing more from the banks or overseas, and, of course, the opposite reactions would serve to sterilise a current account surplus.

The monetarists would naturally protest that the ability to sterilise a balance of payments deficit is strictly limited by the finiteness of foreign reserves, and the limited ability of the government to borrow from abroad. This is obviously true and should be taken into account. However, no such constraint limits the authorities' ability to neutralise a foreign currency inflow, and furthermore, this asymmetry in the practicalities of sterilisation has important implications for the adjustment towards balance of payments equilibrium.

The old Gold Standard system, to which the monetarist approach is often compared, is generally described in terms of symmetrical adjustment. Deficit countries experience a contraction of the money supply and a deflation of the economy, while in surplus countries the money supply automatically increases, and with it the level of demand. In this way the surplus and deficit countries are working together in order to resolve the underlying disequilibrium. With the introduction of the possibility of sterilising inflows but not outflows (except temporarily) this international harmony is no longer guaranteed. Now the whole burden of adjustment is placed on the deficit countries, regardless of the underlying causes of the initial disequilibrium.

It should be added that this argument is only concerned with the practical possibilities of sterilisation, and not with any value judgements concerning the desirability of such actions. It may be the case that certain countries are following excessively inflationary policies, so that the surplus countries may view any ability to neutralise these forces as a necessary means of restraining the inflationary tendencies of the expansionary economies. The justice of the situation need not concern us here, but it should be clear that there are quite likely to exist circumstances in which placing the weight of adjustment upon the deficit countries is inappropriate as a means of resolving the imbalance that may have arisen.

Controlling the money supply

The discussion so far illustrates the problems facing the monetary authorities in employing rates of interest as the main instrument of monetary policy. In the first place, faced with strong demand for loans by the private sector, the banks will compete strongly for deposits. Under these circumstances, moderate increases in the rate of interest on public sector debt may not succeed in curtailing the credit expansion and a temporarily unstable situation may develop. This will be only temporary because the cost of borrowing will also be increasing, even if the banks reduce their borrowing–lending differential. A persistent rise in interest rates must eventually succeed in stopping the expansion, with the likelihood of an evaporation of the previous high level of credit demand. Allowing for lags in response it is probable that a gap will then open up between bank deposit rates and alternative interest rates, so that the demand for money will actually fall. In this case, although the supply of money may appear to be under control, there may still be an excess supply which will continue to affect the rest of the economy. The monetary authorities can therefore succeed in reducing the stock of money but without resolving the underlying disequilibrium. Even if they succeed in changing expectations, it is not clear, given the adjustment process outlined above, that this will reduce the existing excess supply of money, or its effects on the economy. To the extent that the authorities can control only the level of particular interest rates, rather than being able to 'fine tune' interest rate differentials, there is the possibility that short-term control may be difficult to achieve. The control solution in such a case requires a reduction of borrowing from the banking sector, and/or a reduction in the net sterling receipts of the private sector from abroad. Attempting to achieve such control through the banking sector requires a reduction in bank credit to either the public or private sectors, and some rational criteria should be employed in determining which should go short.

An increase in public sector interest rates may also succeed in attracting additional funds from abroad into public sector debt. It is sometimes suggested that this inflow will actually lead to an increase in the money supply. In fact, as should be clear from the discussion above, such *additional* flows make no difference at all unless, that is, they increase confidence in the performance of the economy, and/or the public sector's funding programme, resulting in increased domestic purchases of gilts and a *reduction* in the money supply. Also, if the external inflow into public sector debt has been diverted from the private sector, there will be a reduction in the money supply. So again it will be relative interest rates that will be important, and if all rates move up together it may only succeed in increasing the supply of money.

These control problems are made worse by the possibility that a monetary expansion may reflect only a reallocation of private sector portfolios towards the banks. In this situation, when the demand for and supply of money are changing at the same rate, there may be no immediate problem. It will, however, be difficult to identify exactly what is happening, and the monetary authorities may be forced to try to sell even more public sector debt in response to unfavourable comment, at a time when such action is inappropriate. Such action is anyway unlikely to achieve its objective easily, and may prove unduly disruptive to the private sector of the economy. This is of some importance, since control of monetary conditions generally is only a means to an end and is not an ultimate objective in itself.

Conclusion

The model outlined above was based on *Keynes*-ian foundations, with the money supply changing in response to movements in bank credit (broadly defined) and external flows to the private sector. When combined with a stable demand function this supply mechanism suggests a direct relationship between money and output and prices. The speed of adjustment will depend on, among other things, the use to which the credit is put, and the reaction of the banking sector in bidding for deposits. The discussion has therefore been in terms of a disequilibrium framework with the supply of money being accommodated via channels very similar to those underlying a monetarist explanation, but with the quantity of money not being determined in response to an exogenously determined monetary base.

It was also shown that it is not possible to argue that balance of payments disequilibrium is necessarily related to the non-equality of the domestic demand for money with its supply. Moreover, neither the balance for official financing, nor the implied official definition of 'external and foreign currency finance', provide unambiguous measures of the external influences on the money supply which are independent of domestic credit expansion. The net effects of the foreign account are restricted to the current account of, and net overseas lending to, the non-bank private sector, less the net change in the foreign currency position of the UK private sector with the banks. It is important to understand these relationships if money and the balance of payments are to be reconciled.

An important implication of the general argument is that there are circumstances under which the private sector of the economy is capable of generating its own expansion without the need for an 'exogenous' fiscal stimulus. It does, however, require that the banking system be permitted to meet the increased demands for credit made by the private sector.

Notes

1 That is the balance of payments broadly defined to include current and capital account flows.
2 This obviously does not include that overseas lending which is a counterpart of the official financing requirement, but it does include all other public sector flows entering the capital account of the balance of payments.

4

A Survey of UK Monetary Policy
Since 1945

This chapter is divided into two parts. The first briefly surveys the development of monetary policy since 1945. The second part considers the operation of certain monetary control instruments and important changes to the monetary system in rather more detail. An appendix at the end provides a concise summary of the main changes in economic policy over the period.

The Historical Development of Monetary Policy

The problem of immediate postwar reconstruction fell to the newly elected Labour government.[1] The prime task was clearly defined and the approach adopted was bound to require the extension, for some time at least, of the wartime controls over the allocation of rationing of necessary materials and goods. The attainment of convertibility for the pound also took on the aspect of a major objective, partly, at least, in response to American demands. However, as was to prove the case, in a world of inconvertibility and dollar famine such a move was doomed to disaster.

Responsibility of the government for the state of the economy had already been accepted, with the annual budget seen as the major means of control. Explicit acceptance of this responsibility dates from Kingsley Wood's 1941 budget (see Sayers, 1956; Dow, 1964, and Brittan, 1971). Also, following the wartime government, postwar governments were for a long time to ignore monetary policy altogether and then only to employ it sparingly through direct administrative controls.

The main task of reconstruction entailed the correction of the passive balance of payments, and while some inflationary pressure was expected, it was thought that it would be only temporary. The worry was rather that severe deflationary pressure would soon appear in the world in general, and in the United Kingdom in particular, thus following the pattern of the post-First World War experience.

As the troops demobilized so the economy started the enormous shift of resources to civilian use. During the war the government had dominated economic life (and life itself); now with the coming of peace a massive redirection of economic effort was required.

The first postwar Chancellor of the Exchequer, Hugh Dalton, quickly embarked on a 'cheap money' policy that became a hallmark of this early period. In 1945 Treasury bill rate was halved from 1 to $\frac{1}{2}$ per cent, and over the next two years a great effort was made to reduce the long rate from 3 to $2\frac{1}{2}$ per cent. The objective of these measures was to reduce charges on the National Debt and the cost of public and private borrowing for investment purposes.

At this time, and for some time to come, inflationary pressure was not associated with increases in the money supply, but at least the pressure of demand was thought to be important. So when such pressure was discerned, as in 1947, the result was deflationary fiscal policy; details of fiscal policy changes are given in the appendix. The financing of the public sector deficit was not seen as a problem, and was not even mentioned in economic statements at the time.

Dow (1964, p. 29) concluded that the two-and-a-half years to November 1947, and the end of Dalton's Chancellorship, had witnessed the smooth and practically complete transition from a war to peace economy. The time had now come to build a strong and prosperous economy on the foundations already laid down. The new Chancellor, Sir Stafford Cripps, attempted by means of a combination of exhortation and compulsion to obtain the cooperation of the different sections of the economy in making and maintaining the present sacrifices required to realize future prosperity and security. There were 'voluntary' restraints on dividends and advertising, and on wages – supported by the 'Statement' on wages issued in February 1948. The result was that up until October 1950 wages were effectively restrained to increase less rapidly than retail prices. And so began the direct intervention in the labour market which has continued in much the same way to the present day. (See Appendix to this chapter. Details of Prices and Incomes policies are included in the Appendix because of their perceived importance as an instrument of macroeconomic policy. Such a policy has often been proposed as an alternative to monetary policy for controlling inflation, and sometimes as a supplement, reducing the possible implications for employment of a tight monetary policy.)

The summer of 1949 brought with it a severe exchange crisis, which Dow (1964, p. 42) blamed on the dollar deficit of the overseas sterling area, with speculation essentially playing a secondary role. Despite cuts in dollar imports imposed by the United Kingdom and the Commonwealth in July, the government was forced to devalue on 18 September 1949. The initial devaluation against the dollar was 30 per cent, to $2.80 to the pound, but following the inevitably secondary realignments this was reduced to an average devaluation of 15 per cent (OEEC report, 1950). By the end of 1949 well over half the reserves that had been lost were recovered, and by April 1950 the pre-crisis situation had been re-established and the prospects for the external account were favourable.

Just as the United Kingdom was recovering from the disruption of war so a new disturbance emerged. A combination of rapid world expansion, massive rearmament programmes in the United States and other industrial countries in response to the Korean conflict, and precautionary stockpiling under the assumption of continuing shortages over the long term, resulted in an explosive rise in commodity prices. The price of rubber rose $3\frac{1}{2}$ times within a year; wool and cotton doubled in price; the price of other raw materials rose by 50 per cent, and that of food slightly less. The outcome was that import prices rose by 59 per cent between December 1949 and June 1951, and the price of imported raw materials rose by 115 per cent. This worsened the balance of payments and 'gave ... violent new impetus to the mechanics of internal wage and price inflation' (Dow, 1964, p. 56).

The year 1951 saw the first tentative signs of some form of monetary, or financial, policy. Guidance was given to the Capital Issues Committee on allowable lending, and the clearing banks were requested to moderate their lending. Interest rates were now coming to be used more actively as a policy instrument and in January 1952 hire purchase restrictions were introduced on certain consumer durables (see appendix). Over the next three years there was a definite movement towards a more active monetary policy − by which is meant a policy of direct controls on interest rates and credit availability.

In 1955 there was yet another run on sterling, and in July quantitative restrictions were placed on advances made by the clearing banks. These restrictions remained in force until July 1958, at which time there was a general relaxation of financial policy. In abolishing the lending restrictions the Chancellor of the day, Heathcoat Amory, added that he hoped quantitative requests would not have to be made in the future. Unfortunately, this was not to be and quantitative restrictions on bank lending were in operation from 1965 to 1971 (see appendix for details).

During the latter half of the 1950s, there was a major review of the operation of monetary policy, and the findings were published on 20 August 1959 (Radcliffe Report, 1959). This publication stimulated a wide ranging discussion, which continues today, on the efficacy of monetary policy, and the institutional factors involved. In effect the Report provided justification for the continuation of existing policies. Its direct impact was restricted to increasing the involvement of the Bank of England in policy making, and providing for the collection and publication of much improved financial statistics. Far from the money supply being a major objective, there were, in fact, not even any regularly published statistics for the money supply.

In April 1960, as part of a general tightening of economic policy, special deposits were introduced as a new instrument of monetary policy. Special deposits were deposits made by the London Clearing Banks and Scottish banks with the Bank of England, at the Bank's request. The intention was to restrict the ability of the clearing banks to extend their lending to the private sector. The intention to introduce this new instrument was announced on 3 July 1958, and the proposal was considered by the Radcliffe Committee. From September 1971, with the introduction of Competition and Credit Control (CCC) the number of institutions subject to calls for special deposits was greatly increased. These topics are taken up further below; see also the appendix.

By 1960 the main criticisms of British economic policy had become the slow growth rate in this country compared to our industrial competitors. Concern with economic performance was widespread at the time and heralded a new era in which governments tried to make the economy grow faster. An aspect of this movement was the adoption of a more flexible approach to economic management and a significant extension of horizons (indicative planning). In March 1962 the National Economic Development Council (NEDC) met for the first time, and was an important step in consideration of longer term policy objectives. This organisation came to be associated in particular with the attempt to stimulate growth. In addition the Department of Economic Affairs was established, and the National Plan, when published on 16 September 1965, had the aim of 'accelerating growth by strengthening the foundations of the economy and including an attractive prices and incomes policy' (Economic Report on 1965, 1966).

Although growth was the stated objective it was the balance of payments which actually dominated economic policy in fact. Because of external constraints growth remained low. This is hardly surprising given the extensive restrictions on bank lending, hire purchase controls, high interest rates, tight budgets and persistent prices and incomes policies. It was also announced, in February 1965, that public expenditure would *only* increase at annual average rate of $4\frac{1}{2}$ per cent in real terms over the period up to 1970.

As the 1960s progressed it became clear that it was necessary to devalue sterling. However, within the Cabinet the subject became 'the great unmentionable', and Brittan (1971, pp. 292–300) argued that a feeling was created outside government that party (or personal) dogma had precedence over economic rationality. In July 1966 extensive deflationary measures were taken with the objective of stemming the run on sterling and improving the underlying balance of payments. Beckermann (1972, pp. 62–3) concludes that the failure of the government to devalue at this point constituted their largest and costliest mistake, both financially and with respect to electoral credibility.

The devaluation eventually came in November 1967, when the exchange rate was reduced by 14.3 per cent against the dollar, from $2.80 to $2.40. Devaluation on its own is, however, not sufficient to bring about an improvement in the balance of payments. As Artis (1972, p. 276) points out, 'the change in the exchange rate by itself only gave the opportunity for an increase in exports and for import substitution. Demand management had to ensure that room was made for these developments to take place'. Instead, the public sector borrowing requirement in 1967 rose to more than double the 1966 figure, to £1136 million. Moreover, domestic borrowing grew by a factor of nine to £650 million, of which about a third was financed by the banks, and over the year money supply rose rapidly to end the year 9.8 per cent higher. For the same period there was an expansion of £1758 million in domestic credit.

In order to help rectify this situation cuts in public expenditure were announced in January 1968, and the budget in March 1968 was sharply deflationary, aiming to increase government revenue by £923 million in a full year. However, due to the effective delay of the fiscal measure 'it was in 1969, rather than 1968, which witnessed the largest turn round in the fiscal balance toward restriction' (Artis, 1972, p. 279).

At the time there was great disappointment, and some surprise, with the balance of payments outcome for 1968. At the end of the year the deficit on the current account was practically identical with that for 1967, at just over £300 million, and there had been little change in the long-run capital account which remained in deficit. However, things were not quite as bad as generally presented at the time. In fact, imports had received a boost from the pre-budget consumer boom early in the year, and since then exports had risen strongly on the back of the rapid expansion in world trade which took place in 1968. Even so, imports were maintained at too high a level by the failure of consumer demand to slow down.

Domestic credit was expanding even faster than in 1967 (though not much) at £1898 million and, despite the drain on reserves, money supply rose by 6.6 per cent. The public sector borrowing requirement for 1968 was still as high as £1315 million, but was rapidly reversing about this time under the influence of the fiscal measures taken earlier in the year. The possible importance of domestic credit expansion (DCE) and the money supply was only just beginning to be recognised, and even then, it seemed, only under the influence of the International Monetary Fund (IMF). The Letter of Intent to the IMF, published on 23 June 1969, limited the increase in public expenditure, set a target of £300 million balance of payments surplus for the financial year, and promised to keep DCE below £400 million during 1969/70. It was a lesson that was quickly forgotten with the change in government in 1970.

After a period of extensive consultation and discussion the Bank of England finally announced on 10 September 1971 that a new flexible policy towards the banks and finance houses was to start in six days time, and that all previous ceilings on lending would be removed. Under this new system of competition and credit control (CCC) the clearing banks were to abandon the cartelistic arrangements for fixing deposits and lending rates (which ceased to be tied to Bank rate), and *all banks* were to observe a $12\frac{1}{2}$ per cent minimum reserve ratio, while being liable for calls for special deposits. Also the Bank of England was to continue with its policy of reduced intervention in the gilt-edged market begun in May. The implications of this shift in emphasis are discussed below.

This change can be seen as a movement away from the perceived inefficiencies of selective credit rationing towards the expected benefits that would result from a more general money supply policy, apparently, however, without having any clear conviction that the money supply was important. Hire purchase controls had been abandoned in July 1971 following the Crowther Report (1971) which emphasised the distortions to the consumer credit markets created by such controls. Under the circumstances of the time, and following years of constraint, this reorientation of policy was obviously highly expansionary. And, as if to underline this intention, large increases in public expenditure were announced, in November, to be spread over the next two years (White Paper, 1971).

The year 1971 witnessed a considerable easing of monetary conditions as a result of the expansionary measures. Bank lending expanded strongly in the second half of the year, and particularly with the change to the new credit system in September. The public sector borrowing requirement rose rapidly to £1378 million for the year, and a huge foreign currency inflow of £3,200 million had to be financed. As it turned out, non-bank holdings of gilt-edged rose by a record (at that time) £1,900 million, but even so 'the public sector had to borrow a substantial amount from the bank system' (Financial Statement and Budget Report 1972–3, 1973, p. 4). On top of this the budget on 21 March 1972 was extremely expansionary, particularly considering the previous measures that had already been taken. Revenue was reduced by £1809 million in a full year (or £1211 million in 1972/3), equivalent to an additional $3–3\frac{1}{2}$ per cent in real personal disposable income.

Behind these expansionary policies lay the belief that a sustained level of high demand would raise productive potential and investment, thereby increasing the competitiveness of domestic production, and so improve the external account. When, in 1972, the balance of payments, and pressure on sterling, seemed that it might bring this expansionary phase to an end, the reaction was to allow sterling to float on 23 June. This effectively put an end to the plan to line up sterling with the currencies of the European Economic Community, and when the exchange markets reopened the pound duly floated down. However, as Goodhart (1978b) points out, this was not really a commitment to free floating, and there has remained substantial intervention in the exchange markets.

In October 1972, the Bank rate was replaced by minimum lending rate (MLR)(Bank of England, December 1972, pp. 442–3). The difference was that MLR was to follow the Treasury bill rate instead of being set by decree. The actual formula was $\frac{1}{2}$ per cent above the average rate of discount for Treasury bills at the most recent tender, rounded to the nearest $\frac{1}{4}$ per cent above. The declared intention was to make the rate at which the Bank was prepared to support the discount market more flexible and more sensitive to market forces. The Bank retained the right to overrule the formula, and anyway played a dominant role in determining the Treasury bill rate. In May 1978 the formal link with the Treasury bill rate was broken although the MLR title remained (Bank of England, June 1978, p. 166).

Between end-1971 and end-1973 there was an explosive expansion of bank lending and the money supply. This became of increasing concern to the monetary authorities, and with commodity, particularly oil, prices and domestic inflation increasing rapidly, the Bank of England took the opportunity, in December 1973, to introduce a new supplementary special deposits (SSDs) instrument. Under these new arrangements the banks and finance houses would have to place SSDs (carrying no interest) with the Bank of England if their interest bearing eligible liabilities grew by more than 8 per cent between October–December 1973 and April–June 1974, with the amount to be deposited quickly approaching a penal rate as the gap between the actual and permitted increase in liabilities increased. Changing the emphasis to the liability side of bank balance sheets, leaving the banks free to decide the allocation of their assets, was seen by the authorities as an improvement on direct controls on bank lending to the private sector. The introduction and operation of this new instrument is discussed below.

At the same time, the 'lifeboat' was announced which had the objective of rescuing the secondary banking sector from the consequences of its own explosive growth and high involvement in the highly volatile property market. These secondary banks had been largely unregulated, providing much less information on their activities than the formal banking sector. In the event of impending collapse it was, however, considered necessary to support these intermediaries in order to protect the main banking and financial institutions by maintaining confidence in the whole system. There is, therefore, a paradox that there was, and still is, much better information available on the larger, more conservative, inherently more stable, institutions than there is on those more susceptible to failure. And yet, stability of the system would seem to require the stability of each of the individual components.

Also at this time the country was faced with an energy crisis brought on by the miners' strike which reduced the country to three-day working. As argued in Chapter 3, with this combination of circumstances it was not surprising that bank lending to the private sector, and the growth of the broad money supply, were substantially reduced.

The final development in this period, in the area of monetary policy, was the official adoption of money supply targets. The first indication of this movement, apart from the DCE limits imposed by the IMF in 1969, came in the budget speech in April 1976 in which the Chancellor stated that

> I aim to see that the growth of the money supply is consistent with my plans for the growth of demand expressed in current prices. If it became clear that this aim were not being achieved, I would be ready to use the appropriate mix of policies — not necessarily monetary policy alone — to redress the situation. After two years in which M3 has grown a good deal more slowly than money GDP, I would expect their respective growth rates to come more into line in the coming financial year. (Hansard, 6 April, 1976, col. 237)

This policy was quantified in July when it was announced that 'for the financial year as a whole money supply growth should amount to about 12 per cent' (Hansard, 22 July 1976, col. 2019).

The Governor of the Bank of England has recently claimed that control of the money supply has been a major policy objective since the introduction of SSDs at the end of 1973.

> Since then, emphasis has continued to be placed on controlling the growth of the monetary aggregates as a specific proximate target for policy. Only since 1976 has this taken the form of publicly declared quantitative targets. Before that it constituted an internal aim: I think it is not therefore entirely accidental that during each of the three years 1974–76 the growth of sterling M3 was about 10%, well below the rate of expansion of national income at current prices. (Richardson, 1978)

And, of course, increased importance of the money supply had been an aspect of CCC. The introduction of SSDs can be seen to have left this and most other aspects of the new system unchanged.

In the years that have followed the monetary target policy has been further refined. In 1978, for example, a form of rolling targets was adopted. A target for the money supply was to be set for the first six months, when it would be replaced by a new twelve month target.

Control was still to be achieved through the manipulation of interest rates, and if this did not work, then through the imposition of SSDs. Future developments are likely to centre on the question of how to improve control within a market environment.

Major Developments in Monetary Policy

The objective in this section is to consider some of the major developments in the instruments of monetary control, and the environment within which monetary policy must operate. In particular, it is hoped to give some indication of how these developments may be incorporated into a formal econometric model of the monetary system, and how they have been treated in the past. The four aspects of policy which will be considered are special deposits, quantitative controls on bank lending, the introduction of competition and credit control and, finally, supplementary special deposits.

There is no general discussion of hire purchase (HP) controls although they should obviously be considered in any complete econometric model. HP controls have been found to have some effect on durable goods expenditure (see, for example, Ball and Drake, 1963; and Allard, 1974). This effect is particularly noticeable in the short run and may not persist. Moreover, even in the macroeconomic models that have been estimated, there seems to have been no real effort to identify offsets in other forms of expenditure or alternative sources of finances. For example, it may be that expenditure on durable goods is substituted for current consumption and/or that individuals sell, or reduce purchases of, financial assets to replace hire purchase facilities. These possibilities should all be considered in any complete analysis of the effect of HP controls.

Special Deposits

The introduction of the special deposits (SDs) scheme was announced in July 1958, but the first call was not made until 28 April 1960. The scheme originally applied only to the London Clearing Banks (LCBs) and the Scottish banks, and required them, upon request from the Bank, to place funds at the Bank additional to their normal balances with the Bank of England. To begin with the Scottish banks were only required to pay half the proportion of SDs requested from the LDBs, but this was abandoned in 1971 when, with the introduction of CCC, the scheme was extended to all listed banks, and at a uniform rate (Bank of England, June and September 1971).

The second call for SDs was made on 3 June 1960, although this time the additional 1 per cent was to be provided in two instalments. From then on both increases and reductions in the SDs rate have generally been made in this way, that is, in two instalments. Between

May and November 1962, SDs were phased out as the monetary authorities created the conditions for general credit expansion. This situation did not last long and a call for SDs was forecast in the 1965 Budget, and made on 29 April. Since then there have been SDs lodged at the Bank up until September 1971, at which time all SDs were paid back as part of the change-over to the new CCC system. However, as noted above the scheme was not abolished but was extended to cover the whole banking system. SDs were called in November 1972 and have effectively remained in existence ever since.

Interest is payable on SDs at the average Treasury bill rate (rounded to the nearest 1/16th per cent at the weekly tender of the preceding week). Interest at this rate is calculated and paid on Mondays, or, where a Monday is a holiday, on the first business day of the week. An exception to this was announced by the Bank on 31 May 1969 when, because of the lack of progress by the banks in keeping within the lending ceiling imposed by the Bank, only half the Treasury bill rate was paid on SDs from 2 June 1969 (Bank of England, June 1969). This punitive measure was lifted in April 1970.

At one time the SDs instrument was subjected to a certain amount of criticism for what, in fact, appear to be unsound reasons. At the time of the Radcliffe Report the entire discussion by the Bank was in terms of the level, or rate of change, of advances made by the banks (Radcliffe Memoranda, Vol. 1, 1960). Although the authorities were aware of the limitations and possible inequity of the system, under the prevailing circumstances they seemed unable to find any way round them.

The Bank did not expect the introduction of SDs to have any dramatic effect, and were fully aware of the dangers of 'portfolio rearrangement' and 'alternative finance', but considered them to be the 'least objectionable device' for the control of advances (Radcliffe Memoranda, Vol. 1, 1960). SDs were seen as a supplement to traditional techniques. But at no stage did the Bank spell out the theoretical assumptions underlying SDs, and commentators have been compelled to make their own assumptions and draw their own theoretical conclusions.

Despite the fact that the whole discussion by the Bank was in terms of the level, or rate of change, of advances made by the banks, the introduction of SDs was initially interpreted as an instrument to control bank deposits. Gibson (1964), building on and developing from a previous study by Coppock and Gibson (1963), found that there was no indication that a shortage of liquid assets put a brake on the expansion of deposits[2] either in 1961 or the first half of 1962 (and any curtailment in advances was, he believed, due to the influence of factors other than SDs). Gibson (1968) later claimed that 'the authorities hoped that the introduction of SDs would make it difficult for the banks to expand their deposits and to grant additional credit to borrowers', adding that, 'there is no reason to believe that SDs which have no effect on the volume of the bank's deposits will reduce advances'.

Crouch (1970) carried out a study into the effect of SDs on deposits, believing that the SDs scheme was 'misconceived in theory' and 'misapplied in practice'. He came to the conclusion that, 'in fact, the outcome can actually be perverse so that an increase in the SDs ratio actually tends to increase the level of bank deposits'. This is, then, an important observation and one the Bank should have taken seriously; however, at the time they were concerned only with controlling advances. Walters (1970) drew attention to a study by Parkin *et al.* (1970), stating that 'the study shows clearly what has been suggested by Crouch, Gibson and others; Special Deposits are a nebulous instrument for controlling deposits since Special Deposits are more than offset by sales of bonds and purchases of bills by the banks'. It should be pointed out, however, that the study referred to took advances as given exogenously.

Compare these views with what *The Banker* (1958) had to say: 'A control over bank liquidity is in principle a means of controlling the volume of bank credit as a whole, as represented by total bank deposits, but the Chancellor's request was not directed to a control of that entirely general kind, what he sought was an additional means of restraining an increase in advances.' *The Banker* was not alone in interpreting the introduction of SDs in this way. Dacey (1967) commented that 'the correspondence between the Chancellor and the Governor (of the Bank) is framed wholly in terms of influencing the volume of lending; there is no reference to the volume of deposits, the supply of money or the general liquidity of the economy'. This does not exclude the possibility that SDs might be used as a means of attempting to reduce the liquidity of the system and so influence total deposits. This would, however, require some form of reserve base control, and it was not with this aim in mind that SDs were introduced, or used.

In examining this question it is assumed that the banks operate as profit maximizers holding diversified portfolios with a trade-off between risk and return. Starting from a position of overall equilibrium this will be disturbed by a call for SDs. Initially there is no necessity for deposits to fall, only a rearrangement of the asset side of the portfolios. It was argued in Chapter 4 that control by the banks has not been operated through manipulation of reserve assets so it is reasonable to assume that the objective was not to reduce the reserves of the banks. Originally the Bank was prepared to intervene in the market to prevent interest rates changing (Radcliffe Memoranda, Volume 1, 1960), but a call for SDs could be used to reinforce an upward movement in interest rates (see for example, O'Brien, 1971).

It is assumed, first of all, that, as a result of the banks selling bonds to accommodate a call for SDs, the bond rate is pushed up. In order to maintain the initial preferred ratio between bonds and advances, the rate on advances must increase, thereby reducing the demand for advances. What should happen as a result of a call for SDs in this case is that deposits remain the same while the quantity of advances falls.

Similar results may be obtained by assuming that the bank fully accommodates the sale of bonds so that there is no change in the rate on bonds. The consequence of the banks selling bonds is that the risk content of the portfolio rises (and the yield on the portfolio falls). In order to restore the previous portfolio position the banks must convert some advances into bonds. So again, a call for SDs had led to a fall in advances while leaving total deposits unaltered. These suggested movements can be explained in terms of the simplified diagram presented in Figure 4.1. There

$$S = \frac{B}{A} \text{ or } \frac{\text{bonds}}{\text{advances}}$$

r_b = yield on bonds (including any non-pecuniary returns)

r_a = yield on advances (including any non-pecuniary returns)

R_b = the subjective risk on holding bonds

R_a = the subjective risk on holding advances

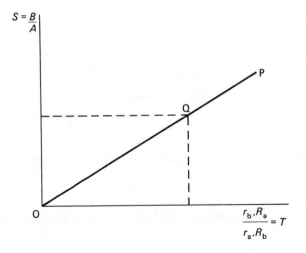

Figure 4.1   *Asset preference, showing the distribution of non-liquid assets in terms of relative rates of return and risks*

In this diagram the line OP, the portfolio preference line, is based on the assumption that the banks are prepared to accept some additional risk for the extra earning power yielded by the riskier assets, that is, advances. Along OP risk and return are in balance and the bank is assumed to be indifferent as between bonds and advances. Any change which shifts the actual portfolio down from, and/or to the right of, OP will be followed by a readjustment of asset holdings in an attempt to re-establish a position on OP.

Maintaining the assumption that the total size of the portfolio, that is, total deposits, remains unaltered it is worth considering the effect of changes in the bank's preferred distribution of the non-reserve portion of the portfolio. The desired portfolio ratio, θ, can be defined as

$$\theta = \frac{A}{A+B} \tag{4.1}$$

so that

$$\theta = \frac{A^*}{(A+B)^*} \tag{4.2}$$

where the asterisk indicates the new desired portfolio distribution following a call for SDs. It is, therefore, possible to write

$$\frac{\theta^* - \theta}{\theta^*} = \frac{(A+B)A^* - A(A+B)^*}{A^*(A+B)} \tag{4.3}$$

The change in $(A+B)$ can be defined as

$$\Delta(A+B) = -kD = -k(A+B+C) \tag{4.4}$$

where

k = the proportionate call for SDs

D = total bank deposits

C = total reserve asset holdings of the banks

Assuming a reserve ratio of α, (4.4) can be rewritten in the form:

$$\Delta(A+B) = -k\left[\left(1 + \frac{\alpha}{1-\alpha}\right)(A+B)\right] \tag{4.5}$$

Given the change in $(A+B)$ it is possible to derive $(A+B)^*$, that is, $(A+B) - \Delta(A+B)$, so that

$$\frac{\theta^* - \theta}{\theta} = \frac{(A+B)A^* - A[1 - k(1+\alpha)/(1-\alpha)](A+B)}{A^*(A+B)} \tag{4.6}$$

$$= \frac{A^* - [A(1-\alpha-k)/(1-\alpha)]}{A^*} \tag{4.7}$$

$$= 1 - \frac{A}{A^*}\left(\frac{1-\alpha-k}{1-\alpha}\right) \tag{4.8}$$

Equation (4.8) relates changes in the desired composition of the portfolio to changes in advances. If there is no change in the desired portfolio ratio (that is, $\theta^* = \theta$) this expression reduces to

$$\frac{A - A^*}{A} = \frac{\Delta A}{A} = \frac{-k}{1-\alpha} \tag{4.9}$$

Advances and bonds have now dropped out of the equation. As long as the banks return to the previous, desired distribution of non-reserve assets, θ, then given k the only thing that the percentage change in advances (and bonds) depends on is the ratio of reserve to non-reserve assets.

At the other extreme, if there is no change in advances (that is, $A^* = A$) then (4.8) becomes

$$\frac{\theta^* - \theta}{\theta^*} = \frac{k}{1-\alpha} \tag{4.10}$$

so that the percentage change in the ratio is exactly the same as the percentage change in advances (and bonds) when the ratio is constant, but with the sign reversed. This particular value can be thought of as a 100 per cent *compensatory change* in θ, that is, the percentage change in θ that will result in no change in advances in response to a call for SDs. If advances fall by $\beta(100)$ per cent, the percentage change in the portfolio balance will then be

$$\frac{\theta^* - \theta}{\theta^*} = 1 - \frac{1}{1-\beta}\frac{(1-\alpha-k)}{1-\alpha} \tag{4.11}$$

It might help to clarify the argument so far to consider a numerical example. Suppose the banks hold a constant reserve ratio of $12\frac{1}{2}$ per cent and SDs equivalent to 2 per cent of deposits are called, that is,

$$\alpha = 0.125$$

$$k = 0.02$$

The percentage change in advances if the balance of the non-reserve portion of the portfolio is to remain constant is given by substituting these values into equation (4.9):

$$\frac{\Delta A}{A} = -\frac{-0.02}{1-0.125} = -0.02286 \qquad (4.9)$$

That is, the percentage fall in advances must be 2.29 per cent. And if there is no change in advances the 100 per cent compensatory change in θ will also be 2.29 per cent.

If advances are, in fact, only reduced by 2 per cent, in other words, $\beta = 0.02$, as a result of this call for SDs, then θ must change by 0.29 per cent or, alternatively, there must be a 12.7 per cent *compensatory change* (0.29/2.29).

When it is realised that a 100 per cent compensatory change requires the whole of a call for SDs to be met by running down bond holdings, and as a result making the asset portfolio more illiquid, such an outcome seems unlikely. Putting the total weight of adjustment on to bond holdings is unrealistic, particularly in the short run, and so, with no change in deposits, SDs are almost certain to have the immediate effect of reducing advances. In this sense the objectives of the Bank were likely to be met at least in part, and their statements in this respect were consistent. However, the conclusion results from a static analysis and there is an important qualification to the use of SDs in a dynamic, short- to medium-term context.

In a situation in which there is a strong demand for bank loans and there is no quantitative limit on reserve assets a call for SDs may actually lead to an increase in bank deposits and the money supply. If the banks are able to increase the yield on advances (and possibly even if they are not) it may well pay them to expand their lending even with the increased 'reserve' requirements imposed by a call for SDs. In fact, the more the monetary authorities engineer an increase in short rates, that is, the Treasury bill rate, in an attempt to restrict the money supply the lower becomes the effective cost of these 'reserves'. It is possible, therefore, that the imposition of SDs may well lead to an *increase* in bank deposits and no *continuing* reduction in advances.

The extent and duration of the effect of a call for SDs is therefore an empirical question, and depends on how the call is reflected in the various asset holdings of the banks, which in turn has implications for bank deposits. It is certainly reasonable to expect some short-run effect on advances resulting from a call for SDs, though the duration of this effect into the longer term is more in doubt. In examining this question it is necessary to look at the total effect on the portfolio, not only on advances. It is in this way that deposits will be affected and it is no use looking for a *direct* relationship between SDs and deposits in the belief that the UK banking sector operates under some form of reserve base/ high powered money regime (tentative empirical support for this view was provided in Coghlan, 1973).

Controls on Bank Lending

Directives have frequently been given to the banks on the form and size of their lending to the private sector. These instructions have frequently been very specific, including an ordering of priorities. Lending to support exports has always had a high priority, and lending for shipbuilding and housebuilding has often figured prominently. Since the explosion of property and land prices in the early 1970s lending to finance property and financial transactions has been discouraged. Lending to the personal sector has always been frowned upon. These directives have not been aimed specifically at controlling the overall quantity of bank lending, and some would argue that they have had little success in influencing the direction of lending (see, for example, Gowland, 1978). Of more importance have been the instructions to the banks to restrict the quantity of their lending, and it is these which are the subject of this section.

The first occurrence of quantitative controls, during the period under consideration, was in July 1955. These controls remained in force for three years, until their abolition in July 1958, when the new SDs scheme was also introduced. At the time the Chancellor of the Exchequer stated that he hoped quantitative guidance on bank lending would not be required in the future. This view was simply wishful thinking, and in May 1965 quantitative controls were reintroduced and remained in force until 1971, with only partial relaxation in 1967 which was quickly reversed the same year. The year 1971 marked the inauguration of a new competitive system in which selective controls of a quantitative nature were rejected; this is dealt with below.

The major problem with this form of control was that quantitative restrictions that were introduced as a temporary measure then became difficult to remove. One reason why removal was difficult was that

> ... a lifting of instructions from the banks would be followed by a fairly rapid growth in bank deposits, and therefore, money supply. What is more, this growth does not require any additional incentives for 'competition' but results directly from the removal of an artificial barrier, and simply reflects the banks' return to a more 'natural' level. (Coghlan, 1975, p. 189)

This 'catching-up' effect has been largely ignored, particularly in empirical work, and not one of the models referred to in Chapter 2 included a variable to reflect the removal of quantitative controls. It is probably the case that certain of the models have approximated such an effect by including a CCC dummy in 1971; this possibility is discussed further below.

The way in which controls on bank lending have been included in econometric studies has, in fact, tended to understate the importance of quantitative controls and overstate the effect of qualitative controls. This is because both forms of control have generally been included together in the same dummy variable; employing 0 when no controls existed, 1 when qualitative guidance was issued and 2 when quantitative restrictions were in force. A variable such as this has been widely employed; see Norton (1969), Coghlan (1975) and Chapter 2 above. This approach is, however, most misleading; quantitative controls are not simply a more severe form of qualitative guidlines, but are different in kind. Moreover, as noted above, some allowance should also be made for the removal of quantitative restrictions.

Quantitative controls were unpopular not only with the banks, but also with the Bank of England who were responsible for their implementation. The Radcliffe Report (1959) also criticised this form of control. To the extent that such controls were effective this would be reflected in increasing inefficiency, penalising the efficient banks and supporting the inefficient. For this reason the Radcliffe Report (1959, para. 527) preferred 'a restriction of the *proportion* of advances to deposits' (italics added), but even then only in an emergency. In addition, restriction of the conventional sources of credit encourages the growth of alternative, less efficient, sources of finance. One result of this development is that the controlled totals are devalued as indicators of the demand for, and supply of, credit:

> The extent to which direct controls on banks lead to a diversion, as compared with a net reduction, in ultimate borrowing is, however, not known. The authorities have little idea of the overall effect of their actions when they introduce credit rationing, and the selection of this or that figure for, say, the maximum level of interest rates or the maximum expansion of loans to the private sector is an arbitrary process involving little or no economic justification.
>
> The maintenance of ceiling controls, particularly when these are set in terms of some quantitative limit to the total volume of loans, cumulatively distorts the allocation of funds. It also becomes that much harder to use the rate of growth of the affected aggregates as an indicator, or monitoring device, of economic developments, particularly when the controls are introduced or relaxed. (Goodhart, 1975c, p. 161)

Moreover, the system of controls was complicated and time consuming for the officials charged with implementing and monitoring them.

It is quite clear that quantitative controls on bank lending were effective in achieving their immediate objective (see Figure 4.2). It is, however, much less clear to what extent alternative sources of credit were available to substitute for bank lending, and, therefore, what the implications for the macroeconomy were (see, for example, Goodhart, 1975b). This is an empirical question and has an important bearing on the nature of the financial system. If markets are efficient and financial aggregates are perfect substitutes, as is sometimes suggested, then these controls should have had very little effect on total credit, or the economy in general. If, on the other hand, markets are segmented (see, for example, Robinson, 1951) so that particular financial institutions and instruments are highly individual and not particularly substitutable then the effect on total credit could be substantial. These two market regimes are not necessarily totally exclusive, and it is possible to believe in a fair degree of market segmentation in the short-run, but that substitutes will evolve over time. The relevant question then becomes the time taken for this evolution; this could well be a lengthy process. The apparent dramatic effect of the removal of quantitative restraints on bank lending (see Figure 4.2 and the argument in Chapter 3) suggests that short-run segmentation may really be quite significant.

The actual structure of the financial system is important for interpreting the past and for the implementation of monetary policy in the present. Thus it will be interesting to see whether there is any evidence that the imposition, and lifting, of quantitative restrictions had any effect on the aggregate economy. In this context it is an advantage to employ annual data so that the period includes the 1950s and gives two examples of this type of control. Even with the limited degrees of freedom available it may be possible to consider sub-periods in order to ascertain whether the effects were similar in both cases.

Competition and credit control
It has already been noted that there was fairly general dissatisfaction with the system of quantitative controls, and this was evident in a speech by the Governor of the Bank of England on 28 May 1971:

We in the United Kingdom have in fact been operating a system of bank lending ceilings with declared official priorities almost continuously since 1965. We have, however, been increasingly unhappy about the effects of operating monetary policy in this way over a prolonged period. In this audience I do not need to labour the ill effects. It is obvious that physical rationing of this kind can lead to serious misallocation of resources both in the economy and in the financial system, and that inhibiting competition between banks can do much damage to the vigour and vitality of the entire banking system. (O'Brien, 1971, p. 5)

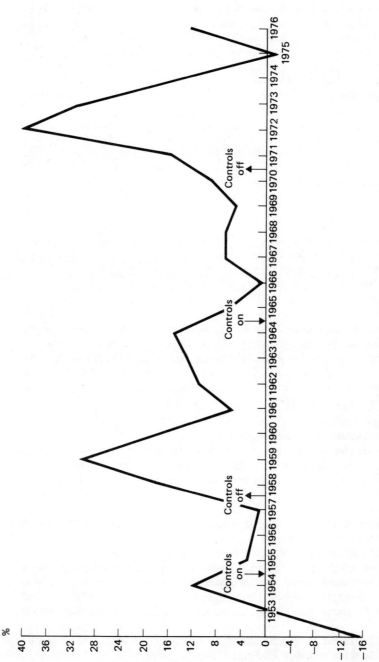

Figure 4.2   *The rate of growth of bank lending to the private sector*

The new system of CCC was seen as 'a major change in our approach to monetary policy', moving over to 'a system under which *allocation of credit is primarily determined by its cost*' (O'Brien, 1971). The main changes introduced by the new system (see Bank of England, June, September and December 1971) were as follows:

(1) Up to this point the clearing banks had been subject to an 8 per cent cash ratio and a 28 per cent liquid assets ratio, while the other banks were not required to hold any particular set of assets as reserves. This system was replaced by a uniform minimum reserve ratio of $12\frac{1}{2}$ per cent of eligible liabilities. Eligible liabilities were defined as the sterling deposit liabilities of the banking system as a whole, excluding deposits having an original maturity of over two years, plus any sterling resources obtained by switching foreign currencies into sterling. Finance houses were to hold a minimum reserve ratio of 10 per cent of eligible liabilities.

(2) Eligible reserve assets were defined to include balances with the Bank of England (other than special deposits), British government and Northern Ireland government Treasury bills, certificates of tax deposit, money at call with the London money market, British government stocks with one year or less to final maturity, local authority bills eligible for rediscount at the Bank of England and Commercial bills eligible for rediscount at the Bank of England, up to a maximum of 2 per cent of eligible liabilities. Notes and coins held by the banks were excluded from the definition of reserve assets.

(3) Special deposits were to be called at a uniform rate from both the banks and finance houses. The possibility was included to call a higher rate of SDs from the finance houses, and also for different rates of call relating to overseas deposits.

(4) The clearing banks agreed to abandon their collective agreements on interest rates.

(5) After 14 May 1971 the Bank of England adopted a more flexible approach to the management of the gilt-edged market in that they no longer felt obliged to provide, as in the past, outright support for the gilt-edged market in stocks having a maturity of over one year.

(6) Members of the discount market were required to hold at least 50 per cent of their funds in selected categories of public sector debt, defined as British government and Northern Ireland government Treasury bills, local authority bills and bonds, and British government, British government guaranteed and local authority stocks with not more than five years to maturity. These arrangements were modified after 19 July 1973, changing the 50 per cent rule to a requirement that limited the aggregate holdings of

'undefined' assets by each discount house to a maximum of twenty times its capital and reserves (Bank of England, September 1973). These undefined assets were all assets other than those defined as public sector assets for the purposes of the previous 50 per cent ratio. There was also a restriction on total assets of each discount house as a proportion of their capital and reserves which effectively set a limit to the expansion of the discount market.

(7) The discount market would continue to cover the Treasury bill tender each week, but no longer at an agreed price. In return, the Bank continued to operate as lender of the last resort to the discount market.

(8) The discount houses were required not to engage in very short-term transactions with the banks designed to substitute 'window-dressing' arrangements for genuine observance of their minimum reserve ratio obligation.

It should be emphasised that the purpose of the new uniform reserve ratio was not to impose a reserve-base system of control on the banks. Certainly attention was directed towards monetary aggregates, but control was to be achieved through manipulation of interest rates. This was made clear by the Governor of the Bank of England in 1971:

> It is not expected that the mechanism of the minimum asset ratio and special deposits can be used to achieve some precise multiple contraction or expansion of bank assets. Rather the intention is to use our control over liquidity, which these instruments will reinforce, to influence the structure of interest rates. The resulting changes in relative rates of return will then induce shifts in the asset portfolios of both the public and the banks. (O'Brien, 1971, p. 6).

It is perfectly fair to claim, as some have done (for example, Griffiths, 1973), that the authorities' objectives would be easier to achieve had they adopted a monetary base control system. It would, however, be quite wrong to suggest that this was the type of system that the authorities adopted in 1971. This was also made clear in Chapter 3 above.

It was seen in Chapter 2 that financial models of the 1970s have made fairly extensive use of the dummy variable representing the introduction of CCC. There is, however, some difficulty in providing a convincing explanation of why this development should have brought about a dramatic change in banking sector behaviour, and in the behavioural responses of the private sector. While the development of non-bank financial intermediaries is perfectly capable of changing the demand for money, and therefore the equilibrium velocity of circulation of money, this should be measurable. The difficulty with CCC is that it is not clear why it should necessarily have changed the behavioural responses within the system. It made a lot of difference to the business conducted by the clearing banks, but it probably had less of an impact on the operations of the total banking sector. The traditional clearing bank business — current accounts and retail deposit accounts — was already rapidly declining as a proportion of total banking deposits.

It is sometimes argued that the new competitive environment in-augurated and encouraged, by CCC resulted in banks operating as 'liability managers', that is, adjusting their liabilities (predominantly deposits) in order to accommodate the asset side of their portfolios. CCC must surely have contributed to an increase in this method of operation but it is easy to over-emphasise the extent of this shift. Although there has been a tendency to analyse bank portfolio be-haviour by taking deposits as given, it was pointed out in Chapter 3 that Keynes had described banks operating as liability managers as long ago as the 1930s.

Another argument is that the introduction of CCC resulted in an increase in reserve assets, which made banks more aggressive in their lending activities. However, if, as has been argued here, reserves were not controlled in such a way as to restrict bank lending, it is difficult to see why the creation of excess reserves should have resulted in an expansion of bank lending — except, that is, to the extent that relative interest rates were changed. But then that influence should be picked up by existing equations — it does not represent a change in behaviour. Moreover, it is easy to exaggerate the increase in reserves made available as a result of the change over to the $12\frac{1}{2}$ per cent reserve ratio. For example, the reserve ratio for October 1971 was only 15.9 per cent, and what is more, this *rose* over the next three months, mainly as a result of an increase in money at call; see Table 4.1. In percentage terms, the main excess reserves were held by the non-clearing banks which had not previously been subjected to reserve control at all. Thus it is difficult to argue that the reduction of reserve requirements on the clearing banks resulted in the creation of substantial excess reserves.

If it was not CCC, as generally supposed, what was responsible for the substantial increase in bank lending and deposits between 1971 and 1974? As we have seen, bank lending to the private sector rose by over 100 per cent between end-1971 and end-1973, and this was certainly

Table 4.1   *Reserve Ratio of the Banking Sector*

	Month	*Reserve Ratio*
1971	October	15.9
	November	15.7
	December	17.4
1972	January	19.1
	February	16.1

exceptional. The answer which has already been suggested is that the main cause was the lifting of restrictions on bank lending to the private sector. These restrictions were removed in 1971, just as the CCC era was about to begin, having been in force since 1965. In examining this question it is also important to take into account the experience of the 1950s when similar controls were in force. This second example has been almost entirely neglected in empirical work.

Supplementary Special Deposits

Supplementary special deposits (SSDs) were introduced on 17 December 1973 as a means of controlling money growth and credit expansion without suffering very high interest rates. When the Bank had changed over to the CCC system they had hoped to control monetary aggregates through the manipulation of interest rate differentials, thereby moving the private sector along a stable demand for money schedule (Goodhart, 1975b, pp. 6–7). In the event things did not work out so smoothly and the banks were able to bid for deposits by raising their own rates because of the strong demand for bank credit. This situation could not continue forever and it is probably helpful to see the problem as one of disequilibrium, for eventually as costs increase for borrowers and the banks, so pressure to reduce lending must increase. The problem was in large part the result not of CCC but the abolition of lending ceilings which took place at the same time. At the time the Bank felt that they had lost control over the money supply through market operations, particularly given the political sensitivity of interest rate rises.

The way the instrument was to operate was that the banks were required to pay non-interest bearing SSDs to the Bank of England if their interest-bearing eligible liabilities grew faster than some specified rate. These SSDs were calculated as a percentage of the excess deposits; to begin with for an excess growth of 1 per cent or less, the rate was 5 per cent of the excess, for more than 1 per cent up to 3 per cent it was 25 per cent, and anything above that required 50 per cent. The three tranches above the allowable rate of growth were widened in November 1974 to 0–3 per cent, 3–5 per cent and over 5 per cent, with the same progressive penalties applying. These widened bands applied to all subsequent use of the SSDs instrument.

The way in which the authorities expected the system to work was clearly explained by the Bank of England:

> The rate of growth of interest-bearing liabilities depends in part upon the rates of interest offered by the banks. Strong bidding for funds by the banks while the scheme is activated could result in their eligible liabilities rising faster than the allowable rate, and thus incurring a progressively larger penalty in the form of non-interest-bearing

supplementary deposits. The arrangements should, therefore, restrain the pace of monetary expansion, including the pace at which banks extend new facilities for bank lending, without requiring rises in short-term interest rates and bank lending rates to unacceptable heights. (Bank of England, March 1974).

The fact that the banks retained the freedom to allocate their assets as desired, within the overall constraints imposed, was seen by the Bank as a great improvement over the previous quantitative controls on bank lending, 'or indeed most other schemes for reinforcing credit control which have been canvassed' (Bank of England, March 1974). The main disadvantage was that the scheme imposed a rigid structure on the banking system, and, as with lending restrictions, supported the inefficient at the expense of the efficient. For this reason it was hoped that this system of control would be employed infrequently and not remain in force for extended periods. It was in fact suggested that the mere existence of the SSDs instrument might be sufficient to deter excessive growth lest it be reimposed. The instrument, therefore, has more the characteristic of an emergency measure than providing a long-run solution to the problem of controlling monetary aggregates.

SSDs did not represent a change in emphasis from the CCC regime introduced in 1971, but rather an expedient to maintain control of the money supply while preserving the main characteristics of the existing system. After all it was CCC that directed attention to the monetary aggregates: 'As far as possible, the supplementary scheme is intended to maintain the main structural benefits to the banking system of the reforms introduced in 1971' (Bank of England, March 1974).

CCC had introduced a uniform reserve structure and had aimed to improve competition in banking. One way of achieving this latter objective was by removing the clearing bank cartel on interest rates. The introduction of SSDs was actually accompanied by an attempt to make this competition more effective. This was done by obtaining an agreement from the clearing banks to relate an increasing volume of their lending to market rates instead of base rates (Bank of England, March 1974). Thus, it seems incorrect to argue that the introduction of SSDs marked the end of CCC (see, for example, Gowland, 1978, and Artis *et al*. 1978). It did indicate the difficulty of achieving control through changes in interest rates, but the structure remained and even that objective was not discarded, only temporarily suspended.

SSDs were considered necessary, particularly because it was CCC that was seen as the main cause of the rapid growth in money and credit over the early 1970s. It has been argued here that in fact the main cause of this apparent instability was the removal of the rigid controls on bank lending in the 1960s. The growth, while excessive, was temporary, and had anyway just about blown itself out by the time SSDs had been introduced. If this hypothesis is correct then the authorities may have been able to avoid the extremes of this period by recognising the potential growth that might result from this pent-up demand. Instead CCC was introduced at a time when the Bank considered there was 'relatively slack demand for loans' (O'Brien, 1971, p. 6).

Within the period considered here, up to 1976, SSDs were only employed once and it is unlikely that it will be possible to identify any significant effect. The type of effect expected is a reduction in bank advances, possibly with some lag because of the flexibility of the scheme. In a more detailed study it would be necessary to investigate the effect of SSDs on interest rate relativities (see Coghlan 1979b for a preliminary discussion of this question).

Appendix

Non-Market Controls: Instructions to the Banks and Other Financial Instructions

During the war, the commercial banks had been subject to loose 'voluntary' controls over advances which emphasised the priority of essential production and the general need to keep down prices.[3] After the war the Bank of England Act of 1946 established a possible chain of direct control over advances from the Treasury, via the Bank of England, to the commercial banks, or directly from the Bank of England with Treasury consent. To begin with the requests were very general, and it was not until the mid-1950s that they became more precise. Also the number of institutions covered by instructions has increased with time, from only clearing banks and finance houses to include many other financial institutions. This gradual increase in the area of control was consolidated with the introduction of Competition and Credit Control in September 1971.

1947
Dec 2	Vague requests to the clearing banks to exercise restraint on the granting of credit.[4]
1949 Oct 26	

1951
April 10	Clearing banks requested to show restraint in their lending and, in particular, when the finance was required to finance speculation, non-priority capital expenditure or investment.
July 26	Strong request for the banks to 'restrict any extension of bank credit for any but essential purposes'.
1953	During the year a more relaxed attitude towards advances become apparent although no explicit reference can be quoted.

1955
- Feb 25   Bank of England and the Capital Issues Committee asked to limit finance for hire purchase and credit sales.
- June 30   Committee of London Clearing Bankers said banks would have to continue a stringent attitude to advances, in accordance with government policy.
- July 27   Chancellor asks for a 'positive and significant reduction' in bank advances — interpreted by the banks as a 10 per cent reduction.

1956
- Feb 17   Request by Chancellor for banks 'to continue their efforts to reduce the total of their advances'.
- July 25   Contraction of credit to be resolutely pursued; no relaxation in present attitude towards application for bank finance.

1957
- Feb 7   Announced that no relaxation meant by the cut in the bank rate.
- Sep 19   Clearing banks told that the average level of bank advances over the next 12 months was not to exceed the average level over the previous 12 months, that is, £2076 million.

1958
- July 3   All restraint on bank advances to be abolished from 31 July 1958. The Chancellor added that he hope quantitative requests would not have to be made in the future.

1961
- July 25   The impact of the new call for special deposits to fall on advances. The recent rate of rise in advances to be greatly reduced; any continued rise in bill finance which would weaken this declared to be undesirable. The clearing banks to limit finance for personal consumption, hire purchase and speculative property development. Other banks, accepting houses and insurance companies asked to observe similar restraint.

1962
- May 31   'Limited relaxation of restraints', but priority still to be given to finance for exports.
- Oct 3   All selective restrictions on lending by banks and other financial institutions abolished, while all institutions reminded of the priority of export and development area finance.

1964
- Dec 8   Letter from the Governor of the Bank of England to clearing banks, other banks, insurance companies, building societies and finance houses 'suggesting' a reduction in the rate of increase of lending with priority to be given to exports, manufacturing industry and developing areas.

1965

May 5   The Bank of England requests the banks and other financial institutions (including finance houses) to restrict their lending (to include bill finance) to the private sector to 5 per cent over the year ending March 1966, while giving priority to finance for exports.

June 27   Reminder of advances restraint.

1966

Feb 1   Existing limits on advances and commercial bills to be retained until further notice.

July 12   Present advances ceiling of 105 per cent of the March 1965 level to remain in force at least until the end of March 1967.

Aug 8   Strong reminder from the Bank of England to the clearing banks to observe the 105 per cent ceiling.

Nov 1   Lending for exports to be given priority by the banks, 'followed by lending in support of productive investment by manufacturing industry and agriculture'. Also bridging finance for house purchase to be considered of special importance.

1967

Feb 6   Chancellor announces that lending by the banks to finance housebuilding to take high priority.

Apr 11   All lending restrictions removed from the clearing banks but retained on other banking institutions and finance houses until a comparable instrument to special deposits formulated.

Nov 18   Bank lending (advances and commercial bills) to be restricted to the level of the latest published figures, but with the exception of lending for exports and shipbuilding.

1968

May 23   Bank lending (with no exemptions) limited to 104 per cent of the November 1967 level (that is, the May level), and the finance houses to bring their lending within 100 per cent of the end of October 1967 level.

Aug 30   Statement issued by the Bank of England re-emphasising the need for further reductions in bank advances for non-essential purposes.

Nov 22   New lending ceiling for the clearing banks set at 98 per cent of the November 1967 level, to be achieved by March 1969, but excluding finance for exports and shipbuilding. Other banks and discount houses to limit lending at end-March 1969 to 102 per cent of the level of November 1967.

1969

Jan 31   The Bank of England issues a reminder on the current lending target.

Apr 15   Further reminder of the requests for advances restraint.

June 2   As a result of the lending by the London clearing banks exceeding the target, the Bank of England halves the rate of interest paid on special deposits until compliance achieved. (The penalty continued, in fact, until 15 April 1970.)

1970

Apr 14   Clearing bank and finance house lending permitted to rise by 5 per cent over 12 months to March 1971 and other banks allowed to increase lending by 7 per cent over the same period, with priority still given to lending that would go towards further improving the balance of payments.

July 27   The Bank of England warns the clearing banks to slow down the growth of advances.

1971

Mar 30   Clearing bank lending for the second quarter of 1971 restricted to $107\frac{1}{2}$ per cent of the March 1970 level.

Sep 15   All lending ceilings abolished as part of the extensive changes made as part of the new system of 'Competition and Credit Control'.

1972

Aug 7   The Bank of England ask the banks to restrict lending for property and financial transactions and to give priority to financing industrial expansion.

1973

Sep 11   The Bank of England reminds the banks and finance houses to exercise 'significant restraint' on the provision of credit for persons, other than for house purchase. The banks were also requested not to pay more than $9\frac{1}{2}$ per cent on deposits under £10,000

Oct 8   No interest paid on that proportion of special deposits representing current account liabilities (that is, the same proportion of special deposits as the percentage of current accounts to eligible liabilities). This measure was introduced in order to reduce 'endowment' profits, and it remained in force until 12 November 1974.

Dec 17   Banks and finance houses requested to restrict personal loans for consumption purposes. Also a new 'incremental' special deposits instrument was introduced whereby the banks would have to make supplementary special deposits with the Bank of England, quickly reaching penal rates, if their interest-bearing liabilities (IBELs) grew by more than 8 per cent between October–December 1973 and April–June 1974. Banks with IBELs of less than £3 million were exempted.

1974

Apr 30   Supplementary special deposits scheme (SSDs) extended until December 1974 on the basis of a three month moving average growth of $1\frac{1}{2}$ per cent per month. The level for May-July was therefore $9\frac{1}{2}$ per cent above the base.

Nov 12   SSDs extended to June 1975.

1975

Feb 28   Bank of England removes SSDs. The limit of $9\frac{1}{2}$ per cent placed on the rate paid by banks on small deposits was withdrawn.

Dec 17   Chancellor of the Exchequer announces that the Bank of England is to restate qualitative guidance to banks, urging priority for lending to manufacturing industry for exports, import saving, industrial investment and working capital needs.

1976

Jul 22   Notice issued by the Bank of England emphasising the need for banks to keep lending to the personal sector, property companies and to finance purely financial transactions under control.

Nov 18   Supplementary special deposit scheme reintroduced. Maximum allowable growth in IBELs between August–October 1976 and February–April 1977 was to be 3 per cent, and $\frac{1}{2}$ per cent thereafter. At the same time qualitative guidance on bank lending was re-emphasised.

Special Deposits

Special deposits are deposits made by the banks with the Bank of England upon request, and which do not count as reserve assets. The scheme was first proposed on 3 July 1958 and was considered by the Radcliffe Committee. To begin with special deposits were only called from the London Clearing Banks and the Scottish banks, the latter paying only half the percentage of the former. After 15 September 1971, and the introduction of Competition and Credit Control, the requirement to pay special deposits at a uniform rate was extended to all banks subject to the new $12\frac{1}{2}$ per cent reserve ratio (apart from the Northern Ireland banks) and the major finance houses. The first part of Table 4A.1 below refers only to the London Clearing Banks, while the post 15 October 1971 figures refer to the total of special deposits called.

Bank Rate and Minimum Lending Rate Changes

Bank rate had remained at 2 per cent since 26 October 1939, when it was lowered from 3 per cent. Bank rate (or minimum lending rate) is the minimum rate at which the Bank of England, in its capacity as lender of last resort, stands ready to lend to discount houses which have access to the discount office of the Bank either by rediscounting bills of approved quality or by lending against the security of such bills or of short-dated government securities. Bank rate was traditionally announced every Thursday morning.

The weekly announcement of Bank rate ceased on 13 October 1972. Instead the Bank of England announced the 'minimum lending rate' every Friday, which is $\frac{1}{2}$ per cent above the average Treasury bill

Table 4A.1   *Special Deposits*

Date of Announcement	Paid by or on	Percentage of gross deposits	£ million	Cumulative total percentage	£ million
1960					
Apr 28	June 15	1	70	1	70
Jun 23	July 20	$\frac{1}{2}$	35	$1\frac{1}{2}$	105
	Aug 17	$\frac{1}{2}$	38	2	143
1961					
Jul 25	Aug 16	$\frac{1}{2}$	38	$2\frac{1}{2}$	185
	Sep 20	$\frac{1}{2}$	36	3	221
1962					
May 31	June 12	$-\frac{1}{2}$	36	$2\frac{1}{2}$	185
	June 18	$-\frac{1}{2}$	36	2	149
Sep 27	Oct 8	$-\frac{1}{2}$	38	$1\frac{1}{2}$	113
	Oct 15	$-\frac{1}{2}$	38	1	75
Nov 29	Dec 10	$-\frac{1}{2}$	39	$\frac{1}{2}$	38
	Dec 17	$-\frac{1}{2}$	38	—	—
1963					
1964					
1965					
Apr 29	May 19	$\frac{1}{2}$	44	$\frac{1}{2}$	44
	June 16	$\frac{1}{2}$	43	1	87
1966					
Jul 14	July 20	$\frac{1}{2}$	47	$1\frac{1}{2}$	140
	Aug 17	$\frac{1}{2}$	49	2	189
1967					
1968					
1969					
1970					
Apr 14	May 6	$\frac{1}{2}$	51	$2\frac{1}{2}$	247
Oct 29	Nov 11	1	108	$3\frac{1}{2}$	366
1971					
Sep 10	Sep 15	$-3\frac{1}{2}$	389	—	—
1972					
Nov 9	Nov 30	$\frac{1}{2}$	119	$\frac{1}{2}$	119
	Dec 14	$\frac{1}{2}$	119	1	238
Dec 21	Jan 3	1	238	2	476
	Jan 17	1	238	3	714
1973					
Jul 19	Aug 6	$\frac{1}{2}$	122	$3\frac{1}{2}$	854
	Aug 15	$\frac{1}{2}$	134	4	1073
Nov 13	Nov 28	$\frac{1}{2}$	144	$4\frac{1}{2}$	1294
	Dec 12	$\frac{1}{2}$	145	5	1439
	{ Dec 27[a]	$\frac{1}{2}$		$5\frac{1}{2}$ }	
	{ Jan 2[a]	$\frac{1}{2}$		6 }	
Dec 17		-1		5	1439
1974					
Jan 31	Jan 31	$-\frac{1}{2}$	150	$4\frac{1}{2}$	1354
Apr 4	Apr 8	$-\frac{1}{2}$	150	4	1201
	Apr 16	$-\frac{1}{2}$	150	$3\frac{1}{2}$	1051
Apr 18	Apr 22	$-\frac{1}{2}$	150	3	900

Table 4A.1 (*continued*)

Date of Announcement	Paid by oron	Percentage of gross deposits	£ million	Cumulative total percentage	£ million
1976					
Jan 15	Jan 19	− 1	324	2	654
	Feb 10	1	327	3	980
Sep 16	Sep 28	$\frac{1}{2}$	175	$3\frac{1}{2}$	1226
	Oct 6	$\frac{1}{2}$	176	4	1411
Oct 7	Nov 2	1	361	5	1806
	Nov 15[b]	1		6	

[a] The special deposits called for on 13 November and required by 27 December and 2 January were never actually made as they were cancelled on 17 December.
[b] The special deposits called for on 7 October and required by 15 November were deferred on 5 November to 14 December, and again on 10 December to 28 January 1977. This call was eventually cancelled on 13 January.

rate, rounded up to the nearest $\frac{1}{4}$ per cent. The rationale of the officially declared Bank rate had been eroded by time, and really became obsolete in September 1971 when the rates charged by the clearing banks ceased to be tied to it. The Bank of England could, however, still manipulate the market rate and retained the right to make discretionary changes. On 25 May 1978 the Bank of England announced that in future minimum lending rate would once more be determined by administrative decision.

Table 4A.2   *Minimum Lending Rate Changes*

			Rate	Change in rate	Percentage change in rate
1945			2		
1951					
	Nov	8	$2\frac{1}{2}$	$\frac{1}{2}$	25.0
1952					
	Mar	13	4	$1\frac{1}{2}$	60.0
1953					
	Sep	17	$3\frac{1}{2}$	$-\ \frac{1}{2}$	-12.5
1954					
	May	13	3	$-\ \frac{1}{2}$	-14.3
1955					
	Jan	27	$3\frac{1}{2}$	$\frac{1}{2}$	16.4
	Feb	24	$4\frac{1}{2}$	1	28.6
1956					
	Feb	16	$5\frac{1}{2}$	1	22.2
1957					
	Feb	7	5	$-\ \frac{1}{2}$	$-\ 9.1$
	Sep	19	7	2	40.0
1958					
	Mar	20	6	-1	-14.3
	May	22	$5\frac{1}{2}$	$-\ \frac{1}{2}$	$-\ 8.3$
	June	19	5	$-\ \frac{1}{2}$	$-\ 9.1$
	Aug	14	$4\frac{1}{2}$	$-\ \frac{1}{2}$	-10.0
	Nov	20	4	$-\ \frac{1}{2}$	-11.1
1959					
1960					
	Jan	21	5	1	25.0
	June	23	6	1	20.0
	Oct	27	$5\frac{1}{2}$	$-\ \frac{1}{2}$	$-\ 8.3$
	Dec	8	5	$-\ \frac{1}{2}$	$-\ 9.1$
1961					
	July	26	7	2	40.0
	Oct	5	$6\frac{1}{2}$	$-\ \frac{1}{2}$	$-\ 7.1$
	Nov	2	6	$-\ \frac{1}{2}$	$-\ 7.7$
1962					
	Mar	8	$5\frac{1}{2}$	$-\ \frac{1}{2}$	$-\ 8.3$
	Mar	22	5	$-\ \frac{1}{2}$	$-\ 9.1$
	Apr	26	$4\frac{1}{2}$	$-\ \frac{1}{2}$	-10.0
1963					
	Jan	3	4	$-\ \frac{1}{2}$	-11.1
1964					
	Feb	27	5	1	25.0
	Nov	23	7	2	40.0
1965					
	June	3	6	-1	-14.3
1966					
	July	14	7	1	16.7
1967					
	Jan	26	$6\frac{1}{2}$	$-\ \frac{1}{2}$	$-\ 7.1$
	Mar	16	6	$-\ \frac{1}{2}$	$-\ 7.7$
	May	4	$5\frac{1}{2}$	$-\ \frac{1}{2}$	$-\ 8.3$

Table 4A.2 (*continued*)

			Rate	Change in rate	Percentage change in rate
	Oct	19	6	$\frac{1}{2}$	9.1
	Nov	9	$6\frac{1}{2}$	$\frac{1}{2}$	8.3
	Nov	18	8	$1\frac{1}{2}$	23.1
1968					
	Mar	21	$7\frac{1}{2}$	$-\frac{1}{2}$	-6.3
	Sep	19	7	$-\frac{1}{2}$	-7.1
1969					
	Feb	27	8	1	14.3
1970					
	Mar	5	$7\frac{1}{2}$	$-\frac{1}{2}$	-6.3
	Apr	15	7	$-\frac{1}{2}$	-6.7
1971	Apr	1	6	-1	-14.3
	Sep	2	5	-1	-16.7
1972					
	June	30	6	1	20.0
	Oct	27	$7\frac{1}{2}$	$1\frac{1}{2}$	25.0
	Dec	29	9	$1\frac{1}{2}$	20.0
1973					
	Jan	26	$8\frac{3}{4}$	$-\frac{1}{4}$	-2.8
	Mar	30	$8\frac{1}{2}$	$-\frac{1}{4}$	-2.9
	Apr	27	$8\frac{1}{4}$	$-\frac{1}{4}$	-2.9
	May	25	$7\frac{3}{4}$	$-\frac{1}{2}$	-6.1
	June	29	$7\frac{1}{2}$	$-\frac{1}{4}$	-3.2
	July	20	9	$1\frac{1}{2}$	20.0
	July	27	$11\frac{1}{2}$	$1\frac{1}{2}$	16.7
	Oct	19	$11\frac{1}{4}$	$-\frac{1}{4}$	-2.2
	Nov	16	13	$1\frac{3}{4}$	15.6
1974					
	Jan	4	$12\frac{3}{4}$	$-\frac{1}{4}$	-1.9
	Feb	1	$12\frac{1}{2}$	$-\frac{1}{4}$	-2.0
	Apr	5	$12\frac{1}{4}$	$-\frac{1}{4}$	-2.0
	Apr	11	12	$-\frac{1}{4}$	-2.1
	May	24	$11\frac{3}{4}$	$-\frac{1}{4}$	-2.1
	Sep	20	$11\frac{1}{2}$	$-\frac{1}{4}$	-2.1
1975					
	Jan	17	$11\frac{1}{4}$	$-\frac{1}{4}$	-2.2
	Jan	24	11	$-\frac{1}{4}$	-2.2
	Feb	7	$10\frac{3}{4}$	$-\frac{1}{4}$	-2.3
	Feb	14	$10\frac{1}{2}$	$-\frac{1}{4}$	-2.3
	Mar	7	$10\frac{1}{4}$	$-\frac{1}{4}$	-2.4
	Mar	21	10	$-\frac{1}{4}$	-2.4
	Apr	18	$9\frac{3}{4}$	$-\frac{1}{4}$	-2.5
	May	2	10	$\frac{1}{4}$	-2.6
	July	25	11	1	10.0
	Oct	3	12	1	9.1
	Nov	14	$11\frac{3}{4}$	$-\frac{1}{4}$	-2.1
	Nov	28	$11\frac{1}{2}$	$-\frac{1}{4}$	-2.1
	Dec	24	$11\frac{1}{4}$	$-\frac{1}{4}$	-2.2
1976					
	Jan	2	11	$-\frac{1}{4}$	-2.2

(Table 4A.2 (*continued*)

		Rate	*Change in rate*	*Percentage change in rate*
Jan	16	$10\frac{3}{4}$	$-\frac{1}{4}$	$-$ 2.3
Jan	23	$10\frac{1}{2}$	$-\frac{1}{4}$	$-$ 2.3
Jan	30	10	$-\frac{1}{2}$	$-$ 4.8
Feb	6	$9\frac{1}{2}$	$-\frac{1}{2}$	$-$ 5.0
Feb	27	$9\frac{1}{4}$	$-\frac{1}{4}$	$-$ 2.6
Mar	5	9	$-\frac{1}{4}$	$-$ 2.7
Apr	23	$10\frac{1}{2}$	$1\frac{1}{2}$	16.7
May	21	$11\frac{1}{2}$	1	9.5
Sep	10	13	$1\frac{1}{2}$	13.0
Oct	7	15	2	15.4
Nov	19	$14\frac{3}{4}$	$-\frac{1}{4}$	$-$ 1.7
Dec	17	$14\frac{1}{2}$	$-\frac{1}{4}$	$-$ 1.7
Dec	24	$14\frac{1}{4}$	$-\frac{1}{4}$	$-$ 1.7

Personal Sector Hire Purchase Restrictions

Table 4A.3

12 Effective date[a]	Passenger cars[b] Deposit[c]	Term[d]	Domestic furniture Deposit	Term	Domestic appliances Deposit	Term
1952						
Feb 1	33.3	18	x[e]	x	33.3	18
1953						
1954						
July 14	x	x	x	x	x	x
1955						
Feb 25	15	24	15	24	15	24
July 26	33.3	24	15	24	33.3	24
1956						
Feb 18	50	24	20	24	50	24
Dec 21	20	24	20	24	50	24
1957						
May 29	33.3	24	20	24	50	24
1958						
Sep 16	33.3	24	x	x	33.3	24
Oct 29	x	x	x	x	x	x
1959						
1960						
Apr 29	20	24	10	24	20	24
1961						
Jan 20	20	36	10	36	20	36
1962						
June 5	20	36	10	36	10	36
1963						
1964						
1965						
June 4	25	36	10	36	15	36
July 28	25	30	10	36	15	30
1966						
Feb 8	25	27	15	30	25	24
July 21	40	24	20	24	33.3	24
1967						
June 8	30	30	20	24	33.3	24
Aug 31	25	36	15	30	25	30
Nov 20	33.3	27	15	30	25	30
1968						
Nov 2	40	24	20	24	33.3	24
1969						
1970						
1971						
July 20	x	x	x	x	x	x
1972						
1973						
Dec 17	33.3	24	20	24	33.3	24
1974						
1975						
Dec 17	33.3	24	20	30	20	30

(*Footnotes to Table 4A.3*)

[a] From 1947 to April 1953 hire-purchase terms were also controlled by hire purchase and credit sale agreements (maximum prices and charges) orders, which stipulated certain maximum and minimum requirements.

[b] From 12 April 1967 excluding three-wheel vehicles.

[c] Minimum deposits as a percentage of final selling price.

[d] Maximum term of contract in months.

[e] x = no control or control removed.

Industrial Sector Hire Purchase Controls

Table 4A.4

		Commercial Vehicles[a]		Shop and Office Furniture		Plant and Machinery	
Effective date		Deposit	Term	Deposit	Term	Deposit	Term
1952							
	Feb 1	33.3	18	33.3	18	x	x
1953							
1954							
1955							
1956							
	Feb 18	50	24	50	24	50	24
1957							
	May 29	33.3	24	33.3	24	33.3	24
1958							
	Sep 16	x	x	33.3	24	x	x
	Oct 29	x	x	x	x	x	x
1959							
1960							
1961							
	Jan 20	x	x	10	36	x	x
1962							
	June 5	x	x	20	36	x	x
1963							
1964							
	July	x	x	10	36	x	x
1965							
	June 4	x	x	15	30	x	x
1966							
	Feb 8	x	x	15	24	x	x
1967							
1968							
1969							
1970							
1971							
	July 20	x	x	x	x	x	x

[a] Excluding light vehicles.

Estimated Budge Tax Changes

Table 4A.5 lists the estimated full year effects of all postwar tax changes, with the estimated effect for the remainder of the financial year of the change given in parentheses.

Table 4A.5

		(1) Taxes on Incomes	(2) Taxes on Companies	(3) Taxes on Capital	(4) Taxes on Expenditure[a]	(5) Total (1) + (2) + (3) + (4)
1945	Oct 23	−292	−83	–	−10	−385
1946	Apr 9	−77.5(−34)	−75[b](−)	22(15)	−16.5(−13)	−147
1947	Mar 10	−87(76)	20(1)	9(1)	111(97)	53(174)
	Nov 12	−(15)	57(2)	–	151(33)	208(50)
1948	Apr 6	−103.5(−86)	–	[c](50)	47.5(47)	−56(11)
1949	Apr 6	10(10)	−76(−)	20(11)	−46(43)	−92(64)
1950	Apr 18	−82(−72)	–	–	81.5(74)	−0.5(2)
1951	Apr 10	80.5(72.5)	232.5(5)	–	75(61)	388(138.5)
1952	Mar 11	−230(−180)	100.5(1.5)	–	64(63)	−65.5(−115.5)
1953	Apr 14	−141(122)	212[d](−3)	–	−60(−45)	−413(74)
1954	Apr 6	–	−4[e](−)	−2(−0.5)	−4(−3.5)	−10(−4)

Table 4A.5 (continued)

	(1) Taxes on Incomes	(2) Taxes on Companies	(3) Taxes on Capital	(4) Taxes on Expenditure[a]	(5) Total (1) + (2) + (3) + (4)
1955 Apr 19	−152.5(−131.5)	—	—	−3(2.5)	−155.5(−134)
Oct 26	−0.5(−)	38[f](−)	—	75(15)	112.5(15)
1956 Apr 17	−53.5(−16.5)	30(1)	—	21.5(23.5)	−2(8)
1957 Apr 9	−56(−40)	−46.5[g](−25)	—	−28(−33)	−130.5(−98)
1958 Apr 15	−4(0.5)	−39[h](−)	−1(−)	−64.5(−49.5)	−108.5(−49)
1959 Apr 7	−229(−192)	−12.5[i](−)	—	−128(−103)	−369.5(−295)
1960 Apr 4	−20(−7)	64.5(1)	−2(−1)	29(29)	71.5(22)
1961 Apr 17	−98.5(−12.5)	73(1.5)	—	83(79)	57.5(68)
July 26	—	—	—	210[j](130)	210(130)
1962[					
1963 Apr 9	−(−8)	—	−1(−0.5)	14(−1)	13(−9.5)
1964 Apr 3	−294.5(−221)	−110[k](−12)	−1.5(−1)	−5(35.5)	−460(−269.5)
Apr 14	—	5(3)	—	111(100.5)	116(103.5)
Nov 11	122(−)	—	—	218[l](87)[m]	340(87)
1965 Apr 6	−8.5(−8)	37[n](−)	10[p](−)	181(171.5)	219.5(163.5)
1966 May 3	−[q](63)	240[r](378)	−5(−)	25(7.5)	260(448.5)

Table 4A.5 (continued)

		(1) Taxes on Incomes	(2) Taxes on Companies	(3) Taxes on Capital	(4) Taxes on Expenditure[a]	(5) Total (1) + (2) + (3) + (4)
1967	July 20	—	—	—	150[js]	150
1968	Apr 11	-4(-3)	-10(-4.5)	—	—	-14(-7.5)
	Mar 19	223(165)	250(208)	10(5)	440(396.5)	923(774.5)
	Nov 22	—	—	—	250[j]	250
1969	Apr 15	—(-6)	235(75)	-8(-4)	118(89)	345(154)
1970	Apr 14	-191.5(-150)	14.5[t](-0.5)	2(6)	-12.5(-35)	-187.5(-179.5)
	Oct 27	-350(—)	-100(-60)	—	—	-450(-60)
1971	Mar 30	-279(-184)	-350(-345)	-45[u](-15)	-3(-2)	-667(-546)
	July 19	—	-40(—)	—	-235(-110)	-275(-110)
1972	Mar 21	-1231(-982)	-265(-17)	-138(-71)	-175(-141)	-1809(-1211)
1973	Mar 6	-10(-7)	110(—)	-5(-2)	-162(-108)	-67(-120)
	Dec 17	—(30)	—	80(—)	—	80(30)
1974	Mar 26	430(267)	130(420)	—	747(660)	1307(1347)
	Jul 22	—	—	—	510(140)	510(140)
	Nov 12	-245.5(-10)	-20[v](-775)	-25[w](-15)	199(10)	-91.5(-790)
1975	Apr 15	234(178)	—(40)	—	1235(1033)	1469(1251)

Table 4A.5 (continued)

	(1) Taxes on Incomes	(2) Taxes on Companies	(3) Taxes on Capital	(4) Taxes on Expenditure[a]	(5) Total (1) + (2) + (3) + (4)
1976					
Apr 6	−1224(−932)	—	−116(−58)	370(375)	−970(−615)
Dec 15	—	—	—	50(370)	50(370)

[a] Including Stamp Duty.
[b] The estimated cost of terminating the excess profits tax as from 31 December 1946.
[c] The estimated cost of terminating the excess profits tax as from 31 December 1946.
[c] £50 million estimated for 1949/50, that is, the total estimated return from the 'Special Contribution' less £50 million.
[d] −£58 million estimated for 1954/55.
[e] The estimated cost for 1955/56.
[f] £10 million estimated for 1956/57.
[g] −41.5 million estimated for 1958/59.
[h] −£26 million estimated for 1959/60.
[i] Value estimated for 1960/61.
[j] Estimated effect of a 10 per cent surcharge on existing customs and excise duties and purchase tax.
[k] Estimated cost for 1964/65.
[l] Includes the estimated effect of the import surcharge and tax rebate of exports announced on 26 October 1964.
[m] Assuming approximately the same proportionate effect for the export rebate over the remainder of the year as that suggested for the import surcharge.
[n] Value estimated for 1966/67.
[p] Estimate for 1966/67. This probably underestimates the full effect since the yield was expected eventually to be as high as £125, but also to be very variable.
[q] £26 estimated for 1967/68 and nothing thereafter.
[r] Including Selective Employment Tax (SET) for the first time.
[s] A net figure after allowing for the effect of hire purchase controls and for additional export rebate which will become payable following the increases in oil duty and purchase tax.
[t] This represents one quarter of the total cost of the increase in initial allowances; estimated at £60 million over the next four years.
[u] Including £5.5 million to allow for a cost of £33 million spread over a number of years.
[v] Estimated cost for 1975/76 was £110 million.
[w] The estimate for 1975/76.

Prices and Incomes Policy

Control over a wide range of goods continued after the war along with rationing and some direct allocation. These price controls were particularly relied upon in the crises of 1948 and 1951, but, even so, were largely dismantled by 1952–53.

A strong appeal was made in February 1948 in the White Paper, 'Statement on Personal Incomes, Costs and Prices' (Cmnd 7321), to limit wage increases and for manufacturers to reduce prices. This paper proposed that cost increases due to higher wages should not be passed on in higher prices. This was accepted by unions and largely adhered to up to October 1950.

There was a half-hearted attempt to revive some form of national wage policy in 1952 but this failed to gain any real support and it was not until 1956 that the attempt to directly control prices and incomes became an independent policy instrument.

1956
June   Electricity, coal and gas prices and rail freights and fares pegged for 12 months.

1957
Aug 12   Council on Prices, Productivity and Incomes set up under the chairmanship of Lord Cohen. (First report 21 February 1958.)

1958
1959
Feb 28   End of compulsory arbitration in industrial disputes. (Announced 22 October 1958.)

1960
1961
July 25   Pay-pause. Brake on wages in the public sector in the hope that the private sector would follow suit.

Nov 16   Pay-pause broken by the electricity engineers in obtaining a pay award.

1962
Jan 22   Government requests Dr Beeching not to make the rail unions a pay offer and to refer the claim to arbitration.

Feb 2   White Paper, 'Incomes Policy: The Next Step' (Cmnd 1626), published. It proposed that the average pay increase should be limited to $2-2\frac{1}{2}$ per cent a year.

Mar 31   Pay-pause ends, succeeded by 'guiding light' policy of wage restraint.

May 23   Breaches of 'guiding light' policy condemned by the Prime Minister, but confirms that the government will not intervene directly in private settlements.

Oct 1   National Incomes Commission (NIC) set up under the chairmanship of Mr. Geoffrey Lawrence, Q.C. (Intention first announced on 26 July 1962 – supported by the employers and opposed by the unions.)

1963
>   July   23   NIC recommends in its second report (Cmnd 2098) that any company with productivity rising by more than $3-3\frac{1}{2}$ per cent should cut prices.

1964
>   Dec   16   Joint 'Statement of Intent' on a prices and incomes policy signed by the government, TUC and employers' organisation. (Previously accepted by the TUC Economic Committee on 9 December 1964.)

1965
>   Feb   11   White Paper on the 'Machinery of Prices and Incomes Policy' (Cmnd 2577).
>
>   Mar   17   Mr Aubrey Jones appointed as Chairman of the National Board for Prices and Incomes. (PIB)
>
>   Apr   8   White Paper on 'Prices and Incomes' (Cmnd 2639) sets criteria to be followed by PIB — stability in general level of prices with the norm for income increases fixed at $3-3\frac{1}{2}$ per cent. (Supported by TUC.)
>
>   Sep   22   TUC sets up an 'early warning system' for wage claims.
>
>   Nov   11   White Paper on an 'Early Warning System' (Cmnd 2808) outlining arrangements for voluntary notification of intended price increases and pay claims/settlements.

1966
>   Feb   24   Prices and Incomes Bill published making provision for legal penalties for violations.
>
>   July   20   Voluntary prices and incomes standstill until the end of 1966. (Reluctantly accepted by the TUC.)
>
>   July   30   White Paper (Cmnd 3073) outlines plan for a six-month standstill of prices and incomes.
>
>   Aug   Prices and Incomes Act. Thirty-day early warning of wage and price increases. Three months compulsory standstill if reference made to the PIB.
>
>   Oct   4   Part IV — the 'compulsory' provisions of the Prices and Incomes Act activated.
>
>   Nov   22   White Paper (Cmnd 3150) on wage and price policy during period of severe restraint, with a nil norm for wage and price increases for the six months from January.

1967
>   Mar   21   Prices and Incomes White Paper (Cmnd 3235) proposing a year of moderation after 30 June 1967, with TUC and CBI voluntary vetting system replacing compulsory notification.
>
>   Apr   17   Amendment to the 1966 Prices and Incomes Act giving the Minister of Economic Affairs the power to delay increases for seven months.
>
>   July   1   New policy of voluntary vetting begins.
>
>   Sep   7   Following increases in electricity prices it is announced that in future all major price increases in nationalised industries will be referred to the PIB.

1968

Mar 19 It is announced in the budget that the present wage legislation, ending in July, is to be followed by a $3\frac{1}{2}$ per cent maximum wage and dividend increase over the next year, except for productivity agreements. (Proposal first announced by the Prime Minister on 5 January 1968.)

Apr 3 White Paper on 'Productivity, Prices and Incomes Policy in 1968 and 1969' (Cmnd 3590) proposes legislation to freeze wages for twelve months pending PIB report, to order price reductions and controls of rents and dividends.

Aug 1 Prices and Incomes Act continues the measures of the previous two acts, and extends their delaying powers by five months to a total of twelve months.

Sep 5/30 TUC Congress and Labour Party Conference vote for the repeal of the Prices and Incomes Act.

1969

Jan 17 White Paper, 'In Place of Strife' (Cmnd 3888), published, proposing legislation to curb strikes and impose penalties for 'unconstitutional' strikes, strike ballots, enforceable cooling-off periods and penal provisions. (Rejected by the unions.)

Apr 16 Proposals for the Industrial Relations Bill announced with no strike ballots or imprisonment provisions. (Rejected by TUC.)

June 18 Government drops the proposed Industrial Relations Bill and agrees to support the TUC's voluntary 'Programme for Action'.

Dec 12 White Paper on 'Productivity, Prices and Incomes Policy after 1969' (Cmnd 4237) proposes a $2\frac{1}{2}-4\frac{1}{2}$ per cent range for wage increases. (Rejected by the TUC.)

1970

Mar 16 Bill published to merge the PIB with the Monopolies Commission to form the Commission for Industry and Manpower. And while statutory incomes control will be dropped powers to regulate prices will be retained. (Opposed by the CBI.)

Dec 3 Government published its Industrial Relations Bill. (Opposed by the unions.)

1971

Jan 12 TUC day of protest against the Industrial Relations Bill.

Mar 18 1.5 million workers strike in protest against the Industrial Relations Bill.

Mar 31 PIB wound up.

July 15 CBI ask industry to avoid price increases or limit them to 5 per cent or less up to 31 July 1972, on condition that the government reflate the economy; supported also by the nationalised industries.

Aug 5   Industrial Relations Act 1971 receives royal assent.

1972

July 18   Tripartite talks between Government, CBI and TUC start in an effort to find a solution to the problems of inflation and industrial relations.

July 19   CBI extends voluntary price restraint to 31 October 1972.

Nov 3   Tripartite talks break down.

Nov 6   Counter Inflation (Temporary Provisions) Bill introduced by the Prime Minister included a ninety-day statutory standstill on most increases in pay, prices, rents and dividends – extendable by up to sixty days if necessary.

1973

Jan 11   Report on beef prices suggests control over farmers' profits.

Jan 17   White Paper on the 'Government Proposals for Second Stage for Programme Controlling Inflation' (Cmnd 5205) published. Pay increases restricted to £1 per week plus 4 per cent with rigid control over prices until the Autumn. Pay Board and Price Commission to be established to regulate pay and prices. Counter Inflation Bill to be introduced regulating prices, pay, dividends and rents for three-year period. Pay freeze continues until the end of April.

Feb 26   Green Paper, 'The Prices and Pay Code, a Consultative Document' (Cmnd 5245), published. Pay and dividends freeze to continue to 31 March, prices and house rents to stay frozen until 28 April.

Apr 1   Phase 2 started. Pay Board and Price Commission set up to regulate pay and prices. Pay increases restricted to £1 per week plus 4 per cent of average wage bills, with maximum of £250 a year. Rigid control on prices. Dividend increases restricted to 5 per cent.

May 1   Controls on prices under Phase 2 to be based on allowable costs and profit margins. 1.6 million workers strike in protest against Phase 2.

Nov 7   Stage 3 of the Price and Pay Code comes into operation. (Proposals first announced on 8 October.) Pay increases limited to £2.25 per week or 7 per cent of the average wage bill, with a maximum of £350 a year, plus 1 per cent flexibility margin. Threshold agreements to run for twelve months allowing 40 pence maximum per week if the retail price index rises by 7 per cent over the October 1973 level, plus a further 40 pence per week for every further percentage point rise. Controls maintained on prices.

1974

Mar 8   Residential rents frozen at present levels for the rest of the year.

Mar 25 Consultative document issued announcing a number of amendments to stage 3: (i) distributors' gross profit margins to be reduced by 10 per cent; (ii) minimum interval of three months between price increases; (iii) retailers to be prevented from changing the price of items already offered for sale; (iv) Price Commission to be permitted to order further reductions in gross margins where considered necessary and to make discretionary judgements as to whether any trade should have a higher ceiling than currently allowed.

Apr 30 Trade Union and Labour Relations Bill published to repeal the Industrial Relations Act.

May 24 A 3 per cent rise in the Retail Price Index results in threshold increases of £1.20 per week. Such rises continued throughout the summer. The final threshold payments were triggered on 15 November; in all eleven threshold payments were made.

June 12 TUC leaders back a policy of voluntary wage restraint as a contribution to a 'social contract', to follow the lifting of statutory wage controls.

Nov 12 Chancellor of the Exchequer announced an easing in the Price Code from December. Companies will be allowed to pass on 80 per cent of labour cost increases and $17\frac{1}{2}$ per cent of the cost of fixed capital formation.

Dec 19 Business rent controls to end on 1 February 1975.

1975

Apr 15 Investment relief allowed under the Price Code increased to 20 per cent.

Jul 1 TGWU conference votes in favour of 'social contract' but opposes statutory wage control and seeks to maintain free collective bargaining.

July 11 White Paper, 'The Attack on Inflation' (Cmnd 6151), published; part of the so-called 'social contract'. The main points were:

    (i) a maximum pay rise of £6 per week proposed for those earning less than £8,500 a year. For those earning more than this there were to be no pay rises at all;

    (ii) Local and public transport authorities to have their rate support grant (and ability to borrow) restricted and staff strictly limited if pay limit exceeded;

    (iii) for the private sector and nationalised industry the whole of any pay increase to be disallowed for price increases if the pay limit is breached. Excess pay increases may actually be declared illegal;

    (iv) Price Code extended beyond March 1976;

    (v) price restraint to be imposed on selected products of special importance in family expenditure;

    (vi) food subsidies increased by £70 million in 1976/7;
   (vii) increase in council rents to be held to average of 60p a week;
   (viii) temporary employment subsidy to be introduced as soon as possible, not available to companies breaking the pay limit;
   (ix) cash limits on public expenditure for 1976/7 to be introduced.

Sep 3 TUC annual congress approves £6 a week pay rise limit.

1976

Apr 6 Chancellor of the Exchequer makes tax cuts of over £1000 million conditional on a TUC agreement to a new low pay norm of around 3 per cent for the second stage of the government's incomes policy.

May 5 TUC and government agree $4\frac{1}{2}$ per cent pay limit. Supported by TUC Congress on 16 June.

June 30 White Paper, 'The Attack on Inflation the Second Year' (Cmnd 6507), published. Wage and salary increases limited to £2.50 for those earning between £50 and £80, and to a maximum of £4 a week on all higher levels of earnings.

June 30 Modifications to the Price Code published (Cmnd 6540), increasing somewhat the costs allowable for price increase.

July 28 TUC and Labour Executive formally endorse phase 2 of the 'social contract'.

Oct 11 Change in the Price Code announced to allow companies to pass on 35 per cent of new fixed investment in higher prices compared to the previous limit of 20 per cent.

Notes

1 The election, on 5 July 1945, was won by the Labour Party with a majority over the Conservatives of 190.
2 That is a proposition which is accepted in this study; the point in question here is the relevance of the observation for discussing the effect of SDs.
3 Letter from the Chancellor of the Exchequer to the Governor of the Bank of England, dated 26 September 1939.
4 For example see the statement by Sir Stafford Cripps on 26 October 1949, and quoted by Dow (1964, pp. 236–7).

5

A Monetary Model of the Economy

The objective of this chapter is to develop and estimate a financial model of the UK economy employing the theoretical approach presented in Chapter 3, taking account of the institutional and policy changes discussed in Chapter 4. No empirical model can hope to represent completely the complexity of the real world. Each model must attempt to identify the crucial elements in the argument at the expense of less important influences. Emphasis has been given here to the supply of and demand for money. The importance given to credit creation has resulted in a model that is significantly different from other models that have been constructed, in that it puts endogenous financial markets at the centre, and integrates these with behaviour in all other markets. This model is a first attempt at such construction and should not be thought of as the only possible empirical representation of the theory.

The preliminary nature of the model, together with the constraints on time and space, and the availability and reliability of the data, have resulted in a small model incorporating very few behavioural equations. At this stage in its development the high degree of aggregation makes it easier to understand how it operates, in contrast to the economic behaviour underlying many of the large scale econometric models that have been built. Even in these cases there is generally only a small core of crucial equations and an added mass of detail which may help answer specific questions but which certainly succeeds in confusing understanding of the operation of the model as a whole. The size of this model was not chosen for ideological reasons and a certain amount of further disaggregation should improve the fit of the model, and would be necessary to provide a reasonable forecasting framework.

Model Outline

The model is presented within a flow-of-funds/income/expenditure framework; what would be called a sources-and-uses statement in the United States. It is hoped in this way to illustrate how the financial implications of income/expenditure decisions might come to be ignored, and also why this might be a mistake.

The flow-of-funds statistics are not employed in the form presented in the matrix tables in which the figures are published (for example, Bank of England, 1973 and 1978a). Those tables were constructed to be consistent with national income accounts, and therefore take sector surpluses and deficits as given (see Bain, 1973; Coghlan, 1980b, Ch. 6). However, that presentation is not necessarily the most informative when trying to describe the pattern of economic behaviour.

The danger inherent in using the statistics in their published form is that research has followed the approach adopted for explaining income/expenditure decisions, taking these decisions as given and then explaining the distribution of the sector flows between various assets and liabilities. In the process one or two interest rates may be determined which will then feed back into the 'real' model. This, for example, is the approach adopted by Bosworth and Duesenberry (1973) who constructed a disaggregated flow-of-funds model of the US economy. The financial sector was, however, still treated separately and was not integrated into the rest of the economy in the way suggested by the approach adopted here.

In the present model the economy is made up of four major sectors – the private, banking, public and overseas sectors – rather than the six sectors included in the normal flow-of-funds tables. This simply means that the personal sector, non-financial companies and the non-bank financial intermediaries (NBFI) have been consolidated together to give a single non-bank private sector – for convenience referred to simply as the private sector. The aggregation of the personal and company sectors can be partly justified in terms of the broad relationship that is hypothesised to exist between money/credit and income/expenditure. This degree of aggregation is not a necessary characteristic of the approach and any extension of the model might usefully include some disaggregation of the income/expenditure decisions. It would also be preferable, and perhaps even more important, to separate out behaviour in the financial markets. In this case, however, there are severe limitations to the available data, with many of the categories allocated as residuals and including potentially large errors (see Bank of England, 1973 and 1979).

The separation of the NBFI from the banking sector is justified in terms of the distinctive institutional characteristics of the banks and the assumed stability (but certainly not constancy) of the velocity of circulation of money. For the purposes of this study the NBFI have been aggregated with the rest of the non-bank private sector on the assumption that they can be interpreted as acting as agents for the private sector and, therefore, reflect the same behaviour. To the extent that this assumption, and the other simplifications that have been made, are not strictly valid, the econometric performance of the model will deteriorate. In this respect, including the NBFI separately would seem to represent a potential improvement. The aggregation assumptions do, however, enable the model to be reduced to more manageable and understandable proportions.

The starting point is to write down the sources-and-uses identities (the flow equivalents of their respective balance sheets) for each of the four sectors. These can be written as follows, with the income/ expenditure outcomes on the left-hand side. The notation is the same as that employed in Chapter 3, and all definitions are included in Appendix 2 of this chapter.

Private Sector

$$Y.P - Ty - E.P \equiv \Delta NC + \Delta B + \Delta D + \Delta \$D + \Delta NDL$$

$$- \Delta L - \Delta \$L - \Delta Nf - \Delta PSA$$

$$\equiv NAFA \qquad (5.1)$$

It is assumed that all income accrues to the private sector. This is only approximately correct, although very nearly so, since profits are also earned by public corporations and the banking sector. The identity says quite simply that income less direct tax payments and expenditure on goods and services is equal to the net acquisition of financial assets (NAFA) of the private sector. NAFA is divided into the various claims on and liabilities to the other sectors of the economy.

ΔPSA represents the change in public sector assets reflecting liabilities of the non-bank private sector; public sector bank deposits are included separately. In reality, and in the estimation of the model, ΔPSA is a residual item that includes certain income receipts of the private sector. For this reason, and because some income accrues to the public sector in the form of the profits of public corporations, separate residuals for the private and public sectors have been included in the estimated model; these are NARES and PBRES, respectively. These complications will not change the present argument and consequently have been left out.

Banking Sector

$$0 \equiv \Delta D + \Delta \$D + \Delta Dg + \Delta NDL + (\Delta Df - \Delta Lf)$$

$$- \Delta L - \Delta \$L - \Delta Lg \qquad (5.2)$$

Under the assumption that no income accrues to the banking sector then total deposit, and non-deposit, liabilities must equal total assets.

Public Sector

$$G.P - Ty - TE \equiv PSFD$$

$$\equiv PSBR - \Delta PSA - \Delta Dg$$

$$\equiv \Delta NC + \Delta B + \Delta Bf + \Delta Lg - BOF$$

$$- \Delta PSA - \Delta Dg \qquad (5.3)$$

Again ignoring any profits of the public sector, total current and capital expenditure less direct and indirect tax receipts must be equal to the financial deficit of the public sector (PSFD). If the financial assets of the public sector are added to PSFD (that is, the claims on the banks and non-bank private sector) this gives the public sector borrowing requirement (PSBR). Slightly rearranging identity (5.3) to give the PSBR on the left-hand side results in identity (3.5) in Chapter 3, that is,

$$PSBR \equiv \Delta NC + \Delta B + \Delta Bf + \Delta Lg - BOF \qquad (3.5)$$

Overseas Sector

$$CA \equiv BOF - \Delta Nf - \Delta Bf - (\Delta Df - \Delta Lf) \qquad (5.4)$$

The current account (CA) results in the net financial flows on the right-hand side. To the extent that *market* related capital inflows/outflows differ from the current account deficit/surplus this must be made up by official transactions as represented by the balance for official financing (BOF). BOF represents the change in the stock of official gold and foreign currency reserves (ignoring valuation changes) plus official short- and medium-term borrowing from abroad. Alternatively, this identity can be rearranged to give identity (3.6), which explains BOF in terms of market related transactions in commodity and financial markets.

$$BOF \equiv CA + \Delta Nf + \Delta Bf + (\Delta Df - \Delta Lf) \qquad (3.6)$$

These identities give some indication of the complex financial inter-relationships that exist within the economy between the various sectors. Even so it is possible to understand how these financial considerations could be ignored. This is because financial transactions require both a borrower and a lender, and when the sectors are aggregated together the financial transactions cancel out. In this case we obtain the national income identity (at factor cost) in the form:

$$Y.P \equiv E.P + G.P + CA - TE \qquad (5.5)$$

from which all financial flows have disappeared.

Most macroeconomic models start by explaining the various elements in identity (5.5) allowing only minimal financial influences on behaviour. Having explained the main variables of concern there was/is then little reason to worry about the financial side of the economy. Even the more recent attempts to redress the balance by estimating more involved financial sectors, for example, the Treasury's monetary model — see Chapter 2· above — have tended to start with the sector surpluses derived from the estimation of income and expenditure markets. Although some interaction is included through interest rate changes (either directly and/or through wealth effects) this is not really an adequate approach. The approach adopted here suggests that if anything financial decisions are taken prior to expenditure decisions, and even that the availability of finance will actually determine the outcome in the so-called 'real' markets.

To take an example, the desire to increase *ex ante* investment expenditure will have a different *ex post* outcome depending on the general availability, and cost, of finance. Simply to regress actual investment on those variables representing the desire to invest will at best be a reduced form (if finance is freely available), and will, in general, represent an important mis-specification of the true relationships involved.

It is not possible to translate desires to spend into actual expenditures unless the finance is available, that is, unless demands can be made effective (for example, Clower, 1965; Leijonhufvud, 1968). Effective demand does not, however, simply mean that expenditure is income constrained. Changes in the velocity of circulation of money, or in the supply of money, must also be taken into account. In particular, it is changes in the supply of money through the expansion of bank credit that is of crucial importance in this context.[1] This, as we saw in Chapter 3, was an aspect of economic expansion on which Keynes placed very great emphasis. It is also central to the theoretical approach adopted here.

One aspect of this approach is that it emphasises the simultaneous determination of incomes and expenditures. The traditional approach of taking income as given in explaining expenditure is hardly adequate. Even when simultaneous equation techniques have been employed the degrees of freedom available are unlikely to result in any real improvement. While such techniques may be consistent they will only eliminate simultaneous equation bias as the sample size approaches infinity. Moreover, while there may be a stable equilibrium relationship between income and expenditure the direct regression of one on the other may prove inadequate to identify the relationship existing during the process of change. Such equations suffer from the fact that they leave out the implications of changes in the supply of finance. As noted above, this is seen as an important lacuna in traditional models. Relating aggregate demand directly to the finance available (not only from income) allows a very different approach to be adopted.

The approach adopted here, therefore, attaches much greater importance to the operations of the banking system and gives much greater weight to behaviour in financial markets. It is accepted that the economy cannot really be treated as consisting of two separate 'real' and financial halves. The importance of finance in making demands effective requires a fully integrated approach. It does not follow that simply because financial transactions cancel out when sectors are aggregated together they are unimportant. The method of constructing and presenting economic statistics encourages this myth.

This model take the provision of finance as crucially important and places the banking system at the centre of the analysis. The role of the banks in providing new credit is seen as being sufficiently important to warrant separate treatment, but allowance is also made for changes in the demand for money permitting changes in the velocity of circulation. Velocity can also change because of an excess supply of money created through the banking system (see the arguments in Chapter 3).

It was noted above, in Chapters 3 and 4, that this emphasis on finance, and the crucial role of the banking system, was an important aspect of Keynes' own theoretical approach. Keynes employed the argument of a direct relationship between the *level* of expenditure and a constant pool of finance:

> If investment is proceeding at a steady rate, the finance (or the commitments to finance) required can be supplied from a revolving fund of more or less constant amount, the entrepreneur having his finance replenished for the purpose of a projected investment as another exhausts his on paying for his completed investment. But if decisions to invest are (e.g.) increasing, the extra finance involved will constitute an additional demand for money. (Keynes, 1937a, p. 247)

This is a significant statement, but is potentially misleading in referring to an increase in the demand for credit as an increase in the demand for money. In a sense this is true, as what is borrowed is money and this could easily be thought of as a demand for money. However, demand for money functions have a very precise meaning related to the demand for the deposits of the banks (including notes and coins). The demand for credit may result in new deposits, and the transfer of money balances, but behaviourally it constitutes a demand for the assets of the banks. This behavioural distinction is very important and was emphasised in Chapter 4. Davidson (1978, Ch. 7) failed to recognise this distinction between those factors affecting the demand for money, and those affecting the supply of money, when he discussed Keynes' 'finance motive'. In consequence he failed to appreciate the full importance of the process in adding to the pool of finance and the supply of money.

Concentrating attention on the behaviour of the banking sector suggests an alternative rearrangement of the sector identities. Substituting the public and overseas sector identities into the banking sector identity results in the main identity (3.8) derived in Chapter 3, that is,

$$\Delta \pounds M3 \equiv [(PSBR - \Delta \$Dg) - \Delta B + \Delta \pounds L] + CA + \Delta Nf$$
$$- (\Delta \$D - \Delta \$L) - \Delta NDL \qquad (3.8)$$

Because the model is particularly concerned with the behaviour of the private sector it is wise to define the stock of money including only private sector deposits. This makes sense, as identity (3.8) includes public sector sterling bank deposits on both sides of the identity, $\Delta \pounds Dp$ being included in PSBR. It is therefore logical to deduct this common element from both sides. Aggregating together the private sector's external capital flows and its net foreign currency deposit position produces the identity that stands at the centre of this model, that is,

$$\Delta M \equiv [(PSBR - \Delta Dg) - \Delta B + \Delta L]$$
$$+ CA + \Delta N - \Delta NDL \qquad (5.6)$$

where

$$\Delta M = \Delta \pounds M3 - \Delta \pounds Dg$$
$$\Delta Dg = \Delta \$Dg + \Delta \pounds Dg$$
$$\Delta N = \Delta Nf - (\Delta \$D - \Delta \$L)$$

that is, net borrowing from abroad in sterling — which is a loose interpretation of the net borrowing from abroad, less the net foreign currency deposit/liability position of the private sector with the banking sector.

It is through this identity that new credit creation becomes reflected in aggregate demand. It is, of course, also necessary to take account of any changes in the velocity of circulation of the existing stock of money. Defining the components of the money supply in this way concentrates attention of the main *behavioural* influences on deposit growth. While it is possible to write down alternative identities, for example, in terms of banks' balance sheets (flows of funds) these do not identify the independent influences on changes in the money supply. A crucial element of the model, therefore, has been to determine the behavioural relationships underlying each of the separate components making up the money supply identity.

The expression in square brackets is defined as domestic credit expansion (DCE), and $CA + \Delta N$ is taken as representing the change in reserves, ΔR. The latter assumption is justified on the grounds that this total consists of the external influences on the money supply, that is, external flows to the private sector converted to sterling. For this reason, and because the other components making up the balance for official financing are taken to be exogenously determined within the model, ΔR is also interpreted as representing intervention by the public authorities in the exchange market.

The basic model consists of eight equations explaining total private sector expenditure at factor cost (EFC), the domestic rate of inflation (price level) (P), exports (X) and imports (Z) of goods and services, private sector capital flows (N), the long-term rate of interest (r_b), private sector demand for public sector debt (B), and bank lending (L). In addition, Appendix 4 includes the results of a preliminary attempt to endogenise the exchange rate, e.

It can be seen that the model contains no explicit demand-for-money function. This may at first sight seem rather surprising in a model stressing monetary relationships, as the demand for money function usually stands at the centre of such models. A stable demand function is, however, still a fundamental requirement of the system. In this case, because the stock of money is assumed to be supply determined, it is adjustment through the demand functions that eventually achieves equilibrium. The components of the demand function therefore become dependent variables in the model. These changes do, however, in turn feed back on the money supply, thereby further complicating the process of adjustment.

The supply of money is determined by the combined behaviour in all markets, real and financial, of the four sectors distinguished in the model: the private, public, banking and overseas sectors. These interactions also determine a demand for money. The process of bringing these two relationships into equilibrium provides the dynamics of the system, and the equilibrium properties of these functions determine the long-run properties of the model. These long-run properties are not necessarily anything we should expect to observe, but are more a state of mind, providing some underlying stability to the system. The fact that there is an underlying tendency to return to equilibrium does not mean that short-run stabilisation policies become redundant. This model has the characteristic that substantial disequilibrium can persist for some time, thereby providing possible justification for stabilisation policies, but within a system that is inherently stable.

Before turning to the empirical estimation of the model it is worth recalling the comments that were made in Chapter 4 on the influence of the major institutional and policy changes that have taken place over this period. In particular, it was pointed out there that the frequent inclusion of dummy variables to represent the introduction of competition and credit control (CCC) in 1971 in order to explain behaviour in financial markets was misleading. In this model the rapid increase in bank lending and deposits between 1971 and 1974 is explained largely in terms of the pent-up demand resulting from the previous quantitative controls on bank lending which had been imposed throughout the second half of the 1960s.

The Empirical Model

As already noted, the model is highly aggregative, consisting of only eight equations, and estimated employing annual data from 1952 to 1976. The degree of aggregation is therefore considerable and many elements which might be thought important have been left out. The more important of these are discussed below; any future development of this approach should include attempts to incorporate some of these influences. Even so, these preliminary results provide some interesting insights into how such a credit/financial/monetary model might work.

In a number of equations where there seemed good reason for expecting the short-run behaviour to differ from the long-run, this has been allowed for. The procedure, already well tried (Davidson *et al.*, 1978; Hendry, 1978), has been to specify the dependent variable, and all short-run behavioural influences, in first differences, but also to include some form of equilibrium relationship(s). For example, if the short-run equation is expressed in the form:

$$\Delta X = a_0 + a_1 \Delta Z - a_2 \begin{bmatrix} X \\ Y \end{bmatrix}_{-1} \qquad (5.7)$$

the long-run *static* equilibrium will be derived by setting all changes equal to zero (but also see below) and rearranging, so that

$$X = \frac{a_0}{a_2} Y \qquad (5.8)$$

This approach can be seen clearly in the first equation explaining private sector expenditure.

Estimation results for each of the equations have been included in Appendix 1; ordinary least squares (OLS) and two-stage least squares (2SLS) results are given. The 2SLS results have been obtained under the assumption that both the exchange rate and the level of intervention are endogenous to the model. This is achieved by assuming an *implicit* trade-off relationship between intervention and the change in the exchange rate in which no other predetermined variables enter, other than those already included in the model. Including this assumption, there are a total of fifty-two predetermined variables. With a maximum of twenty-six observations, and more typically only twenty-three, it was not possible to proceed directly to estimate the included current endogenous variables in the first stage of the two-stage process. The approximation employed to get round this problem was to construct principal components from the set of predetermined variables excluded from the equation being estimated, and to employ the main components in combination with the included predetermined variables. In most cases only six principal components were employed. The variables are defined in Appendix 2 and data sources are given in Appendix 3.

It is, however, necessary to repeat the caution given above that 2SLS estimation will only eliminate simultaneous equation bias as the sample size approaches infinity. With small samples, as here, the simultaneous bias may well not be greatly reduced. The advantage is that the 2SLS estimations are consistent whereas the OLS ones are not. It will be noted that the different estimation methods result in little difference in the estimates obtained.

Real Private Sector Expenditure, EFC
The usual approach to the determination of expenditure employs a demand function in which the level of disposable income plays a dominant role. The simultaneity between aggregate expenditures and incomes is often ignored, and saving is treated as a residual. This approach does not generally measure, or enforce consistency with, any particular long-run properties, and there are no constraints on behaviour. It lays emphasis on the determinants of demand and assumes that the supply side of the economy is flexible enough to accommodate any change in demand, though the relationship between actual and potential output sometimes enters as one of the arguments in determining the rate of inflation. Klein (1978), among others, has recently argued that the time has come to pay much greater attention to supply side influences. This is also an important element in the monetarist approach (for example, Friedman, 1968), which suggests that private sector expenditure should be determined over the long run by the real supply potential of the economy, and that the money supply, together with other demand influences, will have only temporary effects.

The absence of supply influences is an important lacuna in the

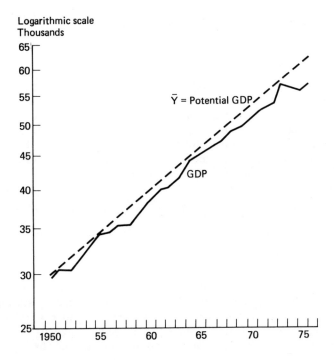

Figure 5.1   *Actual and potential GDP*

majority of econometric models, and it seemed necessary to make some attempt to try to incorporate a self-equilibrating property of the type suggested above into the model. This has been achieved in the simplest way possible by assuming constant exogenous growth rate of potential output (GDP) $\bar{Y}$, close to, but always above, the actual GDP series: the relationship between the two series is illustrated in Figure 5.1. This is obviously an extreme simplification but is possibly not too unreasonable as a first approximation. In any future developments of this type of model, it would be preferable to treat potential output as an endogenous variable. Conventional production functions are probably inadequate for this purpose. Although the stocks of capital and labour are almost certain to be important, the role of new technology and innovation in creating new products, and influencing both potential demand and supply, should not be neglected.

A monetarist might expect private sector expenditure, again at factor cost, EFC ($= E - TE$), in the long run to equal this potential output exactly. This condition has not been imposed since it implies that imports and exports of goods and services should be equal in the long run. Instead, the *static* equilibrium has been freely determined, defined as

$$\text{EFC} = \propto (\bar{Y} - G) \tag{5.9}$$

Various variables were also included to pick up any temporary demand influences, for example, a change in government expenditure, tax rates, foreign demand, changes in the real money supply and interest rates. Interest rates may also be expected to have a more permanent, long-run effect, either through their effect on the expenditure/saving decisions of the private sector, by increasing the perceived real cost of capital accumulation, or changing the demand for money:

$$\Delta \text{EFC} = f_{\text{EFC}} \left\{ K, \Delta(M/P)_{-i}, r_{-i}, \dot{P}_{-i}, \Delta G_{-i}, \Delta t_{-i}, \Delta s_{-i}, \Delta F_{-i}, \left[\frac{\text{EFC}}{\bar{Y} - G} \right]_{-1} \right\} \tag{5.10}$$

The final estimated equations are included in Appendix 1; they are equations A(i) and A(ii). It proved impossible to obtain any significant coefficients for real interest rates or for inflation separately. There is, however, evidence of a long-run effect of nominal interest rates on expenditure. Statistically it makes no real difference whether this long-run effect is related to the long rate of interest or to the short rate. The included equation employs the long rate, as this would seem to imply more reasonable long-run behaviour, although real rates would generally be considered more relevant. The coefficient on the foreign demand variable is not really significant, but is nearly so, and has been retained.

Several of the potential demand influences proved insignificant and have been excluded. Among these was the change in the expenditure tax rate, Δs, implying that expenditure at market prices will increase by the full amount of any increase in expenditure taxes. It is interesting to note that changes in the real money supply have a substantial short-run effect on expenditure, but this disappears in the long run. An increase in the own rate of money, r_m, can be interpreted as increasing the demand for money and thereby reducing the direct effect of money on expenditure. The fit of the equation is fairly good, and the estimated standard error of the equation represents less than 0.5 of 1% of the mean of EFC over the estimation period.

In practice, it is not realistic to calculate equilibrium for a stationary economy since we know that potential income and therefore expenditure are growing over time. The equilibrium values of the equation have therefore been calculated using the mean values of most of the explanatory variables. Changes in the income tax rate are assumed to be zero, as are changes in prices. And if prices are not to change, this implies that the stock of money grows at a rate sufficient to accommodate the increase in expenditure (see the section on prices below, p. 111–3). The resultant long-run equilibrium is given by

$$\frac{\text{EFC}}{\bar{Y} - G} = 1.0380 - 0.0112 r_b \qquad (5.11)$$

If we were to define an equilibrium interest rate as that which produced EFC $= \bar{Y} - G$, it would be 3.38 per cent. This would, in fact, appear to be a very reasonable estimate of an equilibrium long rate. Over the fifty-five years from 1860 to 1914, which was probably a fairly 'normal' period, Bank rate averaged 3.56 per cent and the Consols rate 3.02 per cent. This was a period of relatively stable prices, with, if anything, a tendency for prices to fall. Within the model, to the extent that inflation leads to an increase in r_b, it will reduce private sector expenditure.

The Price Level, P
The obvious long-run property for a monetary model is that the price level should be a function of the money supply, under the assumption that velocity is stable (*not* necessarily constant). And since money has no long-run effect on expenditure (see above), this implies that prices will tend to increase in proportion with the increase in money supply, less the effect of real growth and interest rates on the demand for money.[2] Even so, in the short run, sterling import prices may have a substantial direct impact on the domestic price level. This influence will, however, only be permanent to the extent that the money supply responds to any change in import prices. The actual speeds of adjustment have been kept flexible, and the possibility is also included that velocity may be a function of the own rate of interest on bank deposits and alternative interest rates.
  The basic form estimated was:

$$\dot{P} = f_p \left[K, \dot{P} z_{-i}, \dot{M}_{-i}, \dot{E}_{-i}, \dot{r}_{-i}, \ln r, \ln E_{-1}, \ln (M/EP)_{-1} \right] \qquad (5.12)$$

The fit of the equation is reasonably good, with a standard error below 0.5 per cent of the rate of inflation – see equations B(i) and B(ii) in Appendix 1.
  In the long run with no changes in any of the variables:

$$\ln P = -5.055 + \ln M - 0.4487 \ln E \qquad (5.13)$$

Alternatively, the equation can be interpreted as defining the long-run demand-for-money relationship, so that:

$$\ln M = 5.055 + \ln P + 0.4487 \ln E \qquad (5.14)$$

or

$$\frac{M}{P} = 160.9E^{0.4487} \qquad (5.15)$$

The long-run expenditure elasticity is much smaller than is generally expected for a broad money aggregate. A possible explanation is that it is really due to a trend increase in the velocity of circulation of money, resulting from, for example, an increased integration of industry or the development of non-bank financial intermediaries in competition with the banks. For this reason a trend term was included in the equation as a possible, naive representation of such developments. However, when included with the logarithm of expenditure the trend term was invariably insignificant.

The estimated long-run expenditure elasticity is, in fact, remarkably similar to that obtained by Laidler and O'Shea (1978) employing a very different approach, and estimating the demand-for-money function directly. Their estimate for the elasticity of the demand for money with respect to permanent income was 0.4. It is not clear that values in this range are particularly unreasonable. While there are good reasons to expect saving, that is, non-consumption, to be a luxury good, with an income elasticity greater than unit (and the same may also be true of the acquisition of financial assets), there seems to be much less justification for the demand for money to have this characteristic.

There is no long-run interest elasticity included in the equation. This means that any long-run effect of interest rates on the *supply* of money will be fully reflected in changes in the rate of inflation (or in the price level).

The long-run unitary elasticity relating money and prices was tested by including $\ln P_{-1}$ separately in the equation, in addition to the constraint variable, $\ln (M/EP)_{-1}$. The estimated coefficient was small and not significant.

The inclusion of expenditure and income tax rates failed to produce any additional explanation of movements in prices. The estimated coefficients were always insignificant, and, if added to the reported equations, made no difference to the estimated coefficients on the other explanatory variables.

It was noted above that an increase in the expenditure tax will, in fact, increase expenditure at market prices. This outcome, in combination with a fixed money supply, will have the effect of *reducing* the price level. As it is, the increase in expenditure tax receipts will reduce the PSBR and further reduce the price level. This type of reaction provides a good example of a major difference between Keynesian models, which lay emphasis on fiscal policy, and monetary models in which the transmission of such measures is accomplished through changes in the demand for, and supply of, money. The final equilibrium value is uncertain, as interactions with the rest of the model must also be taken into account. Even so, the path to equilibrium will almost certainly be in the opposite direction to Keynesian models which would assume that an increase in expenditure taxes would be passed on, at least in part, to prices. The expenditure tax rate was included in the bank lending equation but this did not result in a positive effect that might offset the process just described.

Exports, X
The position of the United Kingdom as a relatively small country competing in large world markets suggests that one might expect reasonably high price elasticities of demand implied by such an assumption. In fact it seems almost impossible to identify high elasticities even in markets where substitution is known to be virtually perfect. Identification of high price elasticities is not helped by employment of the composite price indices determined by the small scale of the model. In addition, if domestic prices adjust to changes in import prices in the long run, as is necessary if the so-called 'law of one price' is to hold, then the change in relative prices must result in changes in the domestic money supply unless the exchange rate is to adjust. This is because in the long run domestic prices are determined by the money supply. Changes in relative prices therefore need to influence the current account so that this in turn will change the supply of money. However, this does not necessarily require high price elasticities. As long as the balance of payments (and the money supply) change in the desired direction, this flow will continue until price equilibrium is restored. Therefore, given certain minimum conditions, the size of the price elasticities is only important for the speed of adjustment not for the equilibrium conditions.

Equations were estimated in both linear and log-linear form to allow for the possibility that the estimated elasticities had varied over time. To begin with the evidence quite clearly supported a linear format for imports, thereby allowing elasticities to vary over time; in the case of exports the actual specification made little difference. It was later decided to examine the effect of the dramatic change in the relative price of oil which took place in 1973. This was done very simply by introducing a 0,1 dummy variable in the import equation, putting unity from 1974. The effect of this new variable was to produce a greatly improved logarithmic equation. Not surprisingly, this suggests that the price elasticity of oil is substantially different from most commodities included in the aggregate import function.

Consequently, it is the logarithmic equations which are reported here. Disaggregation of the import and export functions would be required before this model could provide a reliable forecasting framework. As it is these equations adopt a fairly standard approach and improving their performance would also improve the performance of the model as a whole.

The explanatory variables included in the export equation reflect relative prices, the exchange rate, foreign and domestic demand pressure:

$$\ln X = f_{\ln X} [K, \ln E_{-i}, \ln G_{-i}, \ln F_{-i}, \ln P_{-i}, \ln Pz_{-i}, \ln e_{-i}] \quad (5.16)$$

Prices were included separately in order to permit different patterns of response, given the diverse markets involved. It also allows for any differences in the basis upon which the indices have been constructed. As it turned our (see equations C(i) and C(ii) in Appendix 1) the estimated price coefficients were sufficiently similar to allow the price differential to be employed with no loss of significance. The various expenditure elasticities are large and significant and there are no lags in adjustment. The exchange rate was not significant.

Imports, Z
The same basic approach was adopted in explaining imports. In this case exports were included as a separate demand influence, and the oil price increase in 1973 was allowed for by including the oil price dummy, OILD, discussed above.

$$\ln Z =$$

$$f_{\ln Z} [K, \ln E_{-i}, \ln G_{-i}, \ln F_{-i}, \ln X_{-i}, \ln P_{-i}, \ln Pz_{-i}, \ln e_{-i}, \text{OILD}]$$
$$(5.17)$$

Exports have quite a substantial effect on imports — equations D(i) and (ii) in Appendix 1 — far in excess of the import content of commodity exports which is about one-seventh of total value (implying a long-run elasticity of under 0.15), and should be even less when, as here, services are included. No significant role could be identified for foreign demand, at least as measured in this study. The long-run relative price elasticities are very similar, though adjustment to changes in import prices seems to take longer.

Net overseas lending to the private sector in sterling, N
This aggregate is the net result of all forms of private sector external borrowing and lending, and reflects every variety of portfolio choice both here and abroad. There are, therefore, any number of potential behavioural influences on the final outcome. Apart from trying to

identify significant interest-rate effects the main emphasis has been placed on DCE, relative to nominal expenditure, EP, in the United Kingdom and the United States. The effect could work both through direct substitution for capital flows, and through the influence on exchange rate expectations which such changes might have. The rate of change and level of the exchange rate are included to represent expectations. The value of these net external flows must to a large extent reflect the preferences of the rest of the world and should be taken as given when the private sector decides on the final composition of its overall portfolio. For this reason, it would be unlikely to find a significant effect for the lagged stock of money, representing the long-run stock equilibrium behaviour of the private sector (as explained below in the section on the private demand for public sector debt). Even without the lagged money stock, the estimated equation still has reasonable long-run properties.

The change in the value of the current account, ΔCA, has been included in order to measure accommodating financial movements generated by changes in trade flows. Such an influence has been suggested, and employed in empirical estimates of short-term capital flows for the United Kingdom, by Hodjera (1972), Branson and Hill (1971), and Fausten (1975). It would also be possible to justify the inclusion of the level of the current account, or the cumulated total, to reflect expectations of possible exchange rate movements, in which case a positive sign on the coefficient would be expected. Kouri and Porter (1974), however, have produced an alternative argument suggesting a negative sign on the current account. The sign to be expected on the level of the current account is therefore unclear, although there are reasonable grounds for expecting capital flows to be more sensitive to exchange rate expectations than to relative interest rates alone. Capital flows may well be highly elastic with respect to returns available internationally. These returns, however, are not given simply by the rates of interest quoted, but are likely to be dominated by expected exchange rate movements, particularly in the short run.

The basic implicit equation was:

$$\Delta N = f_N$$

$$[K, DCE_{UK-i}, EP_{UK-i}, DCE_{US-i}, EP_{US-i}, M_{-1}, CA, \Delta CA, e, \dot{e}]$$

$$(5.18)$$

The level of the current account, and the lagged stock of money, turned out to be insignificant — see equations E(i) and (ii) in Appendix 1. It is possible to replace the exchange rate by the constant term and get practically the same result, but it is not possible to include both variables, presumably because the exchange rate has itself been so close to a constant over the estimation period. Including the level of the exchange rate as well as the rate of change does, however, produce a stable long-run response of net overseas lending.

This equation is a fairly good fit and has reasonable statistical properties, particularly considering the variability of the series and the usual difficulties encountered in trying to identify capital flow equations for this country. The inclusion of the expenditure variables in the form of changes was not an imposed restriction but resulted from freely estimating the equation employing levels of expenditures. This result is, however, consistent with the rest of the equation and provides what is, in effect, the first difference of a stock adjustment relationship.

The interest rate on public sector debt, r_b

Because the United Kingdom is a relatively small country within the context of world markets, and given the obvious importance of foreign interest rates for domestic rates, the possibility should be considered that r_b is linked in some way to foreign rates, allowing, of course, for *expected* exchange rate movements. In the long run, assuming no balance of payments deficit, or expectations of exchange rate movements, and no change in domestic short rates, the long-run property of such an equation could be defined as:

$$r_b = k + r_{fb} \qquad (5.19)$$

In the short run, r_b is assumed to be influenced by changes in the domestic short rate, Δr_m, and variables influencing expectations regarding future exchange rate changes. This latter group of variables includes the external currency flow to the private sector, ΔR, relative rates of inflation, $\dot{P} - \dot{P}_{US}$, and the percentage change in the exchange rate, $\dot{e}$:

$$\Delta r_b = f_{r_b}[K, \Delta r_{m-i}, \Delta R_{-i}(\dot{P} - \dot{P}_{US})_{-i}, \dot{e}_{-i}, (r_b - r_{fb})_{-i}] \qquad (5.20)$$

Some considerable effort was put into trying to identify a role for the PSBR or the domestic financing requirement (approximately PSBR + CA + ΔN) but this proved quite unsuccessful. An alternative hypothesis – that the long rate is related to the short rate in the long run – was tested by adding the constraint variable $(r_b - r_m)_{-1}$ to the best equation, but this was not significant.

The fit of the equation is quite good, with a standard error which is only one-fifth of 1 per cent of the rate of interest – see equations F(i) and (ii) in Appendix 1. All included variables have the correct *a priori* sign and are significant. Unfortunately, the inflation differential was not significant, and the same was true for the current rate of change of the exchange rate. As far as the domestic rate of inflation is concerned, it is changes in the rate that seem to be important. In the long run, with no changes in any of the independent variables, and no external currency flows to the private sector:

$$r_b = 0.980 + r_{fb} \qquad (5.21)$$

The short rate of interest is taken to be a policy instrument of the monetary authorities. No equation is included for the short rate, but any future developments would need to include work on estimating a reaction function for this variable. For the time being, it is of interest to examine what effect the authorities might have on the economy, within the context of this model, through manipulation of the short rate of interest.

Separate interest rates have not been identified to measure both the borrowing and lending rates for banks. These are assumed to move in line with the official short rate, at least over the period of a year, which is the frequency of observation employed here. Given the close correspondence between these two rates and the difficulty in observing the actual marginal rate on bank credit, this may not be too unreasonable as a first approximation. It does mean that we cannot examine the influence of round-tripping (the 'merry-go-round'), but this may not be a great loss as this phenomenon was probably only a temporary one.

Private sector demand for public sector debt, B
The natural dependent variable, given that the objective is to explain the financing of the PSBR, is net private sector transactions in public sector debt. It does not, however, follow from this that there is no long-run adjustment towards a stock equilibrium. Equations incorporating such a process could be specified along the lines already employed in the estimation of expenditure and prices above, and this form has been employed by Friedman (1977b), incorporating the stock of assets and private sector wealth, as well as the changes; however, see also the criticism in Ando (1978).

In this study, a somewhat different approach has been adopted. It is an approach suggested by the theoretical model employed, and by the assumed characteristics of monetary disequilibrium, but one that is also supported by the fact that there are no really reliable series available for wealth holdings. The nominal money stock relative to nominal expenditure, M/EP (the inverse of velocity), lagged one period, has been included in the equation to pick up any disequilibrium effect − in this case, disequilibrium between the stock of money and the stock of bonds. Bank lending also remains to be explained in similar fashion. In order to ensure a long-run stock equilibrium, it is necessary to include at least one of these two stocks − bank lending or public sector debt. For present purposes, mainly to avoid the problems of trying to measure the relevant stock of public sector debt, the lagged stock of bank lending was included in both equations. In fact, this variable was only significant in the equation explaining public sector debt.

In the short run, flow adjustments are very important, and this can be justified in terms of the institutional nature of the gilt-edged market which is dominated by the large long-term investment institutions – insurance companies and pension funds – which have massive annual funds to allocate and presumably long, planned holding periods.

A common feature of all the equations explaining financial asset and liability demands in the model which should be emphasised, is that they do not represent the allocation of predetermined saving. Instead the separate transactions in assets and liabilities need to be aggregated in order to arrive at a total for saving. This view, that the accumulation of financial wealth is not independent of the forms it takes, is important. An interesting by-product of this approach is that it permits the value of private sector income to be derived without directly considering the markets within which incomes are generated.

The dependent variable is defined as total net purchases of public sector debt by the non-bank private sector divided by nominal private sector expenditure, $\Delta B/EP$. If preferred, it can be thought of as real transactions divided by real expenditure. Various interest rates were included, with lags to allow for the effect of levels and changes. In addition, a number of other variables were incorporated to reflect exchange rate expectations. These include relative rates of inflation, $\dot{P}_{UK}/\dot{P}_{US}$, and total external flows to the private sector (current account flows) divided by nominal expenditure, $\Delta R/EP$. This last variable may also incorporate a direct effect of external flows into public sector debt on top of any influence on expectations.

$$\frac{\Delta B}{EP} = f_B \left\{ K, r_{-i}, \left[\frac{\dot{P}_{UK}}{\dot{P}_{US}}\right]_{-i}, e_{-i}, \left[\frac{\Delta R}{EP}\right]_{-i}, \left[\frac{M}{EP}\right]_{-1}, \left[\frac{L}{M}\right]_{-1} \right\} \quad (5.22)$$

The fit of the equation is reasonable, and does at least identify various interest rate effects – see equations G(i) and (ii) in Appendix 1. The short rate, r_m, only appears as a first difference, indicating that it has no long-run effect. At first sight this may seem somewhat strange, but it is, in fact, consistent with the long-run properties of the implicit demand-for-money function which is independent of any interest rate differential between money and public sector debt. There is also a long-run effect of any increase in r_b which is not directly accounted for by substitution out of other financial assets. According to the rest of the model, these transactions will be financed partly by reducing expenditures and partly by additional borrowing from the banks. The long-run properties of this equation are crucially dependent on the effect of the lagged money supply and stock of bank lending. The sign on this latter variable is consistent with rational portfolio behaviour in that the higher the stock of bank lending the lower the purchase of public sector debt, bearing in mind that there is also a positive effect of an increase in bank lending on public sector debt sales coming from the effect on the money supply. Reducing purchases of, or selling, public sector debt is an alternative means of obtaining finance. If bank lending is regarded as a negative asset of the private sector, then the estimated relationship clearly helps to restore the natural balance of the portfolio.

Bank lending to the private sector, L
When quantitative restrictions have been placed on banks, a period of credit rationing should be expected during which it would not be possible to observe points along a demand curve for bank credit. It had originally been the intention to split the period up in this way, but there are, in fact, insufficient degrees of freedom to allow this. The alternative adopted has been to estimate a demand function including a dummy for those periods when quantitative restrictions were in force. This has the effect of shifting the whole demand function down at such times, but still assumes that the other behavioural determinants have the same influence as before. This is unfortunate and is likely to lead to an underestimate of the true effects of these variables during uncontrolled periods.

As was noted above (Chapter 4) most previous empirical work that has attempted to take account of the effect of quantitative controls has included this influence only in combination with qualitative instructions to the banks; this has been done by employing a 0, 1, 2 dummy. Such an approach is, however, inadequate. Qualitative instructions and quantitative controls are not differences in degree, they are differences in kind. Separate dummies have therefore been included for each of these policy options; ID and QD, respectively.

There is also another weakness associated with using a single dummy variable to represent quantitative controls (whichever way it is defined). If quantitative controls really do result in banks rationing credit to the private sector, as surely they must, then the longer these controls are in force the greater must become the pressure of pent-up demand for bank credit. In order to capture this effect, a pressure variable, PR, which reflects the duration of the quantitative controls, has been included at times when quantitative restrictions have been removed.

The other explanatory variables included in the specification are: the rates of change of real private expenditures, $\dot{E}$, and prices, $\dot{P}$, to represent both an acceleration in financing needs and expectations about the future; various interest rates; the percentage of special deposits called from the banks, SD; a dummy variable, JD, to capture the effect of the introduction of supplementary special deposits; the lagged stock of money relative to nominal expenditure so as to pick up the disequilibrium stock effects, the stock of banks' loans to the private sector relative to private sector money balances lagged one period $[L/M]_{-1}$ for similar reasons, and the change in the current account plus external capital flows to the private sector divided by nominal expenditures, $\Delta R/EP$, in order to capture any direct substitution between inflows from abroad and the need to borrow from the banks. To the extent that these foreign inflows influence expectations, this might be expected to be in a favourable direction and therefore result in the opposite sign in the equation, that is, to increase bank borrowing. This suggests that perhaps other variables should be considered which might influence exchange rate expectations, for example, the actual rate of change of the exchange rate, $\dot{e}$.

The basic form estimated was:

$$\frac{\Delta L}{EP} = f_L \left[K, \dot{E}_{-i}, \dot{P}_{-i}, \left[\frac{\Delta R}{EP} \right]_{-i}, \dot{e}_{-i}, r_{-i}, JD_{-i}, QD, PR_{-i}, SD_{-i}, \right.$$
$$\left. \left[\frac{M}{EP} \right]_{-1}, \left[\frac{L}{M} \right]_{-1} \right] \tag{5.23}$$

The only significant interest rate effect was obtained for the long rate – see equations H(i) and (ii) in Appendix 1. Unfortunately it was impossible to obtain a significant coefficient for the own rate of interest, r_m. This may be because the rate used was an inadequate measure of the bank lending rate. Another possibility is that the inability to separate controlled and uncontrolled periods (see above) has obscured the interest rate sensitivity of unrestricted demand for bank credit. Although it might be reasonable to expect that there is some level of interest rates that will reduce the demand for bank loans it is important to recall the argument put forward in Chapter 3 (for example, Tobin, 1978) that there is likely to be persistent excess demand for bank advances, that is, advances are quantity constrained. To the extent that this is the case it will not be possible to observe reasonable interest rate elasticities. Moreover, interest rate changes will have other effects within the model which then feed back into the lending equation, and these must be taken into account when determining the net effect of any change.

Instructions to the banks to restrict credit appear to have no effect. Quantitative restrictions, on the other hand, significantly reduce bank lending, but the value of this appears to be more than offset subsequently by the force of the excess demand that builds up and is accommodated once the controls are removed. The imposition of special deposits also has the effect of reducing bank lending, but this is only temporary and there is no significant long-run effect. The introduction of supplementary special deposits appears to have a significant negative effect but only with a lag. While this result can be explained in terms of the time taken before the restriction starts to bite, there has only been a single example within the estimation period, which is insufficient to conclude conclusively that the correct influence has been identified.

An increase in the value of the exchange rate seems to result in a temporary increase in bank lending. This will at least produce a stable response, increasing the money supply, and tending to offset any further increase in the exchange rate. A possible explanation of this effect could be the favourable influence on expectations referred to above, and/or a temporary decline in profitability not compensated for by any fall in import prices.

The Durbin–Watson statistic is rather high, but this is a poor indication of first-order autocorrelation given the size of the sample and the limited degrees of freedom available. Inspection of the residuals, in fact, indicates no evidence of negative first-order autocorrelation. As with the demand for public sector debt, the stock of money is an important determinant of bank lending in the long run.

Conclusion

The equations of the model have been estimated without the aid of dummy variables for strikes, prices and incomes policies, union organisation, unemployment or the introduction of CCC. It is perfectly possible that some of these variables have had a short-run influence, but it has still been possible to explain prices and expenditure, etc., quite well without them. If nothing else, these equations demonstrate the possibility of explaining movements in important economic aggregates in terms that are very different from those usually employed. There is, therefore, some tentative support for the integrated monetary/ credit approach proposed here.

The next stage is to simulate the model. This will provide evidence on the dynamic properties of the model, that is, its stability and the dynamic effects of changes in exogenous variables. The results of these experiments are given in Chapter 6.

Appendix 1

Table 5A.1 OLS and 2SLS Estimation Results[a]

A. Private sector expenditure, EFC

The dependent variable is the change in private sector expenditure at factor cost, Δ EFC.

	K	$\Delta(M/P)$	$\Delta(M/P)_{-1}$	$\Delta(M/P)_{-3}$	r_{b-1}	Δr_{m-1}	Δr_{m-2}	Δt_{-1}	ΔF_{-1}	$(EFC/(\bar{Y}-G))_{-1}$
A(i) OLS	10563.4 (7.28)**	0.1844 (4.27)**	0.3889 (7.80)**	0.3049 (3.31)**	−112.54 (3.25)**	−343.77 (7.71)**	−90.07 (1.73)	−19659.6 (3.05)*	0.01075 (1.63)	−9906.39 (6.67)**
						$\bar{R}^2 = 0.982$	s.e. = 149.71	D.W. = 2.012	d.f. = 12	
A(ii) 2SLS	10579.0 (7.28)**	0.1773 (3.63)**	0.3915 (7.81)**	0.3004 (3.24)**	−111.31 (3.19)**	−348.14 (7.62)**	−92.33 (1.77)	−19763.7 (3.06)*	0.01124 (1.69)	−9930.9 (6.68)**
						$\bar{R}^2 = 0.982$	s.e. = 149.97	d.f. = 12		

B. Prices, P

The dependent variable is the rate of change of $P = \dot{P} = \Delta \ln P$

	K	$\dot{P}_z$	$\dot{P}_{z-1}$	$\dot{P}_{z-2}$	$\dot{M}$	$\dot{M}_{-2}$	$\dot{E}$	$\dot{E}_{-1}$	$\dot{E}_{-2}$	$\ln \dot{E}_{-1}$	r_{m-1}	$\ln (M/EP)_{-1}$
B(i) OLS	−1.009 (4.05)**	0.0931 (3.86)**	0.2426 (7.56)**	0.2221 (9.11)**	0.09541 (3.46)**	−0.1781 (3.83)**	−0.5505 (5.33)**	0.3050 (4.38)**	0.1041 (2.64)*	0.1155 (4.45)**	−0.0503 (4.64)**	0.2095 (7.60)**
							$R^2 = 0.994$	s.e. = 0.00427	D.W. = 2.701	d.f. = 11		
B(ii) 2SLS	−1.059 (3.97)	0.0782 (2.45)*	0.2280 (6.41)**	0.2279 (8.70)**	0.09816 (3.00)*	−0.1935 (3.87)**	−0.6264 (4.54)**	0.3346 (4.23)**	0.1001 (2.37)*	0.1310 (4.31)**	−0.0559 (4.11)**	0.2284 (7.19)**
							$R^2 = 0.994$	s.e. = 0.00447	d.f. = 11		

C. Exports, X

The dependent variable is the natural logarithm of exports of goods and services measured at constant prices, $\ln X$.

	K	$\ln F$	$\ln G$	$\ln E$	$\ln (P/P_z)$			
C(i) OLS	7.949 (9.08)**	0.9866 (17.35)**	−0.3404 (4.54)**	−0.7303 (5.98)**	0.5061 (8.15)**	$R^2 = 0.997$	s.e. = 0.0155	
						D.W. = 2.320	d.f. = 18	
C(ii) 2SLS	7.660 (7.54)**	0.9753 (15.49)**	−0.3401 (4.52)**	−0.6918 (4.71)**	0.5182 (7.49)**	$R^2 = 0.997$	s.e. = 0.0159	d.f. = 18

Table 5A.1 (continued)

D. Imports, Z

	K	Time	$\ln E$	$\ln E_{-1}$	$\ln G$	$\ln X$	OILD	$\ln P$	$\ln Pz$	$\ln Pz_{-1}$	$\ln Pz_{-2}$
D(i) OLS	-10.885 (2.92)*	-0.04161 (2.65)*	1.5800 (6.91)*	-0.6519 (2.69)*	0.3609 (3.09)*	0.8330 (4.77)**	0.2016 (2.34)**	1.1861 (3.19)**	-0.7651 (2.47)*	-0.2039 (1.27)	-0.1964 (1.70)
D(ii) 2SLS	-9.627 (2.27)*	-0.03986 (2.18)	1.4725 (5.77)**	-0.7091 (2.69)*	0.3465 (2.68)*	0.7962 (3.97)**	0.1949 (2.24)*	1.2007 (2.96)*	-0.6826 (2.35)*	-0.2714 (1.61)	-0.2367 (2.06)

D(i): $R^2 = 0.998$ D.W. = 2.380   s.e. = 0.0139   d.f. = 12

D(ii): $R^2 = 0.998$ s.e. = 0.0142   d.f. = 12

E. Private Sector capital flows, N

The dependent variable is the flow of net overseas lending to the private sector, ΔN.

	e	DCE_{UK}	DCE_{UK-1}	ΔEP_{UK}	DCE_{US}	ΔEP_{US}	ΔCA	$\hat{e}$
E(i) OLS	-95.336 (4.24)**	-0.4080 (9.09)**	0.1893 (6.71)**	0.1718 (4.36)**	0.01544 (5.23)**	-0.006482 (2.14)*	-0.2104 (3.29)**	5025.1 (5.10)**
E(ii) 2SLS	-95.552 (4.21)**	-0.4107 (8.87)**	0.1889 (6.53)**	0.1825 (4.37)**	0.01540 (5.08)**	-0.006514 (2.11)*	-0.2496 (3.48)**	5086.0 (5.09)**

E(i): $R^2 = 0.884$ s.e. = 155.8   D.W. = 2.146   d.f. = 16

E(ii): $R^2 = 0.883$ s.e. = 156.3   d.f. = 16

F. Long rate, r_b

The dependent variable is the change in rate of interest on public sector debt, Δr_b

	K	Δr_m	Δr_{m-1}	ΔR	$\Delta \dot{P}_{-1}$	$\hat{e}_{-1}$	$(r_b - r_{tb})_{-1}$
F(i) OLS	0.2958 (4.74)**	0.4930 (13.09)**	0.1614 (4.40)**	-0.0003009 (4.72)**	5.2549 (2.28)*	-4.1606 (2.43)*	-0.3271 (4.39)**
F(ii) 2SLS	0.2776 (4.20)**	0.5137 (12.05)**	0.1495 (3.82)**	-0.0002426 (2.91)*	5.6148 (2.37)*	-3.6715 (2.04)	-0.2833 (3.35)**

F(i): $R^2 = 0.956$ s.e. = 0.2061   D.W. = 1.487   d.f. = 16

F(ii): $R^2 = 0.954$ s.e. = 0.2124   d.f. = 16

Table 5A.1 (continued)

G. Private sector demand for public sector debt, B

The dependent variable is the net transactions in private sector holdings of public sector debt, excluding notes and coins, divided by nominal private sector expenditure, $\Delta B/EP$.

	r_b	r_{fb}	Δr_{fb}	Δr_m	$(M/EP)_{-1}$	$(L/M)_{-1}$		
G(i) OLS	0.01420 (4.68)**	-0.006248 (1.71)	-0.02336 (4.20)**	-0.005353 (2.77)*	0.04918 (4.17)**	-0.09324 (2.86)**	$R^2 = 0.625$	s.e. = 0.0120
							D.W. = 2.143	d.f. = 19
G(ii) 2SLS	0.01462 (4.67)**	-0.006386 (1.86)	-0.02358 (4.22)**	-0.005403 (2.78)*	0.04931 (4.21)**	-0.09357 (2.90)	$\bar{R}^2 = 0.624$	s.e. = 0.0120
								d.f. = 19

H. Bank lending to the private sector, L

The dependent variable is the flow of new bank lending to the private sector divided by nominal private sector expenditure, $\Delta L/EP$.

	$\hat{E}$	$\hat{E}_{-1}$	r_b	QD	PR	PR_{-1}	ΔSD	JD_{-1}	$\hat{e}_{-1}$	$(M/EP)_{-1}$
H(i) OLS	0.2692 (7.30)**	0.1464 (4.38)**	0.006956 (14.99)**	-0.01316 (5.31)**	0.004915 (4.06)**	0.01127 (9.10)**	-0.006623 (4.62)**	-0.03019 (4.29)**	0.1698 (3.68)**	0.05082 (8.68)**
					$R^2 = 0.972$	s.e. = 0.00540	D.W. = 3.016	d.f. = 15		
H(ii) 2SLS	0.3171 (6.82)**	0.1426 (3.98)**	0.007204 (14.25)**	-0.01362 (5.27)**	0.004435 (3.87)**	0.01067 (8.61)**	-0.006788 (4.51)**	-0.03106 (4.17)**	0.1752 (3.59)**	0.05524 (8.54)**
					$\bar{R}^2 = 0.970$	s.e. = 0.00545	d.f. = 15			

[a] The econometric results are given with the relevant t statistic in parentheses below each coefficient. The other statistical measures reported are: the coefficient of determination corrected for degrees of freedom, $\bar{R}^2$; the standard error of the equation, s.e.; the Durbin–Watson d statistic, D.W.; and the degrees of freedom, d.f., for the equation. The t statistic associated with each coefficient is starred to indicate whether it is significant at the 5% level* or the 1% level**. These significance levels are given for a two-tail test. In those instances for which we have some a priori expectation of the sign to be expected the criteria employed will understate the significance of the coefficients.

Appendix 2

Identities and definitions

$$Y \equiv \text{GDP} \equiv E + G + X - Z$$

$$Pz \equiv Pz\,\$/e$$

$$Ph \equiv \frac{P(Y + Z) - ZPz}{Y}$$

$$E \equiv \text{EFC} + (\text{TE}/P)$$

$$Yp \equiv E + (Ty + \text{NAFA})/P$$

$$\text{NAFA} \equiv \Delta \text{NC} + \Delta \text{B} + \Delta \text{D} + \Delta \text{NDL} - \Delta \text{L} - \Delta \text{N} + \text{NARES}$$

$$t \equiv Ty/Yp.P$$

$$s \equiv \text{TE}/\text{EFC}.P$$

$$\text{EFC} \equiv E - \text{TE}/P$$

$$\text{PSBR} \equiv G.P - Ty - \text{TE} + \text{PBRES}$$

$$\text{CA} \equiv X.P - Z.Pz + \text{CARES}$$

$$\text{DCE} \equiv \text{PSBR} - \Delta \text{Dg} - \Delta \text{B} + \Delta \text{L}$$

$$\Delta \text{R} \equiv \text{CA} + \Delta \text{N}$$

$$\Delta \text{M} \equiv \text{DCE} + \Delta \text{R} - \Delta \text{NDL}$$

$$\equiv \text{PSBR} - \Delta \text{Dg} - \Delta \text{B} + \Delta \text{L} + \text{CA} + \Delta \text{N} - \Delta \text{NDL}$$

$$D \equiv M - \text{NC}$$

Variables included in the model

(i)   *Endogenous variables*

B = net private sector lending to the public sector

CA = nominal value of the current account of the balance of payments

D = private sector sterling-denominated bank deposits

DCE = UK domestic credit expansion

E = total private sector expenditure at constant 1970 market prices

EFC = total private sector expenditure at constant 1970 factor cost

L = bank lending in sterling to the private sector

Lg = bank lending to the public sector; in sterling, £Lg, and foreign currency, $\$Lg$

M = private sector sterling-denominated money balances

NAFA = net acquisition of financial assets by the private sector including the residual error in the flow of funds accounts (identical to the residual in the national income/expenditure accounts)

N = net external liabilities of the private sector in sterling

NC = private sector holdings of notes and coins

p = price deflator of total final expenditure

Ph = domestic costs of production, that is, the GDP deflator

Pz = price deflator of the sterling value of imports

PSBR = public sector borrowing requirement

R = net foreign reserves, defined as $\sum_{0}^{T} (\text{CA} + \Delta \text{N})$

r_b = domestic long-term rate of interest defined as a thirteen-month weighted average of the value, as at the last working day of the month, of the average redemption yield on five-year gilts

TE   = total expenditure tax receipts minus subsidies

Ty = total income tax receipts less transfer payments (but not including net interest payments)

X = exports of goods and services valued at constant 1970 prices

Y = gross domestic product at constant 1970 market prices

Yp = private sector income at constant 1970 market prices

Z = imports of goods and services at constant 1970 prices

(ii)   *Exogenous variables*

CARES = residual making up the current account identity, and consisting of the current value of net property income and transfers from abroad

DCE_{US} = domestic credit expansion in the United States, as defined in the IMF's *International Financial Statistics*

Dg   = public sector bank deposits, in sterling, £Dg, and foreign currency, $Dg

e = sterling/dollar exchange rate

EP_{US} = nominal private sector expenditure in the United States

F = an index of world demand; the constant 1970 dollar value of world exports, as listed in the IMF's *International Financial Statistics*, excluding the United Kingdom

G = public sector expenditure on goods and services valued at 1970 expenditure prices

ID = 0, 1 dummy variable to represent qualitative instructions to banks to restrict lending to the private sector

JD = a dummy variable representing the introduction of the Supplementary Special Deposits scheme. This variable takes a value of unity when the controls are introduced and zero at all other times

NARES = residual making up NAFA by the private sector, essentially made up by public sector lending to the private sector

NDL   = non-deposit liabilities of the banking sector; equity and reserves

P_{US} = United States GNP deflator

$Pz\$$ = foreign currency price of imports

PBRES = residual making up the PSBR, made up of grants and transfers not already included, e.g. net interest payments, and changes in financial assets of (lending by) the public sector

OILD   = a dummy variable reflecting the sharp increase in the price of oil during 1973. The variable takes a value of zero up to 1973, $0-1$ in 1973, and unity for all following years

PR = a dummy variable to reflect the removal of quantitative restrictions on bank lending when its value is the number of years controls were imposed, and zero at all other times

QD = 0, 1 dummy variable to represent quantitative controls (ceilings) on bank lending to the private sector

r_{fb}	=	overseas long-term rate of interest; defined as the US corporate bond rate (total), average of daily figures
r_m	=	rate of interest on bank deposits and loans; pre-1964 this is Bank rate, post-1971 it is the inter-bank rate, and between these dates it is a weighted average of the two
SD	=	percentage of special deposits called from the banks, daily average
s	=	average expenditure tax rate
t	=	average income tax rate
T	=	time trend
$\bar{Y}$	=	potential GDP at constant 1970 factor cost

Variables included in component identities but not included in the final model equations and identities

BF	=	net overseas lending to the public sector, including all public sector flows entering the capital account of the balance of payments, but excluding that overseas lending which is a counterpart of the official financing requirement
BOF	=	balance for official financing
Df	=	bank deposits held by the overseas sector
$D	=	foreign currency bank deposits of the private sector
Lf	=	bank lending to the overseas sector
$L	=	bank lending in foreign currency to the private sector
Nf	=	net external claims on the private sector

Additional definitions

$\dot{x}$	=	$\Delta \ln x$
Δ	=	first difference operator
x_{-1}	=	the ith period lag of x

Appendix 3

Data Sources
Most of the data series were obtained from CSO and Bank of England data tapes, at least for the more recent years. Some of the earlier figures are estimates obtained directly from the CSO or Bank of England, and many had to be estimated employing imperfect information.

The data sources listed in Table 5A.2 give the most readily available current published series. Detailed sources of, and the methods of construction for, the money supply series are also given. This provides an illustration of some of the problems involved in constructing consistent series.

Money Supply Data
(1)   M = the stock of private sector sterling M3 balances
The total is built up employing the stock figure for 1963 taken from revised figures supplied by the Bank of England, less the stock of public sector bank deposits (£345 million) taken from SA No. 1,T12/1.

Table 5A.2

Notation		Definition	Source[a]
ΔB	=	purchases of public sector debt by the non-bank private sector (£ million)	(QB T11.3)
CA	=	current account of the balance of payments (£ million)	(BB T1.7)
ΔDg	=	change in public sector deposits in sterling and other currencies (£ million)	(QB T6)
DCE_{US}	=	domestic credit expansion in the US ($ million)	(IFS)
e	=	exchange rate; annual average of monthly spot $/£ rate	(QB T19)
E	=	(nominal private sector expenditure) $\div P$; (consumers' expenditure + private sector fixed capital formation and value of physical increase in stocks and work in progress) (£ million)	(BB T1.1) (BB T10.1) (BB T12.4)
EP_{US}	=	nominal private sector expenditure in the US (private sector consumption + gross domestic fixed capital formation) (£ million)	(IFS)
F	=	(nominal value of world exports/price of world exports) − (Nominal value of UK exports/price of UK exports) (£ million)	(IFS)
G	=	(nominal government expenditure) $\div P$; (general government final consumption + gross domestic fixed capital formation of the general government and public corporations + value of physical increase of stocks and work in progress of central government and public corporations) (£ million)	(BB T1.1) (BB T10.1) (BB T10.1) (BB T12.4) (BB T12.4)
L	=	$L_{1963} \mp \Delta L$	
ΔL	=	change in bank lending in sterling to the private sector (£ million)	(QB T11.3)
M	=	$M_{1963} \mp \Delta M$	
M_{1963}	=	$£M3_{1963} - £Dg_{1963}$	(see below)
ΔM	=	change in private sector sterling money balances; $\Delta £M3 - \Delta £Dg$ (£ million)	
$\Delta £M3$	=	change in sterling M3 (£ million)	(QB T11.3)
ΔN	=	change in net external sterling liabilities of the private sector (£ million)	(see below)
ΔNDL	=	change in non-deposit liabilities (£ million)	(QB T11.3)
P	=	TFE (nominal) $\div$ TFE (real)	
P_Z	=	Z (nominal) $\div Z$ (real)	
PSBR	=	public sector borrowing requirement (£ million)	(QB T11.3)
r_b	=	annual average of monthly redemption yield on short-dated (5 years) government stocks	(QB T9)
r_{fb}	=	US corporate bond rate	(FRB)
r_m	=	annual average of three months inter-bank rate (see Appendix 2 for details of earlier figures)	(QB T10)
SD	−	annual average percentage of actual special deposits	(FS T6.2)
T	=	income taxes less grants; (total income tax payments + national insurance contributions + capital taxes − grants to the personal sector − capital grants) (£ million)	(BB T6.3 and T 9.1)

Table 5A.2 (*continued*)

Notation	Definition	Source[a]
T_E	= nominal expenditure taxes minus subsidies (£ million)	(BB T1.1)
TFE	= total final expenditure (nominal) (£ million)	(BB T1.1)
	(real) (£ million, 1970 prices)	(BB T2.1)
X	= (nominal exports of goods and services) $\div P$ (£ million)	(BB T1.1)
Y	= gross domestic product at constant 1970 factor cost (£ million)	(BB T1.1)
$\bar{Y}$	= potential gross domestic product at constant 1970 factor cost; obtained by fitting a straight line to the logarithms of Y at 1955 and 1964, so that $\log \bar{Y} = 10.294 + 0.029$ Time (£ million)	
Z	= imports of goods and services (nominal)	(BB T1.1)
	(real) (£ million, 1970 prices)	(BB T2.1)

[a]BB   = National Income and Expenditure Blue Book
BEQB = Bank of England Quarterly Bulletin
FF   = Flow of Funds Handbook (Bank of England, 1972 and 1978)
FRB   = Federal Reserve Bulletin
FS   = Financial Statistics
IFS   = International Financial Statistics, published by International Monetary Fund
SA   = Bank of England Statistical Abstract No. 1 and No. 2 (Bank of England, 1970 and 1975)

(2) ΔM = the change in the private sectors' sterling M3 balances

         $\Delta £Dg$ = public sector sterling bank deposits; this is, of course, also subtracted from the right hand side of the identity

£M3
    1976–1963   Bank of England data supplied
    1962–1952   SA No. 1, T12/3. These changes are for total M3, and are used under the assumption that UK residents' foreign currency deposits, $D, remained constant over this period at £105 million

$\Delta £Dg$
    1976–1952   FF 1972 and 1978, assumed to be zero before 1963

(3)   PSBR = public sector borrowing requirement
    1976–1963   Bank of England data supplied
    1963–1952   SA No. 1, T12/2

(4) ΔB = total take up of public sector debt by the non-bank private sector
    1976–1963   Bank of England data supplied
    1962–1952   various national income and expenditure Blue Books

(financial accounts), with the breakdown of Treasury bills and government securities sales taken from FF 1972 T4 (8) personal sector, T4 (9) industrial and commercial companies, T4 (11) financial institutions other than banks and public corporations' debt (as per T13.10 in 1977 Blue Book) supplied by CSO. Note: FF 1972 does not identify Northern Ireland Debt

(5) ΔL = the change in bank lending in sterling to the private sector, including the take up of commercial bills by the issue department

1976–1974   BEQB March 1968 T11/3

1973–1964   SA No. 2, T11/4 for bank lending in sterling; SA No. 2, T12/3 for issue department figures (zero before 1971)

1963–1952   FF 1972; T4 (10) banking sector; columns 16 (Bank lending to domestic sectors) + 18 (Loans for house purchase) + T4 (6) public sector, column 16 (Bank lending to domestic sectors). Changes in foreign currency lending are assumed to be zero

(6)   CA = current account, CSO data bank as of March 1978

(7) ΔN = net capital flows from overseas to the non-bank private sector less the net foreign currency deposit/ liability position of the private sector with the banking sector

1976–1952   the possible ways of trying to identify private sector capital flows (converted to sterling) are given in Table 6A.3 with definitions below

IFF = identified flows of funds; FF 1972 and 1978 – line 11 (personal sector + industrial and commercial companies + other financial institutions) + lines 14, 23 and 24 (overseas sector)

I + UFF = identified + unidentified flow of funds; IFF + the unidentified item on flow funds (= balancing item on balance of payments)

RES = residual. Employing the money supply identity given in Chapter 4 it is possible to calculate a residual for ΔN either by subtracting the current account from, and adding bank lending in sterling to overseas to, the figure for external and foreign currency finance published by the Bank of England, or, equivalently, when these figures are not available, simply by using the complete money supply identity, which is

$$\Delta N = \Delta M - PSBR + \Delta B - CA - \Delta L$$

$$+ \Delta NDL + \Delta\$Dg$$

Table 5A.3   *Possible net capital flow series (ΔN)*

1951	IFF	I + UFF	RES
2	− 113	− 47	− 139
3	− 122	− 90	− 39
4	− 130	− 73	− 85
5	− 11	110	70
6	− 132	− 90	− 126
7	− 184	− 104	− 136
8	− 162	− 95	− 104
9	− 163	− 194	− 246
1960	− 34	255	180
1	1	− 34	− 37
2	− 5	60	− 6
3	− 115	− 206	− 240
4	− 280	− 318	− 360
5	− 68	− 69	− 81
6	− 104	− 177	− 282
7	− 296	− 65	− 137
8	− 432	− 548	− 544
9	− 69	343	334
1970	92	102	337
1	515	787	855
2	− 609	− 1,289	− 1,085
3	− 312	− 128	193
4	1,373	1,696	807
5	296	329	171
6	− 730	− 139	− 1,149

This residual series is the one employed since it is also the one about which there is least information

(8)   ΔNDL = the change in non-deposit liabilities of the banking sector

1976–1970   BEQB March 1978 T6/3
1969–1963   SA No. 2, T12/3
1962–1952   SA No. 1, T12/3

Appendix 4

An Endogenous Exchange Rate

In estimating the main model it was assumed that the exchange rate was endogenous, but no specific assumption was made. However, for the sake of completeness, and because of the present interest in flexible exchange rates it seemed worth trying to estimate an explicit relationship.

The main economic variables considered are relative prices, relative interest rates, unemployment, the current account position and the change in foreign reserves. The dependent variable is the rate of change of the exchange rate, $\dot{e}$,

Table 5A.4 Money Supply and its Components

	(1) MS	(2) ΔM	(3) ΔDg	(4) PSBR	(5) ΔB	(6) ΔL	(7) CA	(8) ΔN	(9) NDL
1951	7,909						−369		
2	8,144	235	0	794	216	−332	163	−139	35
3	8,411	267	0	593	329	−24	145	−39	79
4	8,679	268	0	371	299	245	117	−85	81
5	8,431	−248	0	470	641	63	−155	70	55
6	8,512	81	0	573	552	41	208	−126	63
7	8,740	228	0	487	321	24	233	−136	59
8	9,014	274	0	491	807	432	344	−104	82
9	9,592	578	0	571	765	946	155	−246	83
1960	9,774	182	0	710	1,083	729	−245	180	109
1	10,036	262	0	704	510	250	22	−37	167
2	10,311	275	0	547	832	537	128	−6	99
3	11,066	755	10	842	594	715	131	−240	89
4	11,695	629	10	989	504	957	−356	−360	87
5	12,573	878	39	1,205	486	432	−26	−81	127
6	12,999	426	13	961	262	34	104	−282	116
7	14,233	1,234	13	1,863	665	511	−300	−137	25
8	15,219	986	23	1,281	−11	538	−287	−544	10
9	15,527	308	67	−466	354	429	440	334	8
1970	17,030	1,503	44	−18	101	829	710	337	210
1	19,446	2,416	39	1,371	2,104	1,627	1,074	855	368
2	24,293	4,847	80	2,034	1,006	5,510	126	−1,085	652
3	30,895	6,602	100	4,195	2,290	5,972	−883	193	485
4	34,219	3,324	−69	6,375	3,165	3,435	−3,515	807	682
5	36,268	2,049	281	10,520	5,603	−384	−1,614	171	760
6	39,809	3,541	24	9,410	6,085	3,463	−1,107	−1,149	967

$$\dot{e} =$$

$$f_e \left[K, \dot{P}z\$_{-i}, \dot{P}_{-i}, \text{DEV}, \left[\frac{\text{EFC}}{\bar{Y} - G} \right]_{-i}, r_{d-i}, \left[\frac{\text{CA}}{\text{EP}} \right]_{-i}, \left[\frac{\Delta \text{R}}{\text{EP}} \right]_{-i}, \dot{e}_{-1} \right]$$

$$(5\text{A}.1)$$

Relative prices are important because of the concern of the authorities with the competitiveness of British industry in international markets, and the effect of rising import prices on the domestic price level. A reasonable expectation would therefore be that a rise in domestic prices creates the desire to reduce the exchange rate in order to try to maintain competitiveness, but at the cost of adding to the rise in domestic prices. Alternatively, an increase in foreign import prices would *ceteris paribus* induce the opposite reaction of trying to protect the domestic economy from the full extent of the increase, but reducing the possible gain in competitiveness. The extent of such movements will reflect the authorities' trade-offs between these two objectives, and their perception of the way the economy behaves. The included variables are the proportional rates of change of the dollar import price, $\dot{P}z\$$, and domestic prices, $\dot{P}$.

It is also reasonable to assume that the authorities may wish to prevent the long interest rate rising substantially above its long-run equilibrium level. Within the model such deviation will reflect the expectation that the exchange rate is overvalued and will fall. The authorities may, therefore, act directly by reducing the exchange rate in order to allow interest rates to fall. The variable included, r_d, is based on the equilibrium properties of the estimated interest rate, r_b, equation:

$$r_d = r_b - 0.98 - r_{fb} \qquad (5\text{A}.2)$$

Minimising unemployment is an obvious economic objective of the central authorities. In terms of the variables included in the model this has been measured by the deviation of private sector expenditure from potential output, that is, $\text{EFC}/\bar{Y} - G$. One apparent way of improving employment prospects, at least in the short run, is by reducing the exchange rate. This is the argument that was central to the so-called Cambridge 'new school'. We should, therefore, expect a positive relationship between unemployment, as measured, and the rate of change of the exchange rate.

A great deal of attention is directed at the current account, and it is only natural that the behaviour of this variable should be of concern to the authorities. The variable employed is weighted by nominal expenditure in order to abstract from the distorting effects of inflation and growth over time, that is, CA/EP. The worse the current account the more likely the authorities are to reduce the exchange rate. Therefore, we should expect a positive relationship between this variable and the rate of change in the exchange rate.

Changes in the stock of foreign reserves should, however, represent an alternative to changes in the exchange rate. If the external position deteriorates the authorities have the choice of either allowing the outflows/inflows that would otherwise occur, or of allowing the exchange rate to change. The change in reserves (suitably weighted) might, therefore, be expected to have a negative coefficient of unity.

The lagged dependent variable has been included in order to allow for lags in adjustment. A positive coefficient between zero and unity indicates smooth adjustment towards equilibrium, and a negative coefficient between zero and minus unity indicates a stable long-run response but with temporary overshooting.

The equation has been estimated over the full period, 1952–76. Because it has been necessary to estimate over a period during which the exchange rate was 'fixed', a devaluation dummy has been included for 1967–68. This dummy simply reflects the actual change in the exchange rate at that time.

The OLS estimates are given in Table 5A.5. The constant term was not significant, and when included made the coefficient on EFC/ $(\bar{Y} - G)$ insignificant. The results given here therefore exclude the constant term.

Equation (ii) of Table 5A.5 includes the change in reserves (current and lagged) as a separate explanatory variable, with an estimated long-run coefficient of -0.88. Because the change in reserves should be an alternative to a change in the exchange rate it is perhaps not surprising that the estimated coefficients are not significant. The next step, therefore, was to impose the restriction that the long-run coefficient should be minus unity. This, in effect, required employing a composite dependent (and lagged dependent) variable consisting of the sum of the rate of change of the exchange rate plus the weighted change in reserves. A statistical test of this restriction is satisfied, with a calculated F statistic of 1.91 compared to a critical value of 3.74, at a 95 per cent level of significance.

There would seem to be two possible interpretations of equation (i). The first is that the composite variable could be interpreted as representing 'exchange market pressure', as suggested by Girton and Roper (1977), being determined by the right-hand side explanatory variables. In that case it would not be possible to continue to explain the change in reserves separately, and it would be necessary to take out the equation explaining private sector capital flows, ΔN. In order to explain changes in the exchange rate it would be necessary to make some assumption about government intervention policy, and vice versa to explain reserves.

Alternatively, it could be that equation (i) explains the exchange rate *given* the change in reserves as determined elsewhere in the model. In that case the equation could be added to the existing model.

The results should only be regarded as indicative of the way in which the exchange rate could be endogenised within the context of the model developed here. Given that the model represents a preliminary attempt to examine the feasibility of a particular financial approach to modelling the economy it seemed reasonable to abstract from the problem of trying to explain the exchange rate. Most models encounter

Table 5A.5 Restricted and unrestricted exchange rate equations

(i) $\left[\dot{e} + \dfrac{\Delta R}{EP}\right]$ on

$\Delta \ln Pz\$$	$\Delta \ln Pz\$_{-1}$	$\Delta \ln P$	DEV	$\dfrac{EFC}{\bar{Y} - G}$	r_d	$\dfrac{CA}{EP}$	$\left[\dot{e} + \dfrac{\Delta R}{EP}\right]_{-1}$
0.5794	0.7041	−1.5545	0.5821	0.03132	−0.02167	1.7185	−0.3879
(7.72)	(6.31)	(8.50)	(3.84)	(3.82)	(3.43)	(4.33)	(3.21)

$\bar{R}^2 = 0.923$ s.e. = 0.01757   D.W. = 1.5642   d.f. = 16

(ii) $\dot{e}$ on

$\Delta \ln Pz\$$	$\Delta \ln Pz\$_{-1}$	$\Delta \ln P$	DEV	$\dfrac{EFC}{\bar{Y} - G}$	r_d	$\dfrac{CA}{EP}$	$\dot{e}_{-1}$	$\dfrac{\Delta R}{EP}$	$\left[\dfrac{\Delta R}{EP}\right]_{-1}$
0.5201	0.6233	−1.4176	0.5623	0.03095	−0.02164	1.1275	−0.1605	−0.3668	−0.6532
(5.63)	(5.43)	(7.46)	(3.73)	(3.47)	(2.73)	(1.73)	(0.95)	(0.73)	(1.65)

$\bar{R}^2 = 0.893$ s.e. = 0.01665   D.W. = 1.768   d.f. = 14

problems endogenising the exchange rate, and such problems might only serve to obscure the financial inter-relationships which form the basis of the overall model. A number of different equations would be consistent with the approach adopted.

Notes

1   This discussion is in terms of the pressures created rather than the *ex post* outcome. Consequently the result of extra demand associated with an expansion of bank lending may not be reflected in the money supply if the result was an increase in imports. It is, therefore, necessary to consider the underlying financial pressures. In this case the distinction between DCE and the money supply is important; see Coghlan (1980a).
2   The average growth rate of the money supply over this period has been 6.41 per cent per annum while the rate of inflation has averaged 5.93 per cent per annum.

6
Model Simulations and 1971 Estimates

This chapter is divided into three parts. The first section examines the fit of the model as a whole by considering the within-sample dynamic forecasting performance of the model. Next are given the results obtained when the data period is cut off at 1971. In addition, there is a discussion of the results obtained when these new estimates were used to simulate the model over the full data period (that is, up to 1976). Returning to the original estimates, the model is subjected to a number of exogenous shocks, and the dynamic responses are examined in the third section. These responses give some indication of the potential for policy action, and the policy implications are discussed further in Chapter 7.

Within-Sample Dynamic Simulations

The model has been dynamically simulated (that is, employing the predicted values for all lagged endogenous variables) for the twenty-two years, 1955–76, employing a modified Gauss–Seidel procedure (Kuntsman and Kloek, 1976).[1] The actual and predicted series are graphed in Figures 6.1 to 6.4, and a number of test statistics are included to assist in evaluating the model. These statistics must, however, be treated with a fair degree of caution, as explained below.

Dynamic simulation over a considerable length of time can prove a severe test for any model, because of the problems created by cumulating errors in the lagged endogenous variables. Performance would be improved if the important explanatory variables were assumed to be exogenously determined. Within a monetary model in which money, and/or DCE, play a crucial role, the simulation properties would almost certainly be improved if these variables were taken to be exogenous. The endogeneity of money and DCE in this model therefore increases the chances that the dynamic simulations will go off course.

The main statistics are the inequality coefficient devised by Theil (Theil, 1966), and the separate bias, variance and random elements into which the inequality coefficient can be broken down. The inequality coefficient, U, can be written as

$$U = \sqrt{\frac{(1/n)\sum_{i=1}^{n}(P_i - A_i)^2}{(1/n)\sum_{i=1}^{n}A^2}} \qquad (6.1)$$

where n is the number of observations, P is the *percentage* change of the predicted value, and A is the *percentage* change of the actual observation. This coefficient will have a value of zero if $\Sigma(P_i - A_i) = 0$, but has no upper bound. The critical point is generally taken to be unity, which is the value associated with a prediction of no change, that is, all $P_i = 0$. Any value greater than unity would therefore seem to represent a worse predictive performance than the assumption of no change. In fact, as we shall see below this is not necessarily the case.

It would obviously be possible to eliminate n from (6.1), but in its present form the numerator is the root mean square percentage error, RMSE, which provides the explanatory power of the coefficient. The denominator is simply intended to take account of the scale of the particular variable. The sources of error can be more easily identified if the RMSE is broken down into its various components, in similar fashion to the decomposition of the total sum of square deviations in the analysis of variance, that is,

$$(1/n)\Sigma(P_i - A_i)^2 = (\bar{P} - \bar{A})^2 + (S_P - S_A)^2 + 2(1 - r_{PA})S_P S_A \quad (6.2)$$

where

$$\bar{P} = (1/n)\Sigma P_i \quad \text{and} \quad \bar{A} = (1/n)\Sigma A_i$$

in other words, they represent the means of the predicted and actual percentage changes,

$$S_P = \sqrt{(1/n)(\Sigma P_i - \bar{P})^2} = \text{standard deviation of the predicted values}$$

$$S_A = \sqrt{(1/n)(\Sigma A_i - \bar{A})^2} = \text{standard deviation of the actual values}$$

$$r_{PA} = \frac{\Sigma(P_i - \bar{P})(A_i - \bar{A})}{nS_P . S_A} = \text{the correlation coefficient of the predicted and actual values}$$

Dividing equation (6.2) through by $(1/n)\Sigma(P_i - A_i)^2$ gives

$$1 = UM + US + UC \qquad (6.3)$$

where

$$UM = \frac{(\bar{P} - \bar{A})}{(1/n)\Sigma(P_i - A_i)^2} = \text{measure of bias}$$

$$US = \frac{(S_P - S_A)^2}{(1/n)\,\Sigma(P_i - A_i)^2} = \text{variance error}$$

$$UC = \frac{2(1 - r_{PA})S_P S_A}{(1/n)\,\Sigma(P_i - A_i)^2} = \text{residual error}$$

UM and *US* represent the systematic forecasting errors which it should be possible to correct. *UC* is the unsystematic error, including any observation errors. Obviously, given (6.3), if the systematic errors are very low, that is, close to zero, the unsystematic error must be very large, or close to unity. It will be seen below that the types of errors recorded depend on the form in which the variable is defined, something which must be borne in mind when comparing predictive performance.

The remaining reported test statistics are the unweighted RMSE and the average error. This last statistic is defined as the sum of the actual values minus predicted, divided by the sum of the actual values, all times 100. This provides an additional indication of bias in the predictions, but can be misleading if the sum of the actual errors, and therefore the denominator, can be close to zero, for example, CA and ΔN.

Looking at the charts in Figures 6.1 to 6.4 reveals that the fit of the model appears to be really very good. These charts show the relationship between the actual and predicted series for the main endogenous variables in the model. The correspondence is remarkably close. In most cases the inequality coefficients support this conclusion, although there are times when the *U* statistic is rather high, and in three cases, ΔN, ΔL and $\dot{P}$, there is an apparent conflict in that the *U* statistics exceed unity. However, it should be quite clear that in all three examples the assumption of zero change would not have produced an improved relationship. This apparent ambiguity results from the use of *percentage* errors which has the effect of exaggerating the errors if the value of the series approaches zero.

For most stocks, flows of income and expenditure and price indices there will be no problem, and the inequality coefficient provides a useful indicator of model performance. The problem arises when the series change sign and/or have values close to zero. Under these circumstances there is a real danger that a small actual error will be substantially exaggerated. For example, the percentage error of ΔN (Figure 6.4) for 1962/3 is nearly 5000 and for 1967/8 is nearly 4000, and for ΔL (Figure 6.3) for 1957/8 is over 3000. The actual errors were not, in fact, particularly serious, given the volatility of the series explained, and there can be no doubt that the general assumption of no change would have produced a worse explanation, contrary to the normal interpretation of the Theil inequality coefficient. Other variables

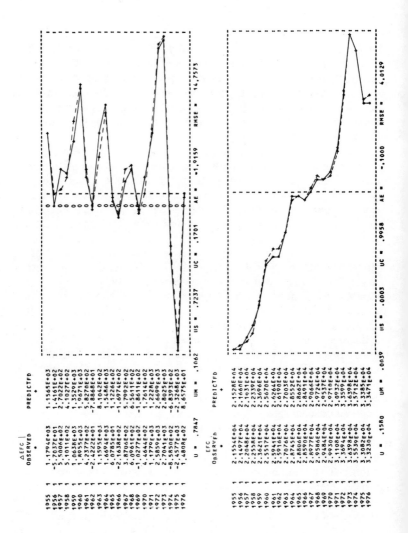

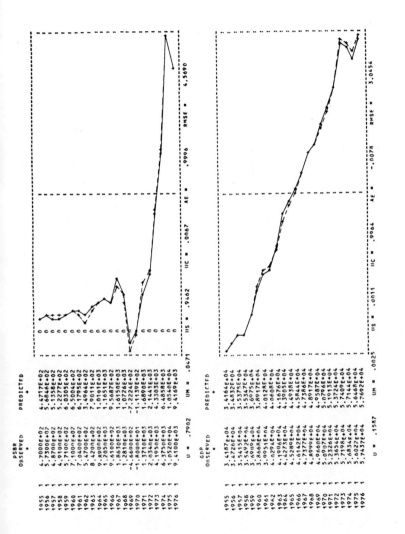

Figure 6.1   Dynamic simulation results 1955–76

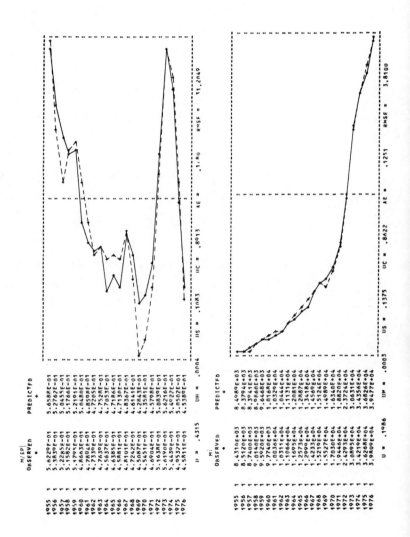

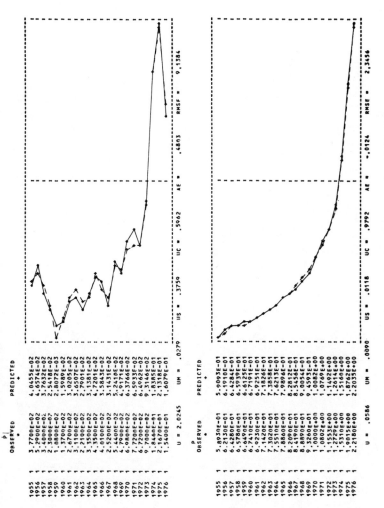

Figure 6.2 Dynamic simulation results 1955–76

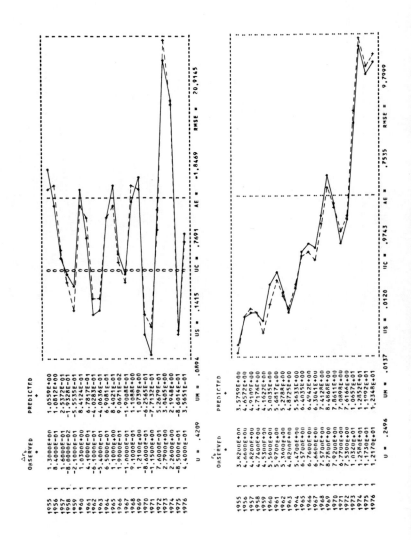

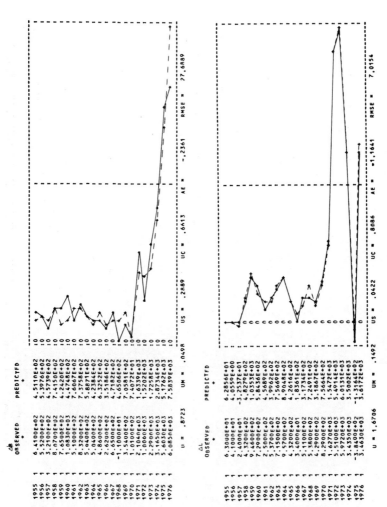

Figure 6.3   Dynamic simulation results 1955–76

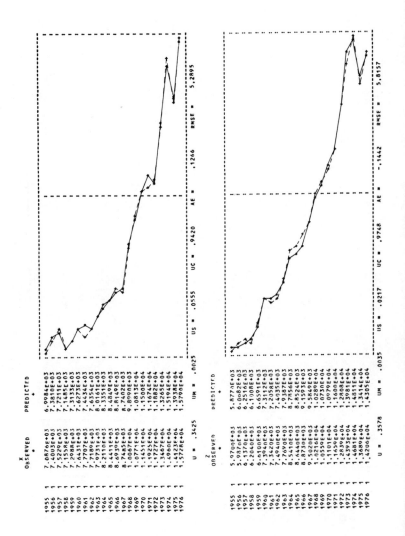

	X OBSERVED *	PREDICTED +
1955 T	7.0870E+03	6.9984E+03
1956 T	7.4003E+03	7.3810E+03
1957 T	7.5229E+03	7.7211E+03
1958 T	7.1558E+03	7.7485E+03
1959 T	7.2988E+03	7.3133E+03
1960 T	7.6431E+03	7.6273E+03
1961 T	7.7707E+03	7.4434E+03
1962 T	7.7180E+03	7.6354E+03
1963 T	7.9731E+03	8.0161E+03
1964 T	8.2111E+03	8.1351E+03
1965 T	8.4474E+03	8.4849E+03
1966 T	8.6939E+03	8.8149E+03
1967 T	8.7485E+03	8.7602E+03
1968 T	1.0067E+04	8.8990E+03
1969 T	1.0771E+04	1.0813E+04
1970 T	1.1451E+04	1.1500E+04
1971 T	1.1925E+04	1.1674E+04
1972 T	1.1727E+04	1.1882E+04
1973 T	1.3467E+04	1.3265E+04
1974 T	1.4060E+04	1.5194E+04
1975 T	1.4423E+04	1.5938E+04
1976 T	1.5728E+04	1.5900E+04

U = .3425   UM = .0025   US = .0555   UC = .9420   AE = .1266   RMSE = 5.2895

	Z OBSERVED *	PREDICTED +
1955 T	5.9770E+03	5.8773E+03
1956 T	5.9870E+03	6.0682E+03
1957 T	6.1370E+03	6.2516E+03
1958 T	6.2040E+03	6.1908E+03
1959 T	6.6100E+03	6.6591E+03
1960 T	7.3946E+03	7.2946E+03
1961 T	7.3420E+03	7.2058E+03
1962 T	7.4940E+03	7.4035E+03
1963 T	7.7690E+03	7.9387E+03
1964 T	8.5410E+03	8.7856E+03
1965 T	8.6440E+03	8.8524E+03
1966 T	8.8730E+03	9.1593E+03
1967 T	9.5020E+03	9.5849E+03
1968 T	1.0216E+04	1.0289E+04
1969 T	1.0559E+04	1.0730E+04
1970 T	1.1101E+04	1.0779E+04
1971 T	1.1459E+04	1.1600E+04
1972 T	1.2359E+04	1.2398E+04
1973 T	1.2397E+04	1.3981E+04
1974 T	1.4681E+04	1.4811E+04
1975 T	1.3689E+04	1.3414E+04
1976 T	1.4206E+04	1.4305E+04

U = .3578   UM = .0035   US = .0217   UC = .9768   AE = -.1442   RMSE = 5.8157

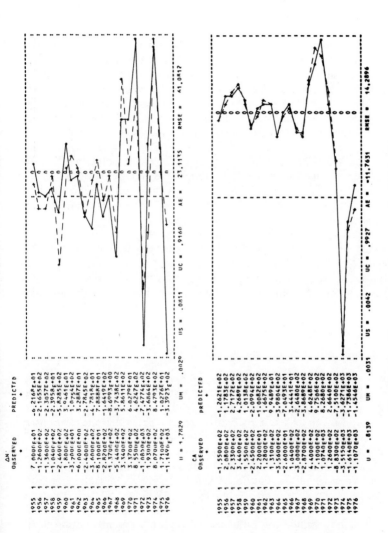

Figure 6.4 *Dynamic simulation results 1955–76*

likely to have been affected in this way are CA, ΔB, PSBR, M/EP, Δr_b and ΔEFC. The problem associated with the RMSE, which is where the difficulty lies, has been noted by Kuh and Schmalensee (1973, p. 13) but seems generally to have been ignored when interpreting the inequality coefficient.

The effect of these distortions should be borne in mind when comparing the predicted values of ΔB, ΔL and ΔN with the actual series. The *stocks* of these composite assets/liabilities would follow a much more stable path and would consequently produce more conventionally acceptable U statistics. To illustrate this point compare the apparent fit of EFC with the first difference of the same series, ΔEFC (Figure 6.1).

It is encouraging that in all cases, except two, the unsystematic component of the error substantially exceeds the systematic component. The two exceptions are ΔEFC and PSBR, for which US equals 0.7237 and 0.9462, respectively. The problem to some extent arises because of the volatility of the series, and in a sense both are first differences. For example, US for EFC is only 0.0003, and the total systematic error $(UM + US)$ is only 0.0042; a less pronounced comparison can be made between $\dot{P}$ and P (Figure 6.1).

Equally, it could be that the stock of public sector indebtedness would be very well explained. In this case the argument is less compelling, as the PSBR is a variable we do need to explain directly. Given the specification of the model the only possible sources of error are the tax functions. It could be that the simplistic tax rate assumptions have caused the problem, and there can be no doubt that further improvements in this direction are possible.

Estimation to 1971 and Simulation to 1976

It was noted in Chapter 2 (pp. 24/5) that the apparent ability to explain price movements in terms of past changes in the money supply had been challenged by the claim that this was only due to the inclusion of data for the 1970s. In particular, it was claimed that the relationship depended on changes in import prices which had varied sharply in a period of floating exchange rates, and that when this influence was taken into account the apparent causality would disappear. This view is representative of the position taken by many Keynesian economists; see, for example, Chapter 2 and Taylor (1979, pp. 89–92). However, perhaps it should be noted at this point that the price equation in this model does include the influence of import prices in addition to the money supply.

Even those models that have emphasised the importance of money in explaining movements in prices have generally assumed that a different model applied to the flexible exchange rate regime of the 1970s than to the period of fixed exchange rates which represented the broad range of experience up to 1972 (see Chapter 2). The period following 1972 is better referred to as one of flexible rates than of floating rates, since, as was noted previously, the level of intervention remained high, and there was little evidence that currencies were being allowed to float freely.

Despite this qualification, and the fact that the price equation in this model does include the influence of import prices in addition to the money supply, it is clear that the 1970s have generally been treated as representing a substantial deviation from the previous trend. An important, and severe, test of the model is, therefore, to estimate it excluding the post-1971 period to see whether the basic relationships are maintained. The difficulties are magnified by the limited degrees of freedom available. The model employing these '1971' estimates has also been simulated dynamically for the whole of the period, up to 1976.

The main events that have been suggested as causing a break in previous behavioural relationships for the UK were the introduction of CCC in 1971 and the adoption of flexible exchange rates in 1972. On top of that there was the massive exogenous rise in oil prices during 1973. Given the aggregate import equation this last influence must have had some effect and needs to be taken into account (see Chapter 5). This is because the level of aggregation does not enable separate import price elasticities to be measured, and this is bound to create problems when there is a major discontinuity in the price of a commodity which has a particularly low price elasticity. However, there is not assumed to be any change in the underlying economic behaviour, so that the basic economic model still holds. It is possible that the sharp increase in the price of oil, combined with the limited availability of substitutes, has reduced the supply potential of the economy. This is a factor that would need to be taken into account in any attempt to endogenise potential output; see Chapter 5. If this were the case, and it may well be that such an influence has been offset by increasing production in the North Sea, then the assumption of a fixed potential growth rate would tend to produce poor results.

The introduction of CCC and a more flexible exchange rate are not expected to make any major difference. The change in policy towards the exchange rate might result in some change in the capital flows equation, and that possibility would seem to warrant further study, employing a longer run of 1970s data, but that should be the main effect; it is not expected to make any difference to the price equation.

The OLS results obtained from estimating the eight equations in the model up to 1971 are presented in Table 6.1, together with the OLS results obtained for the whole period, taken from Appendix 1 in Chapter 5.

It will be seen that there is reasonable consistency between the results for the two periods, and that removing the post-1971 period

Table 6.1 OLS Equations Estimated to 1971 and 1976

A. Private sector expenditure, EFC

	K	$\Delta(M/P)$	$\Delta(M/P)_{-1}$	$\Delta(M/P)_{-3}$	r_{b-1}	Δr_{m-1}	Δr_{m-2}	Δt_{y-1}	ΔF_{-1}	$(\text{EFC}/(\bar{Y}-G))_{-1}$
1976	10563.4 (7.28)	0.1844 (4.27)	0.3889 (7.80)	0.3049 (3.31)	−112.54 (3.25)	−343.77 (7.71)	−90.70 (1.73)	−19659.6 (3.05)	0.01075 (1.63)	−9906.39 (6.67)
						$\bar{R}^2 = 0.982$	s.e. = 149.71	D.W. = 2.012	d.f. = 12	
1971	10501.2 (4.37)	0.3339 (2.78)	0.3433 (1.94)	0.2743 (2.19)	−192.62 (1.95)	−346.07 (3.35)	−50.91 (0.78)	−21483.1 (2.42)	0.02182 (1.95)	−9520.62 (4.23)
						$\bar{R}^2 = 0.947$	s.e. = 144.95	D.W. = 1.945	d.f. = 7	

B. Prices, P

	K	$\dot{P}z$	$\dot{P}_{z-1}$	$\dot{P}_{z-2}$	$\dot{M}$	$\dot{M}_{-2}$	$\dot{E}$	$\dot{E}_{-1}$	$\dot{E}_{-2}$	$\ln E_{-1}$	r_{m-1}	$\ln(M/EP)_{-1}$
1976	−1.009 (4.06)	0.0931 (3.86)	0.2426 (7.56)	0.2221 (9.11)	0.09541 (3.46)	−0.1781 (3.83)	−0.5505 (5.33)	0.3050 (4.38)	0.1041 (2.64)	0.1155 (4.45)	−0.05028 (4.64)	0.2095 (7.60)
							$\bar{R}^2 = 0.994$	s.e. = 0.00427	D.W. = 2.701	d.f. = 11		
1971	−1.048 (4.36)	0.1064 (2.58)	0.2322 (7.44)	0.2662 (5.97)	0.1413 (3.24)	−0.1939 (3.60)	−0.4138 (3.93)	0.3349 (5.97)	0.1514 (3.64)	0.1187 (4.84)	−0.04533 (3.91)	0.2143 (9.07)
							$\bar{R}^2 = 0.973$	s.e. = 0.00306	D.W. = 3.228	d.f. = 6		

C. Exports, X

	K	$\ln F$	$\ln G$	$\ln E$	$\ln(P/Pz)$				
1976	7.949 (9.08)	0.9866 (17.35)	−0.3403 (4.54)	−0.7303 (5.98)	0.5061 (8.15)	$\bar{R}^2 = 0.997$	s.e. = 0.0155	D.W. = 2.320	d.f. = 18
1971	7.995 (6.03)	1.0040 (15.38)	−0.3722 (3.56)	−0.7261 (3.98)	0.5203 (3.63)	$\bar{R}^2 = 0.991$	s.e. = 0.0163	D.W. = 1.756	d.f. = 13

Table 6.1 *(continued)*

D. Imports, Z

	K	Time	$\ln E$	$\ln E_{-1}$	$\ln G$	$\ln X$	OILD	$\ln P$	$\ln P_z$	$\ln P_{z-1}$	$\ln P_{z-2}$
1976	−10.885	−0.04161	1.5800	−0.6519	0.3609	0.8330	0.2016	1.1861	−0.7651	−0.2039	−0.1964
	(2.92)	(2.65)	(6.91)	(2.69)	(3.09)	(4.77)	(2.34)	(3.19)	(2.47)	(1.27)	(1.70)
1971	−9.802	−0.02561	1.3314	−0.7097	0.3700	1.0192		0.8491	−0.9600	−0.1202	−0.1824
	(1.67)	(1.08)	(4.32)	(2.33)	(2.12)	(2.30)		(1.64)	(1.50)	(0.53)	(1.09)

$\bar{R}^2 = 0.998$ s.e. $= 0.0139$ D.W. $= 2.380$ d.f. $= 12$

$\bar{R}^2 = 0.996$ s.e. $= 0.0144$ D.W. $= 2.779$ d.f. $= 8$

E. Private sector capital flows, N

	e	DCE_{UK}	DCE_{UK-1}	ΔEP_{UK}	DCE_{US}	ΔEP_{US}	ΔCA	$\dot{e}$
1976	−95.336	−0.4080	0.1893	0.1718	0.01544	−0.006482	−0.2104	5025.1
	(4.24)	(9.09)	(6.71)	(4.36)	(5.23)	(2.14)	(3.29)	(5.10)
1971	−79.160	−0.4473	−0.007675	0.1201	0.01495	−0.0004908	−0.01815	3529.2
	(3.23)	(3.70)	(0.10)	(1.47)	(2.92)	(0.11)	(1.07)	(2.60)

$\bar{R}^2 = 0.884$ s.e. $= 155.8$ D.W. $= 2.146$ d.f. $= 16$

$\bar{R}^2 = 0.799$ s.e. $= 136.8$ D.W. $= 2.265$ d.f. $= 11$

F. Long rate, r_b

	K	Δr_m	Δr_{m-1}	ΔR	$\Delta \dot{P}_{-1}$	$\dot{e}_{-1}$	$(r - r_{fb})_{-1}$
1976	0.2958	0.4930	0.1614	−0.0003009	5.2549	−4.1606	−0.3271
	(4.74)	(13.09)	(4.40)	(4.72)	(2.28)	(2.43)	(4.39)
1971	0.3093	0.5060	0.1101	−0.0003750	6.8345	−4.5583	−0.3024
	(3.12)	(5.82)	(1.24)	(2.39)	(1.82)	(2.11)	(2.36)

$R^2 = 0.956$ s.e. $= 0.2061$ D.W. $= 1.487$ d.f. $= 16$

$\bar{R}^2 = 0.912$ s.e. $= 0.2253$ D.W. $= 1.463$ d.f. $= 11$

Table 6.1 (continued)

G. Private sector demand for public sector debt, B

	r_b	r_{tb}	Δr_{tb}	Δr_m	$(M/EP)_{-1}$	$(L/M)_{-1}$				
1976	0.01420 (4.68)	−0.006248 (1.71)	−0.02236 (4.20)	−0.005353 (2.77)	0.04918 (4.17)	−0.09324 (2.86)	$\bar{R}^2 = 0.625$	s.e. = 0.0120	D.W. = 2.143	d.f. = 14
1971	0.01280 (2.32)	−0.0003833 (0.78)	−0.03118 (3.91)	−0.005388 (1.44)	0.04809 (3.68)	−0.09872 (2.50)	$\bar{R}^2 = 0.455$	s.e. = 0.0114	D.W. = 2.188	d.f. = 14

H. Bank Lending to the private sector, L

	$\dot{E}$	$\dot{E}_{-1}$	r_b	QD	PR	PR_{-1}	ΔSD	JD_{-1}	$\dot{e}_{-1}$	$(M/EP)_{-1}$				
1976	0.2692 (7.30)	0.1464 (4.38)	0.006956 (14.99)	−0.01316 (5.31)	0.004915 (4.06)	0.01127 (9.10)	−0.006623 (4.62)	−0.03019 (4.29)	0.1698 (3.68)	0.05082 (8.68)	$\bar{R}^2 = 0.972$	s.e. = 0.00540	D.W. = 3.016	d.f. = 15
1971	0.2815 (6.09)	0.1343 (3.01)	0.006501 (8.20)	−0.01198 (3.46)	0.004519 (2.51)	0.009717 (4.67)	−0.006496 (2.96)		0.1548 (2.96)	0.04755 (6.75)	$\bar{R}^2 = 0.893$	s.e. = 0.00587	D.W. = 3.204	d.f. = 11

has made little difference to the coefficient estimates obtained. In particular it should be noted that the price equation is virtually identical to that estimated over the full period (that is, the 1976 result). This is very encouraging since it suggests that *long-run* changes in the price level were equally well explained in terms of both the growth of the money supply and real expenditure over the 1950s and 1960s. Even the long-run expenditure elasticity is approximately the same at 0.4.

Another interesting result is the stability of the bank lending equation. A major advantage of running this equation over a long period that includes the 1950s is that it incorporates another example of the imposition and removal of bank lending controls. The 1971 estimates for the coefficients on these variables are very similar to the 1976 estimates, and the implications of removing bank lending restrictions are quite clear. Estimating this equation, incorporating supply constraints, and employing data available only up to 1971 would very clearly have demonstrated the expansionary dangers inherent in such a policy.

Even where there is some slight deviation from the results previously obtained these do not indicate a reduction in the influence of money — in fact, quite the reverse. Take, for example, the EFC equation; in this case the short-run effect of real money balances on expenditure is slightly higher and more rapid with the 1971 estimates. The private sector capital flows equation is not so well determined but the continuing influence of DCE stands out. The export equation is practically the same, but the import equation is not quite as good, although the same basic characteristics remain. The trend term has changed somewhat, and the price terms are not so well determined; this is not too surprising given the high correlation between the price terms and the reduced degrees of freedom. However, although this equation is needed to complete the model it is not crucial to the approach adopted.

The 1971 model was also simulated over the full period up to 1976, and the results for some of the main endogenous variables are shown in Figure 6.5 and 6.6. In addition to the 1971 model it was also necessary to include the oil price dummy and the SSD dummy together with their previously estimated coefficients. Even at the time it would have been necessary to make some judgemental adjustment to take account of these exogenous changes.

The within-sample performance is again very good, and the predicted values stay close to their actual path for the first three years outside the estimation period, but start to diverge over the last two. The main culprit is the import equation. Because of this the current account goes off course and with it the interest rate and the money supply, thereby feeding into all other equations. The bank lending equation does not provide as good an explanation from 1975 as might have been expected, given the similarity of the equation estimates, but this is probably

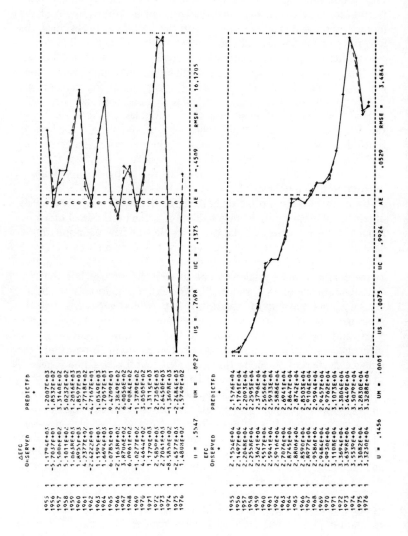

ΔEFC

	OBSERVED *	PREDICTED +
1955	1.1704E+03	1.2007E+03
1956	-5.7037E+02	1.4537E+02
1957	5.5006E+02	3.5140E+02
1958	5.1011E+02	5.0232E+02
1959	1.0653E+03	1.2016E+03
1960	1.8955E+03	1.8597E+03
1961	4.2377E+02	2.7718E+02
1962	-2.4222E+01	-4.7167E+02
1963	1.1595E+03	1.0549E+03
1964	1.6694E+03	1.7057E+03
1965	0.0785E+01	0.4700E+01
1966	-2.1638E+02	-2.3840E+02
1967	6.4006E+02	6.0036E+02
1968	6.4061E+02	4.4084E+02
1969	-1.0277E+02	-3.3809E+02
1970	4.4644E+02	3.3505E+02
1971	1.1779E+03	1.3115E+03
1972	2.5859E+05	2.7305E+03
1973	2.7041E+03	2.6450E+03
1974	-8.5636E+02	-1.3690E+03
1975	-2.4577E+03	-2.2484E+03
1976	1.4803E+02	4.5740E+02

U = .5547   UM = .0027   US = .7698   UC = .1375   AE = -.4509   RMSE = 16.1205

EFC

	OBSERVED *	PREDICTED +
1955	2.1526E+04	2.1576E+04
1956	2.1497E+04	2.1761E+04
1957	2.2048E+04	2.2003E+04
1958	2.2558E+04	2.2595E+04
1959	2.3621E+04	2.3796E+04
1960	2.5517E+04	2.5656E+04
1961	2.5941E+04	2.5933E+04
1962	2.5916E+04	2.5866E+04
1963	2.7076E+04	2.6921E+04
1964	2.8745E+04	2.8647E+04
1965	2.8806E+04	2.8742E+04
1966	2.8590E+04	2.8503E+04
1967	2.8977E+04	2.9104E+04
1968	2.9586E+04	2.9457E+04
1969	2.9488E+04	2.9457E+04
1970	2.9036E+04	2.9762E+04
1971	3.1108E+04	3.1073E+04
1972	3.3694E+04	3.3806E+04
1973	3.5358E+04	3.5388E+04
1974	3.5539E+04	3.5070E+04
1975	3.3082E+04	3.2830E+04
1976	3.3230E+04	3.3288E+04

U = .1456   UM = .0001   US = .0075   UC = .9024   AE = .0529   RMSE = 3.4841

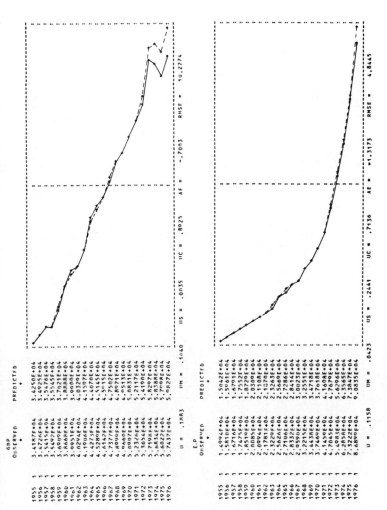

Figure 6.5 Dynamic simulation with 1971 model, 1955–76

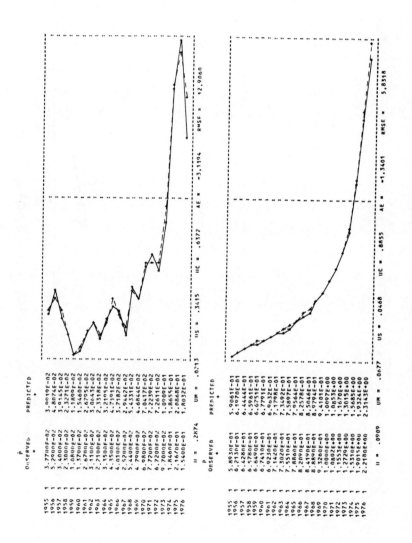

	Ṗ OBSERVED	PREDICTED
1955	3.770E-02	3.001E-02
1956	5.290E-02	4.874E-02
1957	3.400E-02	3.014E-02
1958	3.000E-02	2.327E-02
1959	1.080E-02	1.180E-02
1960	1.370E-02	1.546E-02
1961	2.670E-02	2.679E-02
1962	3.100E-02	3.063E-02
1963	2.710E-02	2.331E-02
1964	3.550E-02	3.210E-02
1965	4.350E-02	4.710E-02
1966	4.010E-02	3.787E-02
1967	2.520E-02	2.942E-02
1968	5.540E-02	4.433E-02
1969	4.790E-02	4.641E-02
1970	6.980E-02	7.061E-02
1971	7.720E-02	7.239E-02
1972	6.720E-02	7.261E-02
1973	9.700E-02	1.090E-01
1974	1.860E-01	1.865E-01
1975	2.160E-01	2.086E-01
1976	1.540E-01	1.803E-01

II = .2874   UM = .0213   US = .3415   UC = .6372   AE = -3.1194   RMSE = 12.9060

	P OBSERVED	PREDICTED
1955	5.893E-01	5.903E-01
1956	6.213E-01	6.197E-01
1957	6.428E-01	6.444E-01
1958	6.578E-01	6.596E-01
1959	6.649E-01	6.277E-01
1960	6.741E-01	6.779E-01
1961	6.925E-01	6.932E-01
1962	7.142E-01	7.179E-01
1963	7.302E-01	7.349E-01
1964	7.551E-01	7.589E-01
1965	7.886E-01	7.956E-01
1966	8.209E-01	8.257E-01
1967	8.419E-01	8.504E-01
1968	8.889E-01	8.779E-01
1969	9.326E-01	9.410E-01
1970	1.0807E+00	1.0007E+00
1971	1.0802E+00	1.0853E+00
1972	1.1553E+00	1.1670E+00
1973	1.2729E+00	1.3015E+00
1974	1.5310E+00	1.5685E+00
1975	1.9015E+00	1.9326E+00
1976	2.2180E+00	2.3143E+00

II = .0909   UM = .0677   US = .0468   UC = .8855   AE = -1.3401   RMSE = 5.8318

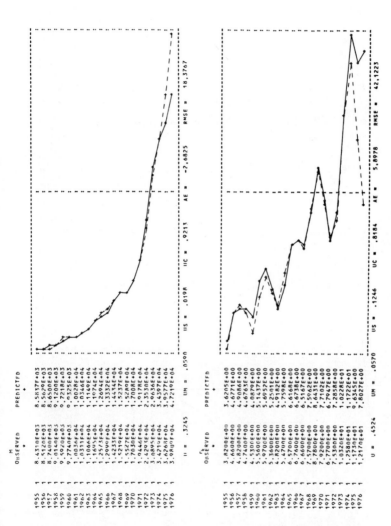

Figure 6.6   Dynamic simulation with 1971 model, 1955–76

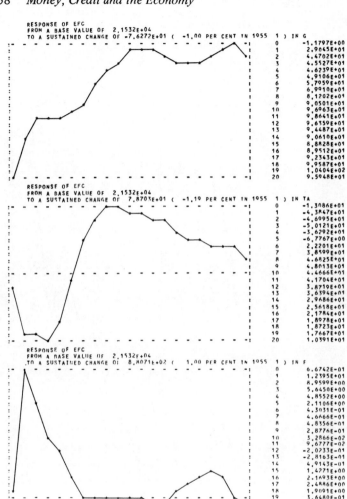

Figure 6.7(A)   *Dynamic simulations: deviations of EFC from base value, 1955–75*

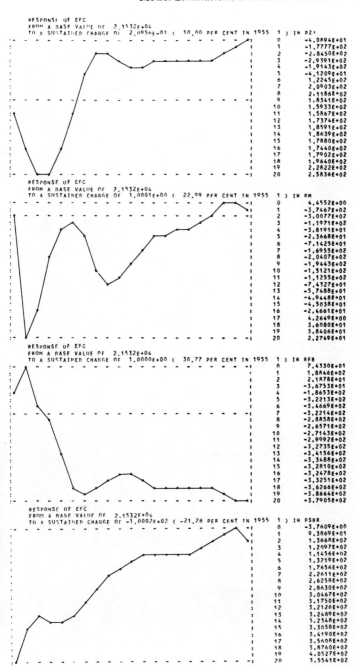

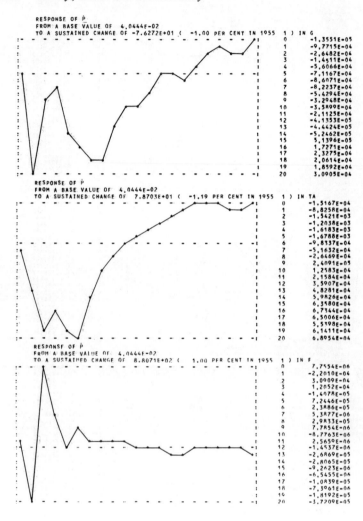

Figure 6.8(B)   *Dynamic simulations: deviations of $\dot{P}$ from base value, 1955–75*

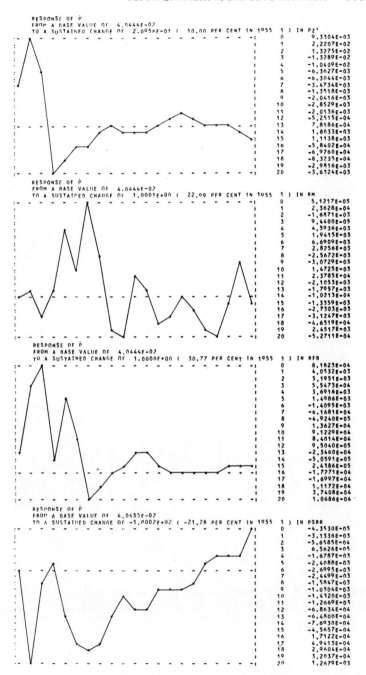

RESPONSE OF $\dot{P}$
FROM A BASE VALUE OF 4.0444E-02
TO A SUSTAINED CHANGE OF 2.0956E-01 (10.00 PER CENT IN 1955 1) IN PZ'

0	9.3304E-03
1	2.2207E-02
2	1.3275E-02
3	-1.3289E-02
4	-1.0409E-02
5	-6.3627E-03
6	-6.3044E-03
7	-3.4734E-03
8	-1.3518E-03
9	-2.0416E-03
10	-2.8529E-03
11	-2.0136E-03
12	-5.2515E-04
13	7.8186E-04
14	1.8033E-03
15	1.1138E-03
16	-5.8402E-04
17	-6.9260E-04
18	-8.3235E-04
19	-2.9816E-03
20	-3.6324E-03

RESPONSE OF $\dot{P}$
FROM A BASE VALUE OF 4.0444E-02
TO A SUSTAINED CHANGE OF 1.0001E+00 (22.09 PER CENT IN 1955 1) IN RM

0	5.1217E-05
1	2.3628E-04
2	-1.6871E-03
3	9.4400E-05
4	4.5936E-03
5	1.9415E-03
6	6.6909E-03
7	2.8256E-03
8	-2.5672E-03
9	-3.0729E-03
10	1.4725E-03
11	2.3785E-04
12	-2.1053E-03
13	-1.7957E-03
14	-1.0213E-04
15	-1.3359E-03
16	-2.7303E-03
17	-3.1247E-03
18	-4.6319E-04
19	2.4517E-03
20	-5.2711E-04

RESPONSE OF $\dot{P}$
FROM A BASE VALUE OF 4.0444E-02
TO A SUSTAINED CHANGE OF 1.0000E+00 (30.77 PER CENT IN 1955 1) IN RFB

0	8.1823E-04
1	4.0532E-03
2	5.1951E-03
3	5.5473E-04
4	3.6916E-03
5	1.4086E-03
6	-1.4095E-03
7	-6.1681E-04
8	-4.9240E-05
9	1.3627E-04
10	9.1229E-04
11	8.4014E-04
12	9.5040E-05
13	-2.3460E-04
14	-5.0591E-05
15	2.4386E-05
16	-1.7271E-04
17	-1.6997E-04
18	1.1172E-04
19	3.7408E-04
20	1.0686E-04

RESPONSE OF $\dot{P}$
FROM A BASE VALUE OF 4.0455E-02
TO A SUSTAINED CHANGE OF -1.0002E+02 (-21.28 PER CENT IN 1955 1) IN PSBR

0	-4.3530E-05
1	-3.1336E-03
2	-5.6585E-04
3	6.5626E-05
4	-1.6787E-03
5	-2.4088E-03
6	-2.6995E-03
7	-2.4499E-03
8	-1.5847E-03
9	-1.0304E-03
10	-1.4320E-03
11	-1.2669E-03
12	-6.8634E-04
13	-6.4800E-04
14	-7.6930E-04
15	-4.5657E-04
16	1.7122E-04
17	4.9413E-04
18	2.9604E-04
19	3.2037E-04
20	1.2679E-03

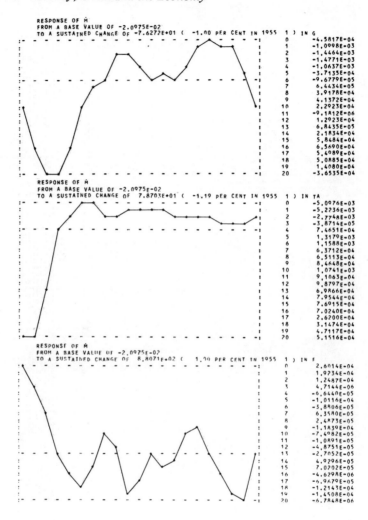

Figure 6.9(C)   *Dynamic simulations: deviations of $\dot{M}$ from base value, 1955–75*

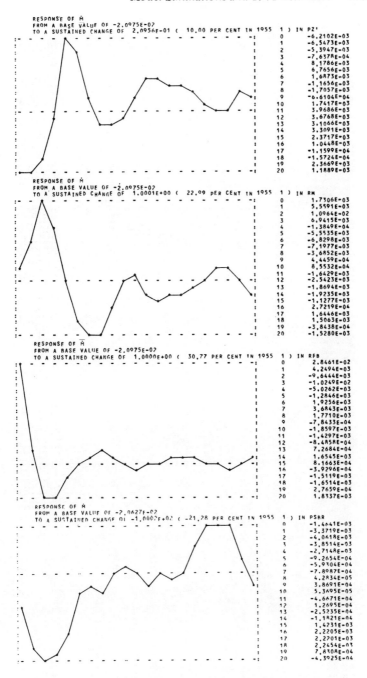

```
RESPONSE OF M̊
FROM A BASE VALUE OF -2.0975E-07
TO A SUSTAINED CHANGE OF 2.0956E-01 ( 10.00 PER CENT IN 1955  1 ) IN PZ'
                                                            0    -6.2102E-03
                                                            1    -6.5473E-03
                                                            2    -5.3947E-03
                                                            3    -7.6378E-04
                                                            4     8.1786E-03
                                                            5     6.7656E-03
                                                            6     1.6873E-03
                                                            7    -1.1656E-03
                                                            8    -1.7057E-03
                                                            9    -6.6104E-04
                                                           10     1.7417E-03
                                                           11     3.9686E-03
                                                           12     3.6768E-03
                                                           13     3.1066E-03
                                                           14     3.3091E-03
                                                           15     2.3717E-03
                                                           16     1.0448E-03
                                                           17    -1.1599E-04
                                                           18    -1.5724E-04
                                                           19     2.3669E-03
                                                           20     1.1889E-03

RESPONSE OF M̊
FROM A BASE VALUE OF -2.0975E-07
TO A SUSTAINED CHANGE OF 1.0001E+00 ( 22.09 PER CENT IN 1955  1 ) IN RM
                                                            0     1.7306E-03
                                                            1     5.5591E-03
                                                            2     1.0964E-02
                                                            3     6.9415E-03
                                                            4    -1.3849E-04
                                                            5    -5.5535E-03
                                                            6    -6.8298E-03
                                                            7    -7.1977E-03
                                                            8    -3.6852E-03
                                                            9     4.4459E-04
                                                           10     8.5532E-04
                                                           11    -1.6629E-03
                                                           12    -2.5423E-03
                                                           13    -1.8694E-03
                                                           14    -1.9235E-03
                                                           15    -1.1277E-03
                                                           16     2.7219E-04
                                                           17     1.6446E-03
                                                           18     1.5063E-03
                                                           19    -3.8438E-04
                                                           20    -1.5280E-03

RESPONSE OF M̄
FROM A BASE VALUE OF -2.0975E-07
TO A SUSTAINED CHANGE OF 1.0000E+00 ( 30.77 PER CENT IN 1955  1 ) IN RFB
                                                            0     2.8461E-02
                                                            1     4.2494E-03
                                                            2    -9.6444E-03
                                                            3    -1.0249E-02
                                                            4    -5.0262E-03
                                                            5    -1.2846E-03
                                                            6     1.9256E-03
                                                            7     3.6843E-03
                                                            8     1.7710E-03
                                                            9    -7.8433E-04
                                                           10    -1.8597E-03
                                                           11    -1.4297E-03
                                                           12    -8.4858E-04
                                                           13     7.2684E-04
                                                           14     1.6545E-03
                                                           15     8.1663E-04
                                                           16    -3.9296E-04
                                                           17    -1.5119E-03
                                                           18    -1.6514E-03
                                                           19     2.7659E-04
                                                           20     1.8337E-03

RESPONSE OF M̊
FROM A BASE VALUE OF -2.0627E-02
TO A SUSTAINED CHANGE OF -1.0002E+02 ( -21.28 PER CENT IN 1955  1 ) IN PSBR
                                                            0    -1.4641E-03
                                                            1    -3.3719E-03
                                                            2    -4.0618E-03
                                                            3    -3.8514E-03
                                                            4    -2.7148E-03
                                                            5    -9.2265E-04
                                                            6    -5.9304E-04
                                                            7    -7.8087E-04
                                                            8     4.2834E-05
                                                            9     3.8691E-04
                                                           10     5.3695E-05
                                                           11    -4.6671E-04
                                                           12     1.2695E-04
                                                           13    -2.5235E-04
                                                           14    -1.1821E-04
                                                           15     1.4231E-03
                                                           16     2.2205E-03
                                                           17     2.2701E-03
                                                           18     2.2454E-03
                                                           19     7.8308E-04
                                                           20    -4.3925E-04
```

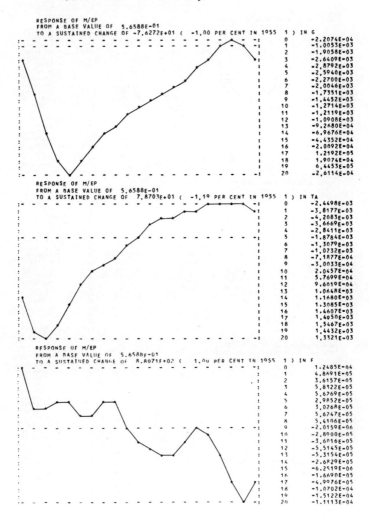

Figure 6.10(D)   *Dynamic simulations: deviations of M/EP ($= 1/V$) from base value, 1955–75*

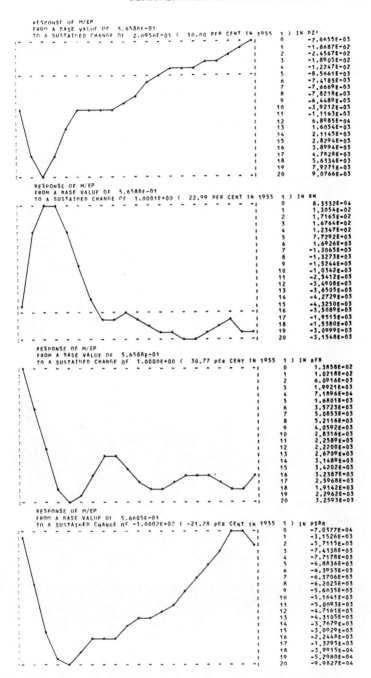

```
RESPONSE OF M/EP
FROM A BASE VALUE OF  5.6588E-01
TO A SUSTAINED CHANGE OF  2.0956E-01 ( 10.00 PER CENT IN 1955   1 ) IN PZ'
                                                                0    -7.6655E-03
                                                                1    -1.8687E-02
                                                                2    -2.4567E-02
                                                                3    -1.8905E-02
                                                                4    -1.2247E-02
                                                                5    -8.5661E-03
                                                                6    -7.6185E-03
                                                                7    -7.6669E-03
                                                                8    -7.8218E-03
                                                                9    -6.6489E-03
                                                               10    -3.9212E-03
                                                               11    -1.1163E-03
                                                               12     6.8985E-04
                                                               13     1.6054E-03
                                                               14     2.1145E-03
                                                               15     2.8294E-03
                                                               16     3.8994E-03
                                                               17     4.7828E-03
                                                               18     5.6134E-03
                                                               19     7.9271E-03
                                                               20     9.0766E-03
```

```
RESPONSE OF M/EP
FROM A BASE VALUE OF  5.6588E-01
TO A SUSTAINED CHANGE OF  1.0001E+00 ( 22.99 PER CENT IN 1955   1 ) IN RM
                                                                0     8.3332E-04
                                                                1     1.3054E-02
                                                                2     1.7165E-02
                                                                3     1.6764E-02
                                                                4     1.2347E-02
                                                                5     7.7292E-03
                                                                6     1.6926E-03
                                                                7    -1.3065E-03
                                                                8    -1.3273E-03
                                                                9    -1.5244E-05
                                                               10    -1.0342E-03
                                                               11    -2.5412E-03
                                                               12    -3.4908E-03
                                                               13    -3.6505E-03
                                                               14    -4.2729E-03
                                                               15    -4.3250E-03
                                                               16    -3.5089E-03
                                                               17    -1.9515E-03
                                                               18    -1.5380E-03
                                                               19    -3.0999E-03
                                                               20    -3.1548E-03
```

```
RESPONSE OF M/EP
FROM A BASE VALUE OF  5.6588E-01
TO A SUSTAINED CHANGE OF  1.0000E+00 ( 30.77 PER CENT IN 1955   1 ) IN RFB
                                                                0     1.3858E-02
                                                                1     1.0218E-02
                                                                2     6.0916E-03
                                                                3     1.9921E-03
                                                                4     7.1896E-04
                                                                5     1.6801E-03
                                                                6     3.5723E-03
                                                                7     5.0853E-03
                                                                8     5.2116E-03
                                                                9     4.0592E-03
                                                               10     2.8316E-03
                                                               11     2.2589E-03
                                                               12     2.2200E-03
                                                               13     2.6709E-03
                                                               14     3.1489E-03
                                                               15     3.4202E-03
                                                               16     3.2387E-03
                                                               17     2.5968E-03
                                                               18     1.9142E-03
                                                               19     2.2962E-03
                                                               20     3.2593E-03
```

```
RESPONSE OF M/EP
FROM A BASE VALUE OF  5.6605E-01
TO A SUSTAINED CHANGE OF -1.0002E+02 ( -21.28 PER CENT IN 1955   1 ) IN PSBR
                                                                0    -7.0377E-04
                                                                1    -3.1526E-03
                                                                2    -5.7115E-03
                                                                3    -7.4338E-03
                                                                4    -7.7178E-03
                                                                5    -6.8836E-03
                                                                6    -6.3953E-03
                                                                7    -6.3706E-03
                                                                8    -6.2025E-03
                                                                9    -5.6035E-03
                                                               10    -5.1641E-03
                                                               11    -5.0093E-03
                                                               12    -4.7161E-03
                                                               13    -4.3105E-03
                                                               14    -3.7679E-03
                                                               15    -3.0929E-03
                                                               16    -2.2448E-03
                                                               17    -1.3295E-03
                                                               18    -3.9015E-04
                                                               19    -5.2980E-04
                                                               20    -9.9827E-04
```

166   *Money, Credit and the Economy*

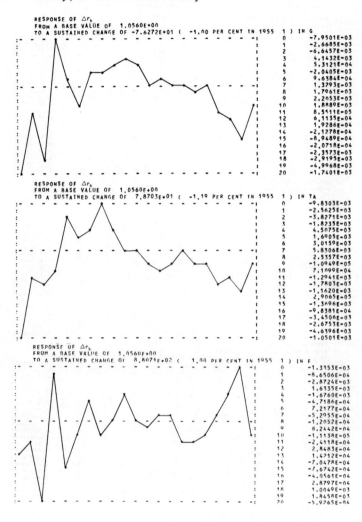

Figure 6.11(E)   *Dynamic simulations: deviations of Δr_b from base value, 1955–75*

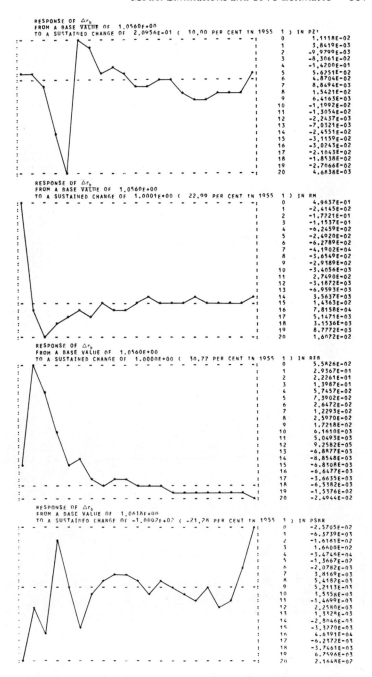

```
RESPONSE OF  Δr_b
FROM A BASE VALUE OF  1.0560E+00
TO A SUSTAINED CHANGE OF  2.0456E-01  ( 10.00 PER CENT IN 1955   1 ) IN PZ'
                                                        0    1.1118E-02
                                                        1    3.8419E-03
                                                        2   -9.9799E-03
                                                        3   -8.3061E-02
                                                        4   -1.4200E-01
                                                        5    5.6251E-02
                                                        6    4.8704E-02
                                                        7    8.8494E-03
                                                        8    1.5421E-02
                                                        9    6.4163E-03
                                                       10   -1.1992E-02
                                                       11   -1.3054E-02
                                                       12   -2.2437E-03
                                                       13   -7.0321E-03
                                                       14   -2.4551E-02
                                                       15   -3.1159E-02
                                                       16   -3.0243E-02
                                                       17   -2.1043E-02
                                                       18   -1.8538E-02
                                                       19   -2.7066E-02
                                                       20    4.6838E-03

RESPONSE OF  Δr_b
FROM A BASE VALUE OF  1.0560E+00
TO A SUSTAINED CHANGE OF  1.0001E+00  ( 22.99 PER CENT IN 1955   1 ) IN RM
                                                        0    4.9637E-01
                                                        1   -2.4145E-02
                                                        2   -1.7221E-01
                                                        3   -1.1537E-01
                                                        4   -6.2459E-02
                                                        5   -2.4920E-02
                                                        6   -6.2789E-02
                                                        7   -4.1902E-04
                                                        8   -3.6549E-02
                                                        9   -2.9389E-02
                                                       10   -3.4056E-03
                                                       11    2.7490E-02
                                                       12   -3.1872E-03
                                                       13   -6.9593E-03
                                                       14    3.5637E-03
                                                       15    1.4363E-02
                                                       16    7.8158E-04
                                                       17    5.1471E-03
                                                       18    3.1536E-03
                                                       19    8.7772E-03
                                                       20    1.6072E-02

RESPONSE OF  Δr_b
FROM A BASE VALUE OF  1.0560E+00
TO A SUSTAINED CHANGE OF  1.0000E+00  ( 30.77 PER CENT IN 1955   1 ) IN RFB
                                                        0    5.5826E-02
                                                        1    2.9367E-01
                                                        2    2.2261E-01
                                                        3    1.3987E-01
                                                        4    5.7457E-02
                                                        5    7.3902E-02
                                                        6    2.6472E-02
                                                        7    1.2293E-02
                                                        8    2.5970E-02
                                                        9    1.7218E-02
                                                       10    6.1610E-03
                                                       11    5.0493E-03
                                                       12    9.2582E-05
                                                       13   -6.8877E-03
                                                       14   -8.8548E-03
                                                       15   -6.8308E-03
                                                       16   -6.6477E-03
                                                       17   -3.6635E-03
                                                       18   -6.5382E-03
                                                       19   -1.5376E-02
                                                       20   -2.4944E-02

RESPONSE OF  Δr_b
FROM A BASE VALUE OF  1.0618E+00
TO A SUSTAINED CHANGE OF -1.0002E+02  ( -21.28 PER CENT IN 1955   1 ) IN PSRR
                                                        0   -2.5705E-02
                                                        1   -6.5739E-03
                                                        2   -1.6181E-02
                                                        3    1.6600E-02
                                                        4   -3.4746E-04
                                                        5   -1.3667E-02
                                                        6   -2.0782E-03
                                                        7    3.8169E-03
                                                        8    5.4182E-03
                                                        9    5.2113E-03
                                                       10    3.5358E-03
                                                       11   -1.4699E-03
                                                       12    2.2580E-03
                                                       13    1.3328E-03
                                                       14   -2.8046E-03
                                                       15   -3.3270E-03
                                                       16    4.6391E-04
                                                       17   -6.2372E-03
                                                       18   -3.7461E-03
                                                       19    6.7596E-03
                                                       20    2.1648E-02
```

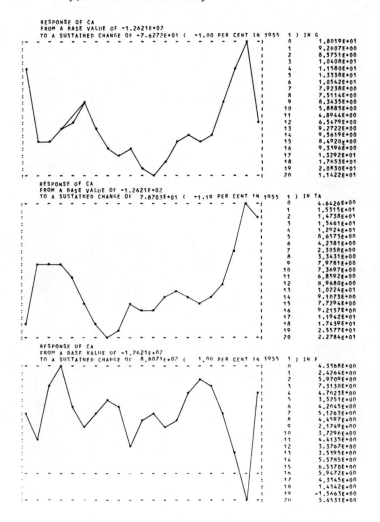

Figure 6.12(F)   *Dynamic simulations: deviations of CA from base value, 1955–75*

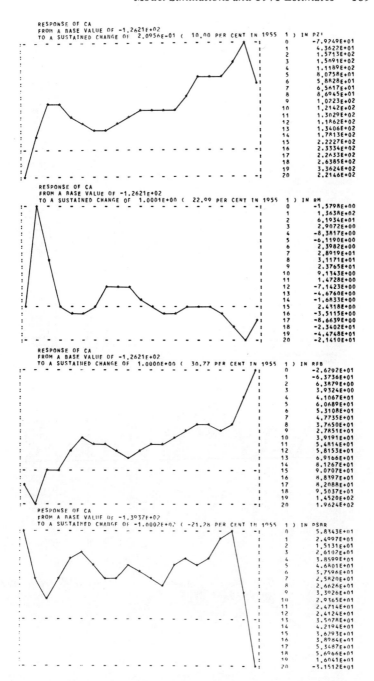

RESPONSE OF CA
FROM A BASE VALUE OF -1.2621E+02
TO A SUSTAINED CHANGE OF 2.0956E-01 (10.00 PER CENT IN 1955   1) IN PZI

0	-7.9749E+01
1	4.3622E+01
2	1.5713E+02
3	1.5091E+02
4	1.1189E+02
5	8.0758E+01
6	5.8828E+01
7	6.5617E+01
8	8.6945E+01
9	1.0223E+02
10	1.2142E+02
11	1.3029E+02
12	1.1862E+02
13	1.3406E+02
14	1.7813E+02
15	2.2227E+02
16	2.3334E+02
17	2.2633E+02
18	2.6385E+02
19	3.3624E+02
20	2.2146E+02

RESPONSE OF CA
FROM A BASE VALUE OF -1.2621E+02
TO A SUSTAINED CHANGE OF 1.0001E+00 (22.99 PER CENT IN 1955   1) IN RM

0	-1.5798E+00
1	1.3638E+02
2	6.1934E+01
3	2.9072E+00
4	-8.3817E+00
5	-6.1190E+00
6	2.3982E+00
7	2.8919E+01
8	3.1171E+01
9	2.3765E+01
10	9.1143E+00
11	1.4728E+00
12	-7.1423E+00
13	-4.6760E+00
14	-1.6833E+00
15	2.4318E+00
16	-3.5115E+00
17	-8.6639E+00
18	-2.3402E+01
19	-4.4748E+01
20	-2.1410E+01

RESPONSE OF CA
FROM A BASE VALUE OF -1.2621E+02
TO A SUSTAINED CHANGE OF 1.0000E+00 (30.77 PER CENT IN 1955   1) IN RFB

0	-2.6292E+01
1	-6.3736E+01
2	6.3879E+00
3	3.9324E+00
4	4.1067E+01
5	6.0689E+01
6	5.3108E+01
7	4.7735E+01
8	3.7650E+01
9	2.7851E+01
10	3.9191E+01
11	5.4814E+01
12	5.8153E+01
13	6.9166E+01
14	8.1267E+01
15	9.0707E+01
16	8.8397E+01
17	8.2088E+01
18	9.5037E+01
19	1.4520E+02
20	1.9624E+02

RESPONSE OF CA
FROM A BASE VALUE OF -1.3937E+02
TO A SUSTAINED CHANGE OF -1.0002E+02 (-21.28 PER CENT IN 1955   1) IN PSRR

0	5.8343E+01
1	2.4997E+01
2	1.5131E+01
3	2.6102E+01
4	3.8599E+01
5	4.6801E+01
6	3.7596E+01
7	2.5820E+01
8	2.4626E+01
9	3.3026E+01
10	2.9365E+01
11	2.4714E+01
12	2.4124E+01
13	3.5078E+01
14	4.2194E+01
15	3.6293E+01
16	3.8984E+01
17	5.3487E+01
18	5.6966E+01
19	1.6041E+01
20	-3.1512E+01

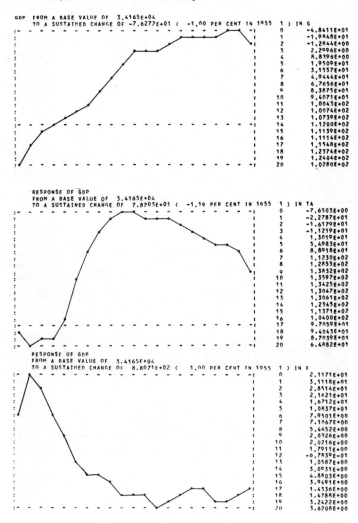

Figure 6.13(G)   *Dynamic simulations: deviations of GDP from base value, 1955–75*

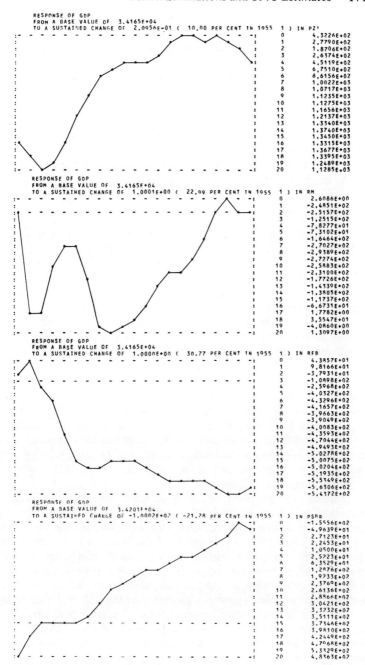

because of the deterioration in r_b at the end of the period. It is a mistake to judge individual equation performance from the simulation of the whole model because of the errors feeding in from the rest of the model.

Considering the volatility of many of these variables over the 1970s following a long period of relatively stable growth, plus the fact that this was a dynamic simulation over the whole period, the performance of the model is reasonably encouraging. The EFC equation is particularly good, with an actual improvement in simulation performance even including the years outside the estimation period. This must mean that errors that resulted towards the end of the period elsewhere in the model largely offset each other in this equation.

Dynamic Multipliers

In this section the model estimated over the full period has been subjected to a number of exogenous shocks, and the responses, in terms of deviations from the base run, of some of the main endogenous variables have been traced out in Figures 6.7 to 6.13.

Before moving on to discuss the multiplier results themselves some preliminary remarks about the procedure involved will be necessary. It is not advisable with this model to calculate the effect of a fiscal policy change *while holding the money supply fixed.* It could be done but it would make little sense, as the money supply is totally endogenous within this model. The authorities can control different instruments that will influence the money supply, but it is not an exogenous variable directly under their control. This is very important, and a great deal of confusion and harm can be created by making such an assumption. It is, in fact, very difficult for the authorities to control money in any meaningful sense. If all that was important was the control of some definition of money (any definition?) that could be easily achieved, but would also be pointless (see Coghlan and Sykes, 1980). This question is discussed further in Chapter 7.

It should be recognised that the base value of the simulation has an important affect on the multiplier results obtained. This is a feature of most macroeconomic models (for example, Ormerod, 1979, pp. 142–3), but there is one aspect of this problem in this particular model which does require further consideration. Consider, for example, the effect of a permanent increase in government expenditure of £100 million in 1955. What we find is that although the deviation of the endogenous variables is generally damped over time, there is a tendency for the deviations to increase towards the end of the period. Given that the effect of a sustained shock can be thought of as the summation of a series of separate spike shocks, the influence of the base value would be least apparent if a single spike shock is considered. However, it is more usual to present simulation results in terms of a sustained shock, and it is in this form that the following results are given.

Ignoring the residual element, the PSBR can be written as:

$$\text{PSBR} = (G - tY_p - s\,\text{EFC}).P \qquad (6.4)$$

Therefore, if the PSBR is positive to begin with, anything that changes the price level will further change the PSBR. An increase in G will increase the PSBR, increase the money supply, increase prices and further increase the PSBR. The extent of this last effect will in turn depend on the initial size of the PSBR. This helps to illustrate how the difficulty of controlling inflation is increased when there is a high PSBR to begin with.

The main stabilising influence under these circumstances would normally be a high marginal income tax rate, as long as taxes are not completely indexed to allow for inflation. This possibility is missing from this model because of the use of a single *average* tax rate. In order to improve the model response in this respect a constant marginal tax rate of 50 per cent has been included in the tax equation,

$$T = TA + 0.5\,(Y.P) \qquad (6.5)$$

where TA is the fixed non-income related component.

This marginal rate, however, is still not high enough to prevent an increase in the price level from further increasing the PSBR during the 1970s, but does at least produce a marginal rate above the average rate. Such a marginal rate is not particularly high given the net definition of income tax receipts employed.

Because the model was originally constructed on the assumption of an exogenous average tax rate this assumption has been retained in the multiplier simulations. In any future work it would be desirable to develop a more sophisticated tax function and include a marginal tax rate in the expenditure equation. Given the aggregate nature of this model, and in particular the *net* definition of income tax, it was virtually impossible to identify a meaningful marginal rate. The average rate, in fact, seemed the best approximation that could be made.

In the experiments discussed here all shocks are sustained for the twenty-one years from 1955 to 1975 and the deviations from the base run are graphed in Figure 6.7 to 6.13.

$\Delta G = -1\%(-\pounds 76.3\ million)$

It makes no real difference whether the exogenous shock is an increase or a reduction since the effects are virtually symmetrical. In this case a reduction is assumed.

The PSBR falls by much less than the drop in government expenditure.

There is virtually no change in EFC in the first period, and the effect over the next twenty years is positive (A1).[2] The new equilibrium value should be an increase of approximately £76.3 million, but less if r_b is above its 'equilibrium' value. The rate of inflation is reduced for most of the period (B1), resulting in a *lower* price level, but the rate of inflation is higher towards the end of the period. Changes in the price level are reflected broadly in changes in the money supply (C1). This latter series falls sharply at the end of the period, but this must be partly due to the fall in the PSBR, which is associated with the sharp increase in the base value over this period. Even so it seems likely that this series would inevitably be moving back towards zero. The stock of money is about £80 million lower at the end of the period.

The velocity of circulation, after rising sharply for the first five years, falls steadily to approximately the base level at the end of the period (D1). This is not particularly related to changes in the long rate of interest (E1) which, given that this is the only endogenous interest rate in the model, also implies a change in all interest rate differentials. The level of r_b remains below the base level throughout the period.

One consequence of the reduced price level is that external competitiveness is increased, so that despite the rise in private sector expenditure exports are increased and imports reduced. However, although the current account improves, the lower *value* of exports means that the improvement is not very great (F1). On the other hand the improvement in the real trade balance does result in a large increase in GDP, with a *negative* mutliplier of − 1.63 after twenty years (G1). However, for the first year GDP is reduced, the multiplier value being 0.63, and the effect remains negative, though reduced, for the next two years. It is not until the eighth year that the positive effect is as high as the negative effect in the first year. On the evidence of a single period spike shock the deviation from the base run of GDP, the money supply, prices and most other variables would eventually return almost to zero, but the lag is likely to be very long and is well outside the range of experience and data available.

The short-term response is not, in fact, inconsistent with the typical Keynesian models that suggest that in the short run GDP will increase as the result of an increase in government expenditure. It is not impossible that at some point *within* the first year the multiplier actually exceeds unity. The fact that this improvement is later reversed creates problems for the use of such changes for the purpose of demand management; these problems for policy are discussed further in Chapter 7.

$\Delta TA = + £78.7 \, million$

The tax change reported here is for a change in the fixed term, TA, in the endogenous income tax revenue function. However, because the average tax rate is exogenous, and performing the role of a marginal tax rate, this has been kept fixed. This example emphasises the consequences for the rest of the model of the resultant changes in the PSBR.[3]

Experiments changing the average expenditure tax rate must be treated with great caution. This again reflects the aggregate nature of the model. Any increase in the expenditure tax rate will automatically tend to increase expenditure at market prices, $E = \text{EFC}(1 + s)$, and, therefore, GDP which is measured at market prices. The failure to include a separate price for factor cost adjustment also means that the change in the price level is not particularly realistic if there is a change in this deflator *relative* to the factor cost expenditure deflator. Even so an increase in the average expenditure tax rate does result in the same broad pattern of adjustment as the change in *TA* discussed here. The effects of a change in the residual element in the PSBR are also practically identical.

For some time following the increase in *TA* private sector expenditure remains depressed (and it is the same for an increase in the expenditure tax rate), and it is not until six years after the change that EFC increases from the base value (A2). After another three years the positive effect approximately offsets the maximum negative value. From then on the positive effect declines slowly but continuously, and is still positive after 21 years.

The rate of inflation is also reduced initially but becomes higher nine years after the shock (B2). The price level remains 0.32 per cent below the base value after twenty-one years. The change in the money supply is not particularly closely related to inflation although it does follow the same broad pattern, as it must (C2). It is interesting to note that although the price level is ultimately determined by the stock of money, taking into account the level of real private sector expenditure the relationship is not necessarily obvious in the short run. One reason for this is that while the velocity of circulation is stable it is not constant, and can vary quite widely (D2). As before this is not related in any systematic way to the change in the rate of interest (E2).

Again exports are increased and imports depressed, and, as before, the lower price level reduces the effect on the current account (F2). GDP increases substantially by a maximum of £138 million, nine years after the initial shock (G2). From then on the deviation declines gradually. For the first four periods (including the initial period) GDP is reduced, but not by very much.

$\Delta F = + 1\%$ (+ $880.7 million)

An increase in foreign demand does not have a very great net effect on the economy. Private sector expenditure is increased to begin with, but only by very little, and within seven years has returned to the base value (A3). Inflation also stabilises quickly (B3). The price level does remain higher, but only by 0.019 per cent above the base value. The rate of change of the money supply and the velocity of circulation seem to move fairly erratically (C3 and D3), but the changes are in fact very small and have been magnified by the scale employed.

The same is also true of changes to the rate of interest (E3) and the current account (F3). The current account, in fact, exhibits a fairly steady but very small increase. Underlying this, both exports and imports have increased steadily, stabilising after about fourteen years at approximately £35 million to £32 million, with the balance in favour of exports. These deviations are, of course, very small in terms of the overall level of trade flows at the end of the period. GDP increases but the peak is the first period after the shock, and the increase is in single figures after seven years (G3).

$\Delta Pz\$ = + 10\%$

In this example the change considered is for the 'average' type of commodity contained in the definition of imports and does not hold in the case of a change in the price of oil, for which is was necessary to include a separate dummy variable. An increase in import prices (measured in dollars) reduces private sector expenditure for the first six years, but subsequently expenditure increases (A4). Inflation is also higher to begin with but declines later on (B4). The price level is higher for the first ten years but then falls. This is yet another example where the long-term reaction is the opposite of the short-term reaction − a type of response that must undoubtedly cause problems for government policy.

Exports are substantially increased but there is an even greater drop in imports, although both series are moving quite sharply back towards the base level after about fifteen or sixteen years. The peak increase in exports is £456 million and the fall in imports is £724 million. However, changes of this magnitude still only represent 4.2 per cent and 5.6 per cent, respectively, of the base period value. By the end of the period these percentages are reduced to 2.10 per cent and 3.88 per cent, respectively. As a result the current account increases substantially (F4), but only after an initial drop in the first year. This drop occurs despite a sharp rise in exports and fall in imports and is due to the rise in import prices. This price effect is subsequently offset as the effects of the change work their way through the economy. The improved real trade balance and the eventual improvement in private sector expenditure results in a greatly improved GDP (G4). The responses are very similar for a devaluation of the exchange rate, the only real difference being a rather better long-term price response.

$\Delta r_m = + 1$ *percentage point*

An increase in the short rate of interest by one percentage point reduces private sector expenditure. The maximum decline is in the first period after the change, and this reduces to approximately zero at the end (A5). The rate of inflation increases to begin with but is lower in the second half of the period (B5). The velocity of circulation *falls* to begin with and only increases after eight years, but by much less (D5). As expected there is an initial increase in r_b, and this remains higher for eight years, but then returns to the base level.

Exports initially increase, and imports decrease, both by about £100 million after one year, but these effects are then damped down and the signs are reversed after about four years. The current account largely reflects these developments (F5). GDP is reduced by a maximum of about £300 million after nine years, and follows the same broad pattern as private sector expenditure (G5).

Over recent years changes in the short rate of interest have generally been employed to push up gilt-edged yields, increasing the sales of gilts by creating the expectation of a fall in interest rates.[4] Such a policy is successful within the context of this model in that it does generate higher debt sales – at least for the first ten years – the actual sales achieved depending on the initial base values at the time of the change.

Moreover, it seems that a perverse response is likely in the bank lending equation in which the short rate of interest is absent, but the long rate is present, with a positive sign. However, although bank lending increases in the first period it does fall in the second and third years (and later on) as a result of the depressing effect on domestic expenditure and output. As indicated in Chapter 5, it may well be that the bank lending equation fails to capture fully the effects of changing interest rates. Even so, the chain of events described above is not inconsistent with the effects of the deflationary policy followed during 1979. The sharp increases in short-term interest rates following the election of the Conservative Government in the spring had little, if any, obvious effect in reducing the level of bank lending. The onset of recession, which will be partly the result of these higher interest rates should, however, reduce bank lending by the second half of 1980.

The net effect of changes in bond sales and bank lending is negative for years one to eight. The expansion in the money supply and, therefore, of prices follows from the increase in the current account and the rise in PSBR resulting from the fall in private sector income and expenditure, and the consequent fall in tax revenues. These effects are reversed after a few years, which is why the price level has returned to the base value after about seventeen years, but the lags are still very long.

$\Delta r_{fb} = +1\ percentage\ point$

An increase in r_{fb}, unlike an increase in r_m, results in a permanent increase in r_b. The increase stabilises about 0.93 of one percentage point after ten years, and there is little change after that (E6). Initially there is an increase in private expenditure, but this is short-lived and the subsequent drop in EFC stabilises at about £300 million from the sixth year (A6). Inflation also increases for the first six years but then fluctuates around, and close to, the base level (B6). The price level increases quite substantially, being 1.56 per cent above the base level ultimately.

The velocity of circulation falls sharply on impact, and, although this fall is quickly reduced, it remains negative (D6). Exports are initially depressed but soon return to approximately the base level. Imports, on the other hand, increase progressively for some time. However, the increase in the price level still allows the current account to increase (F6), and leaves GDP substantially depressed (G6).

ΔPSBR $= -£100$ *million*

The final change considered assumes that the government sets a target for the PSBR and that government expenditure adjusts to satisfy that objective. As a result EFC is increased (A7) and the rate of inflation reduced (B7), and the price level is 1.89 per cent lower than the final base value. The velocity of circulation rises sharply to begin with but then falls steadily and is ultimately close to the base level (D7).

On the external account, exports are increased and imports reduced. The current account maintains a fairly steady and rather small increase, except at the end of the period (F7). GDP declines to begin with by more than the cut in PSBR, but after three years has become positive and follows the pattern of EFC (G7). The initial fall in GDP is larger than the fall in PSBR, as is the fall in government expenditure required. However, GDP rises over the long term, but it is not until the seventh year that the increase offsets the initial fall; it then continues to grow to about three times that value. The fall in government expenditure is substantially greater than the fall in PSBR, reaching $-£300$ million after fourteen years, but is declining very rapidly at the end of that time and is $-£149$ million for the last year.

Notes

1 The actual simulation programme employed was HASH (see Harrison and Smith, 1977).
2 This number refers to the particular figure; all references beginning with A refer to changes to EFC, etc.
3 The PSBR is initially reduced by approximately the full effect of the tax change, and it then returns gradually and smoothly to its base value, which is achieved fifteen years after the shock. There is then a slight deviation from base during the later years, reflecting the higher base PSBR.
4 To the extent that such moves result in a reduction in DCE they will also reduce sterling outflows from the private sector and support the exchange rate.

7
Implications for Monetary Policy and Analysis

In this chapter the opportunity is taken to re-emphasise the main aspects of the financial approach adopted. This has been dealt with at length elsewhere (in particular, Chapters 3 and 5) and need not occupy much space here. In addition, a discussion of the specific policy conclusions following from the model approach and simulation results is included. Finally, the broad conclusions for monetary policy and analysis are presented.

Review of Theoretical Approach

In the approach adopted here money is important as a reflection of aggregate demand. Effective demands require the ability to finance the purchases. Net additional finance can be obtained either through an expansion of credit created by the banks, in which case the money supply increases, or through an expansion of NBFI credit, in which case the velocity of circulation of existing money balances will be increased. The importance of the banking system in this process has resulted in emphasis on the money supply, but with allowance being made for changes in the velocity of circulation. This emphasis on the banks accords with Keynes' own view of their importance in the provision of new finance (see Chapters 3 and 5 above).

It may well be the case that there is a long-run relationship between expenditures and incomes, but simply to relate the former to the latter seems to miss out an important element in the process of expansion — the creation of new finance. New credit can provide the means to finance additional expenditure which will in turn create new incomes. Whether those incomes accrue domestically depends on whether the commodities purchased were imported or not. In addition, a net increase in factor incomes ahead of expenditure will require the availability of new finance. A proper analysis of the financial system is therefore required if the dynamic development of the economy is to be properly understood.

The most suitable definition of money to be employed must depend on the development of the financial system. For reasons outlined in

179

Chapter 3, the definition of private sector sterling M3 seemed to be the most relevant for the purposes of this study. Since the abolition of exchange controls in October 1979 it might be useful to include UK residents' sterling deposits held abroad. There are, however, difficulties in identifying this total. What would be completely inconsistent with this approach, given the emphasis on credit demands and supplies, would be the use of a narrow definition of money, for example, M1. The same basic arguments would be true in the application of this approach to other economies, and the approach should be equally applicable.

In this model the demand for and supply of credit determine the supply of money. Money is, therefore, completely endogenous to the system. The monetary authorities do not have direct control over the money supply, but can only change the cost, or availability, of credit or their own financial demands. The policy choices open to the authorities are discussed further below. The main point to emphasise here is that the supply of money is endogenous, but that it still has important implications for the rest of the economy. Demand (and supply) adjusts in order to bring about equilibrium between the demand for and supply of money.

The existence of disequilibrium between the demand for and supply of money results ultimately from the general acceptability of money as the means of payment, combined with the institutional structure of the banking system. The existence of disequilibrium helps to explain the lags in the process of adjustment, and was referred to above as the 'secondary' effect of money. However, lags will also exist because of the continuing interreactions between the various sectors of the economy to price changes, to the balance of payments, etc., even if demand adjusted quickly to a change in supply. The 'primary' role of money results directly from the process of money creation, and the direct link assumed to exist between credit markets and expenditure markets.

The emphasis on credit, and the importance given to the underlying real forces which result in credit generation, clearly distinguish this approach from the standard monetarist position, and contain many elements of a Keynesian/Radcliffian approach. The limited role given to interest rate changes to influence credit demands is also in line with the conclusions of the Radcliffe Report (1959). The Radcliffe Committee (para 528) recognised the importance of restricting the financial demands of both the private and public sectors, and the banks were seen to be particularly important providers of finance. However, the connection with the money supply was not seen, and attention was concentrated on specific credit flows and on direct quantitative controls to influence these flows. The Committee therefore failed to bring together both sides of the banks' balance sheets, to recognise the problems that might be encountered when these controls were removed, and the distortions that would be created if such controls became a permanent feature of the system.

The other aspect of the model, the relationship between money and the rest of the economy, is more familiar to monetarist models. For example, domestic output is assumed to be supply determined in the long run, and largely independent of any demand influences, although such pressures can be important for some considerable time. Moreover, prices are considered to depend ultimately on the stock of money. This is not a feature normally encountered in Keynesian models of the economy.

Although money plays a central role in the transmission mechanism of changes within the economy it is perhaps better to think of this as a financial or credit model of the economy, lying somewhere between the Keynesian and monetarist extremes.

Recognising the importance of endogenous credit creation for the process of money supply creation also calls into question many of the simple tests that have been applied to demonstrate the importance, or otherwise, of money; see Coghlan (1980b) and Chapter 3 above. One obvious implication of this approach is that causality between money and prices should run in both directions, but that just tends to reinforce the inflationary potential of an exogenous inflationary shock. Moreover, the dynamics of adjustment implied by the monetary approach to the balance of payments are called into question. In this model disequilibrium between the supply of and demand for credit is likely to be a more important determinant of external capital flows than simply the demand for money as a function of a restricted set of explanatory variables (see Chapter 3). The attempt to provide empirical support for this model, therefore, involved a rather different approach from that normally adopted. The conclusions are discussed below.

Empirical Results and Specific Policy Conclusions

The empirical model that was built to test the theoretical approach adopted was kept as small as possible, and consequently abstracts from many important aspects of the real world. It should be viewed as no more than a preliminary attempt to isolate the fundamental characteristics of the theoretical model in an attempt to determine whether there is any empirical support for the approach, and to obtain at least some broad indication of what the implications for policy might be.

The results from the estimated model are very encouraging. The price level does depend in the long run on the stock of money, and the level of real expenditure, but other influences are important in the short run. Although velocity appears to be stable, with a tendency to rise as private sector expenditure increases, it is capable of varying quite widely for some considerable time. Therefore, although the domestic price level is directly related to prior changes in the money supply it is clear from the simulations that there is no obvious one-for-one relationship in the short run between inflation and the rate of change in the money supply. This is an interesting result, as it demonstrates that it does not make sense to look for simple correlations between the two series when such a simple relationship is not observed within a model in which the price level is actually related to the stock of money, but only in the long run.

The supply constraint on output does seem to play an important role in determining private sector output, even with the simple assumption of a constant growth rate. There is a great deal of additional work that could be done to endogenise the supply side of this, and other, models. It should also be emphasised that although certain equilibrium properties are included in the model these only apply in the very long run. The tendency for the economy to return to some equilibrium eventually is not in itself justification for abandoning short-term stabilisation policies. However, as was seen in Chapter 6, and is discussed below, the longer-run responses of the economy do qualify certain types of short-run policy. Not because short-run problems do not exist – they still remain in this model – but rather because short-run policy reactions can succeed in making the problem worse in the long run.

Although the empirical results are very encouraging, and seem reasonably stable over time, it would be misleading at this stage to put too great an emphasis on the particular estimates obtained. No empricial model provides a perfect replication of the real world, and it is a mistake to expect it to do so. In this study the empirical results are interpreted as providing support for the theoretical approach, and providing some broad indication of the magnitudes involved. It is difficult to imagine how a more categorical conclusion could be adopted when subsequent data revisions are capable of causing the original data series to change quite dramatically (see, for example, Balacs, 1972).

In drawing conclusions for policy from the empirical estimates and dynamic multiplier simulations, emphasis is placed on the broad directions of movement rather than the specific estimates obtained. The conclusions might, therefore, be best thought of as depending crucially on the theoretical approach adopted, deriving support from the specific empirical model that has been estimated.

The fact that it proved possible to re-estimate the model employing data only up to 1971, and obtain very similar results, is important in that it provides evidence that the results were not due to the particular circumstances of the 1970s. The price equation was, in fact, virtually identical to the 1976 estimate. This is particularly encouraging in view of the doubts that have been expressed about the relationship between prices and the money supply when the 1970s are excluded. That such a model should hold throughout the 1950s and 1960s is somewhat surprising given the emphasis at the time on Keynesian models in which there was little, if any, accommodation for financial variables (see Chapter 2 above).

The evidence also indicates that some of the worst distortions of the 1970s could have been foreseen had the importance of financial constraint been appreciated at the time. Of particular importance in this respect is the stability of the bank lending equation when estimated up to 1971. This indicated quite clearly that the supply constraints imposed on the banks in the 1950s and 1960s had been effective, and demonstrated that the subsequent relaxation of these constraints in the 1950s had resulted in an explosive increase in bank lending to the private sector as the pent-up demand was released.

As a result, the consequences for bank lending of the sudden removal of bank lending controls in 1971 could have been anticipated. Admittedly, the problem stemmed originally from the imposition of the controls during the 1960s, but had the problems of relaxation been appreciated this could have been accomplished with less drastic consequences. The view expressed at the time (see Chapter 4) that bank lending was likely to remain unchanged was clearly invalid. Moreover, the expansionary fiscal policy of the time was a complete mistake, and tight fiscal policy would have been much more appropriate under the circumstances.

It is tempting to conclude that this example demonstrates the desire of governments to be seen to be in control, and directly determining economic performance. This may indeed be a characteristic of democratic governments, but there is also evidence, referred to above, that the automatic expansionary potential of the private sector was not appreciated by the government, their policy advisors or their econometric models. This, in turn, was dependent on the implicit, and explicit, models of the economy adopted, and neglect of the importance of the underlying financial developments. The explanation for policy error in this case is, therefore, in terms of the perceived view of how the economy works, and this is supported by the fact that even now the general explanation of the post-1971 expansion of bank lending and the money supply is that it was related to the introduction of CCC, with no mention being made of the relaxation of bank lending controls (see Chapters 2 and 4).

The dynamic simulations demonstrate the conflicts that can exist between the short-term effects of a policy change and the longer-run consequences. Short run in this context refers to up to about six years, and is generally what most short-term model builders would refer to as the medium term. These longer-run developments can create problems for short-term policy if the policy horizon is short and the longer-run implications are ignored.

Consider the effects of fiscal policy, as conventionally defined. A reduction in government expenditure, or an increase in tax revenue, will reduce GDP initially, but eventually result in an increase which is then sustained for a long period. This result is not necessarily inconsistent with short-term Keynesian models which emphasise the short-term expansionary role of an *increase* in government expenditure, or reduction in taxes, and conversely for a reduction in government expenditure or increase in taxes. However, recognising the longer-term effects demonstrates that the short-run attempt to maintain GDP at the initially higher level will require ever increasing government expenditure as the longer-run effects begin to dominate in the opposite direction.

Alternatively, a longer-run perspective would support the opposite policy of a reduction in government expenditure or an increase in taxes. In the long run the private sector replaces the fall in demand from the public sector, or the fall in private sector demand caused by the payment of higher taxes, and the improvement in the balance of payments also contributes to the continued improvement in domestic output. This is the type of long-run objective governments have claimed to be trying to achieve in the United Kingdom for most of the period of this study, while at the same time *expanding* the public sector, without ever seeming to recognise the possible inconsistency involved.

The conscious objective of trying to reduce the PSBR by some given amount, by reducing government expenditure by whatever amount is necessary, will result in a correspondingly larger fall in government expenditure and GDP in the initial period. However, GDP will also improve more rapidly than in the case of a fixed change in government expenditure or taxes, even though the fall in government expenditure remains larger for all the period. There is also a reduction in the rate of inflation. Conversely, a policy of increasing the PSBR through changes in government expenditure will increase GDP initially but will very soon result in a reduction, and will be combined with higher inflation. Attempts to try and maintain the initial higher level of GDP will require an ever higher PSBR and accelerating inflation. That is the story told by the model simulations, and is certainly not inconsistent with experience over the 1970s.

These examples also illustrate the problems created in trying to reverse short-term expansionary policies in order to improve the longer-term prospects. The initial costs could be substantial. Continuing short-term expansionary policies, adopted with the best of intentions, will tend to generate their own momentum and become difficult to reverse, eventually leading to long-run instability. The best opportunities for reversing the short-run trend to obtain a long-run improvement arise when there are other changes capable of offsetting the initial depressing effect of reduced government expenditure. A good example would be if there was an increase in the growth of world trade that would provide an increased demand for domestic output, at least for a number of years. Of even more help would be an increase in non-oil import prices, or a fall in world interest rates, which result in a more lasting improvement in domestic output, but at the cost of higher inflation. It is, consequently, not possible to judge the wisdom of individual policy actions without first taking into account the context within which the measures are taken.

There are also problems associated with the policy of devaluation as a means of improving the current account, as indicated by the effect of a rise in the dollar price to imports. The current account deteriorates in the first period as a result of the change but then recovers, although there is an immediate and sustained improvement in the GDP. There is also a cost in terms of higher inflation and lower private sector expenditure for the first few years. Attempts to offset the fall in private sector expenditure, for example, by cutting taxes, would only serve to further increase the rate of inflation and reduce the long-run advantages that would otherwise accrue.

There is, therefore, no easy solution to the problems associated with controlling the economy. There is some undesirable aspect to every policy option open to the authorities. The most consistently favourable policy response would be that following a reduction in the short-term rate of interest, although it would still take a few years before the full benefits were appreciated. The main cost would be in terms of the early deterioration in the current account. Given the way in which the short rate tends to be varied in order to stimulate debt sales to finance the PSBR, the best chances for a fall in r_m would be for a cut in the PSBR.

However, manipulation of the short rate of interest represents a poor way of controlling the money supply, even though, as expected, it does result in higher public sector debt sales. This conclusion undoubtedly partly reflects the failure to capture the full significance of interest rate movements within the model. Even so there would seem to be severe limitations in the use of short-term interest rate changes as a means of achieving monetary control, as argued by the Radcliffe Report (1959). Direct controls on bank lending, and even the introduction of SSDs, seem to have a short-run effect, but this only postpones the problem for the future. That may be of some help as a one-off measure, as long as the longer-run implications are fully appreciated, but it hardly represents an efficient means for controlling the economy, and will become distortionary if incorporated as a regular instrument of policy.

General Conclusions

An interesting feature of the results of this study is the importance of time in any policy decisions. Not only are the lags very long, as a result of the continuing interactions within the model, but also because the long-run effects are quite likely to be different from the short-run effects, not only in terms of the magnitude of the effect but also the sign to be expected. There are, in fact, two types of temporal problem that are likely to arise. The first concerns the problem discussed in relation to the imposition of direct controls on bank lending, and is related to the subsequent abolition of the controls. Similar reactions should also be considered in relation to the imposition of SSD controls over any longer period. If there is some temporary disturbance which is expected to reverse at some future date such one-off controls may be effective, as long as the problem of relaxing the controls is recognised, and as long as the controls do not become a permanent feature of the market. If arbitrary controls are imposed frequently, or continuously, the financial system will adapt, and develop alternative sources of finance. The result is a loss of efficiency and creates problems similar to those that result from a rigid form of monetary base control, and which are discussed below. Such distortions would cause important institutional changes which would be difficult to capture within an emprical model.

The second type of temporal problem relates to the fact that the short-term reactions to certain policy changes would seem to be in a different direction to the longer-term effects. The problems associated with adopting a short-term policy horizon were discussed above. The short-term approach can create a self-feeding cycle which it then becomes very difficult to break out of, and there can certainly be very high initial costs involved in trying to adapt policy to a longer-term view.

The disadvantages of concentrating on the short term have also been recognised by other economists adopting a very different, and much more Keynesian, approach. The results of this model are, therefore, in broad terms consistent with the position taken by the Cambridge Economic Policy Group in evidence provided to the House of Commons' Expenditure Committee:

> The record of demand management during the last twenty years has been extremely poor. Throughout this whole period fiscal policy has been operated in alternating directions to produce periods of strong demand expansion followed by reversals of policy in crises conditions . . .
> The sharp reversals of policy indicate that the outcome of previous phases of policy was not acceptable and had to be corrected. The process in part has been the result of swings in the Government's choice of policy objectives. But the story also suggests that some of the outcomes were not properly foreseen − in particular that the conventional forecasting systems on which policy is based may

underestimate the full effect of changes in policy. Demand, output and the balance of payments might have been more stable than they were had some simple rule been followed through thick and thin such as that a tax yield should be sought as to cover, as nearly as possible, some fixed proportion of public expenditure. (Cripps *et al.*, 1974)

Within the model developed here, control over the supply of money is clearly very important from a policy point of view. However, the means through which control is achieved, and the definition of money employed, are equally important. The objective is not simply to obtain control over some arbitrary definition of the money supply but to influence underlying financial conditions. Money is not exogenously determined, as is generally argued by monetarists, for example, Friedman (1968), or provided by gremlins in the night (Tobin, 1961), and it would be self-defeating to try to make it exogenous, as suggested, for example, by Duck and Sheppard (1978). As long as money is controlled through market mechanisms, without penalising the banks in any way, so that it does not become profitable for new alternative institutions to provide the restricted services, the supply of money will generally provide a good indication of underlying financial conditions.

Another characteristic of many monetarist, and non-monetarist, arguments supporting monetary control is that they are not specific about the particular definition of money to be controlled. The exogenous control of any definition would apparently be sufficient (see, for example, Duck and Sheppard, 1978), but this is not the view taken here. It was argued in Chapter 3 that a broad definition of money is required, reflecting underlying financial conditions within the economy (see also Chapter 5). Moreover, in order to retain its value as an indicator of the financial health of the economy it is important that control is exercised by operating on the causes of monetary growth – and that is not particularly related to the supply of high-powered money, although the price and availability of reserves will certainly have some influence. Monetary growth is a sympton of the underlying financial pressures, and it is through these underlying credit demands and supplies that money should be controlled. This is a direct implication of the approach developed in Chapter 3, and the policy argument has been developed at greater length in Coghlan and Sykes (1980).

This is not an argument that is intended to apply solely to the United Kingdom and should be equally applicable to other countries, after taking account of their particular institutional circumstances. For example, it is now becoming clear that the apparent effectiveness of restrictive monetary policy in the United States in the past has probably had a great deal to do with the limitations placed on interest rates, and the consequent rationing of credit (see, for example, Tobin, 1978, and

Samuelson, 1979). Now that these controls are being dismantled, so the problems of control have become more noticeable. Although monetary policy in the United States has generally been directed at controlling the narrow money aggregates this does not mean that the policy is correct. The *Bank Credit Analyst* has had considerable success in forecasting the rising inflation in the United States over the late 1970s, and the subsequent fall in the exchange rate and rise in the gold price. This analysis was on the basis of looking at broad monetary aggregates and DCE, rather than developments in M1; see, for example, the *Bank Credit Analyst* for August 1979.

Credit demands and supplies will depend on business confidence and expectations generally. Recognition of the forces determining the supply of money also reintroduces the possibility that public sector deficit expenditure will prove a necessary means through which to expand the money supply and aggregate demand. The possible need for policies of this type is reinforced by the fact that it is the supply of money relative to demand that is important. If confidence were so low that the demand for money was very high, and increased in line with the supply of money without ever feeding through into additional expenditure, open market operations would prove ineffective. Expansionary policy would need to be backed by additional expenditure. This is, of course, the argument underlying Keynes' liquidity trap, and, interestingly, was specifically argued by Chicago economists in the 1930s (see Tavlas, 1977).

Within this model it is easy to see, for example, that sharp drops in foreign prices and foreign demand (and perhaps also rising foreign interest rates) could produce an extremely depressed economy, which changes in domestic interest rates, even if these were possible, would do little to rectify. A fiscal expansion could, however, provide temporary relief, even though in the long run it would add to the forces of depression. Such a policy might still be worth considering if it were thought likely that the external depressing forces were only temporary and likely to reverse in the not-too-distant future. Therefore, the way in which the money supply changes is also important within this model, with different causes having different effects. Moreover, it might still be possible to justify sharp increases in the PSBR as a means of stimulating the economy.

It does not follow from this reasoning, however, that the continuing large deficits experienced in the United Kingdom, particularly over the 1970s, have been beneficial in anything but the very short run. It seems more likely, in fact, that, under the circumstances of the time, these deficits have not contributed to the stability of the economy, but have, instead, resulted in higher inflation, larger balance of payments deficits and lower output.

One thing the above argument does indicate is that the PSBR is an important factor influencing DCE and the money supply. In this context it is interesting to note that Hansen (1958) and Blinder and Solow (1974) define fiscal policy as comprising 'all tax and expenditure transactions of governments as they affect the size of the public debt but not its composition' (Blinder and Solow, 1974, p. 4). That is essentially the public sector's financial deficit (PSFD), but is also very close to the PSBR; see Chapter 5. For the moment it is convenient to assume that they are the same. Monetary policy under this definition, therefore, consists of separate policy measures determining the supply of money relative to other public sector debt.

The present approach suggests that this type of dichotomous treatment may be somewhat misleading. In this model monetary policy is largely concerned with influencing the demands for and supplies of credit in the economy, and the PSBR fits naturally within this category. It is, therefore, necessary to consider whether the PSBR might not be better considered as part of monetary policy than of fiscal policy. There is not really any separate exogenous monetary policy under which the authorities can guarantee perfect control of the money supply in any meaningful sense. That is a standard myth of macro-economics, adopted by most monetarists and many Keynesians. The money supply, and consequently aggregate demand, can be much more easily controlled with a low PSBR than a high one. It does depend, however, on the total demands for finance from other sources, and there may well be circumstances, as noted above, when demand is severely depressed, in which an expansionary monetary policy requires the support of an expansionary PSBR.

Within this model, macroeconomic policy, in the sense of aggregate demand management, operates mainly through the supply of money and changes in interest rates. Changes in government expenditure and the income tax rate will also have a separate effect on private sector expenditure, but the money supply and interest rates are the channels through which changes in the PSBR have their effect. It might, therefore, be more sensible to refer to the direct effect of a change in government expenditure or tax rates as fiscal policy, and the extent to which these changes influence the PSBR as part of monetary policy.

This categorisation comes close to defining monetary policy as macroeconomic policy, and fiscal policy as the microeconomic effects of fiscal actions. The net borrowing need of government is a factor influencing the money supply, and changes might reasonably be thought of as part of monetary policy, even though they may have resulted from changes in taxation. The government, by means of taxes, grants and subsidies, and control of the basic infra-structure of the economy and certain basic industries, is in a powerful position to influence allocation and distribution within the economy, and perhaps even the efficiency and growth of the economy. In this respect fiscal policy could prove very important, and possible influences on incentives should be included in any attempt to endogenise potential output. Such influences are obviously of crucial importance, but they will best be achieved within a stable, non-inflationary environment, and that is the province of macroeconomic (or monetary) policy.

In conclusion it should perhaps be repeated that the endogeneity of money, and the process through which money is created, has resulted in an approach rather different to that normally associated with the monetarists. On the other hand, the importance of money in the transmission mechanism clearly distinguishes the approach from the standard Keynesian model. It was suggested above, in fact, that it might be best thought of as a financial, or credit, model of the economy. That may be a rather unimaginative description, but it does at least indicate the influences that are considered to be particularly important. Moreover, although the model has been developed and tested within the context of the UK economy, it is not specific to the United Kingdom and should be relevant in the study of other monetary economies.

References

Allard, R. J., 'An Economic Analysis of the Effects of Regulating Hire Purchase', *Government Economic Service Occasional Papers No. 9*, London, HMSO, 1974.

Allen, W. A. and Enoch, C. A., 'Some Recent Evidence on Short-Run Exchange Rate Behaviour', *Manchester School*, December 1978.

Andersen, L. and Jordan, J., 'Monetary and Fiscal Actions: A Test of Their Relative Importance in Economic Stabilisation', *Federal Reserve Bank of St. Louis Review*, November 1968.

Andersen, L. and Carlson, K., 'A Monetarist Model for Economic Stabilization', *Federal Reserve Bank of St. Louis Review*, April 1970.

Ando, A., 'On Financial and External Sectors of a Macro Econometric Model and Problems of their Estimation', paper presented at the LBS Conference on Economic Model Building, July 3–5, 1978.

Archibald, G. C. and Lipsey, R.G., 'Monetary and Value Theory: A Critique of Lange and Patinkin', *Review of Economic Studies*, October 1958.

Artis, M. J., 'Fiscal Policy for Stabilization', in W. Beckerman (ed.) *The Labour Government's Economic Record 1964–1970* (London: Duckworth, 1972).

Artis, M. J., *et al. Competition and Credit Control*, Submission to the Committee to Review the Functions of Financial Institutions, University of Manchester, August, 1978.

Artis, M. J. and Lewis, M. K., 'The Demand for Money in the United Kingdom', *The Manchester School*, June, 1976.

Artis, M. J. and Nobay, A. R., 'Two Aspects of the Monetary Debate', *National Institute Economic Review*, August 1969.

Bacon, B. R. and Johnston, H. N., 'Statistical Methodology in RBA 76', in Reserve Bank of Australia, *Conference in Applied Economic Research*, December 1977.

Bain, A. D., 'Flow of Funds Analysis: A Survey', *Economic Journal*, December 1973.

Balacs, P. D., 'Economic Data and Economic Policy', *Lloyds Bank Review*, April 1972.

Ball, R. J., Boatwright, B. D., Burns, T., Lobban, P. W. M. and Miller, G. W., 'The London Business School Quarterly Econometric Model of the UK Economy', in G. A. Renton (ed.) *Modelling the Economy*:

192   *Money, Credit and the Economy*

Proceedings of the SSRC Conference in Modelling the UK Economy, held at the London Graduate School of Business Studies in July 1972 (London: Heinemann, 1975).

Ball, R. J., Burns, T., Warburton, P. J., 'The London Business School Model of the UK Economy: An Exercise in International Monetarism', paper presented at the LBS Conference on Economic Model Building, July 3–5, 1978.

Ball, R. J. and Drake, P. S., 'The Impact of Credit Control on Consumer Durable Spending in the United Kingdom, 1957–1961', *Review of Economic Studies*, October 1963, reprinted in H. G. Johnson, (ed.) *Readings in British Monetary Economics*, 1972.

Bank Credit Analyst, August 1979.

The Banker, 'The New Monetary Mechanism', August 1958.

Bank of England, 'Credit Restriction: Press Announcement, 31 May 1969', *Quarterly Bulletin*, June 1969.

Bank of England, *Statistical Abstract No. 1*, 1970.

Bank of England, 'Competition and Credit Control: Text of a Consultative Document Issued on 14th May 1971', *Quarterly Bulletin*, June 1971.

Bank of England, 'Competition and Credit Control: the Discount Market', *Quarterly Bulletin*, September 1971.

Bank of England, 'Competition and Credit Control: Extract from a Lecture by the Chief Cashier of the Bank of England', *Quarterly Bulletin*, December 1971.

Bank of England, *An Introduction to Flow of Funds Accounting: 1952–70*, August 1972.

Bank of England, 'The Change from Bank Rate to Minimum Lending Rate, *Quarterly Bulletin*, December 1972.

Bank of England, 'Competition and Credit Control: Modified Arrangements for the Discount Market, *Quarterly Bulletin*, September 1973.

Bank of England, 'Credit Control: A Supplementary Scheme', *Quarterly Bulletin*, March 1974.

Bank of England, *Statistical Abstract No. 2*, 1975.

Bank of England, *United Kingdom Flow of Funds Accounts: 1963–1976*, May 1978(a).

Bank of England, *Quarterly Bulletin*, June 1978(b).

Beckerman, W. (ed), *The Labour Government's Economic Record 1964–1970* (London: Duckworth, 1972).

Beenstock, M., *The Foreign Exchanges: Theory, Modelling and Policy* (London: Macmillan, 1978).

Bergstrom, A. R., 'Non-recursive Discrete Models as Discrete Approximations to Continuous Systems of Stochastic Differential Equations', *Economitrica*, January 1966.

Bergstrom, A. R. and Wymer, C. R., 'A Model of Disequilibrium Neoclassical Growth and its Application to the United Kingdom', in A. R. Bergstrom (ed.) *Statistical Inference in Continuous Time Economic Models* (Amsterdam: North Holland, 1976).

Bispham, J. A., 'The NIESR Model and its Behaviour' in G. A. Renton (ed.) *Modelling the Economy*: Proceedings of the SRC Conference in

Modelling the UK Economy, held at the London Graduate School of Business Studies in July 1972 (London: Heinemann, 1975).

Blinder, A. S. and Solow, R. M., 'Analytical Foundations of Fiscal Policy', in *The Economics of Public Finance* (Washington: The Brookings Institution, 1974).

Bosworth, B. and Duesenberry, J. S., 'A Flow of Funds Model and its Implications', in *Issues in Federal Debt Management*, Federal Reserve Bank of Boston Conference Series No. 10, June 1973.

Brainard, W. and Tobin, J., Pitfalls in Financial Model Building', *American Economic Review (Papers and Proceedings)*, May 1968.

Branson, W. H. and Hill, R. D., Jr., 'Capital Movements in the OECD Area: An Econometric Analysis', *OECD Economic Outlook, Occasional Studies*, December 1971.

Brittan, S., *Steering the Economy: The Role of the Treasury* (revised edition) (Harmondsworth: Penguin, 1971).

Brunner, K. and Meltzer, A. H., 'Liquidity Traps for Money, Bank Credit, and Interest Rates', *Journal of Political Economy*, January/February 1968.

Brunner, K. and Meltzer, A. H., 'An Aggregative Theory for a Closed Economy', in J. L. Stein (ed.) *Studies in Monetary Economics, Volume 1: Monetarism* (Amsterdam: North Holland, 1976).

Chick, V., 'On the Structure of the Theory of Monetary Policy: Phenotype and Genotype', paper presented at the Association of University Teachers of Economics Conference at Exeter, 26–29 March 1979.

Christ, C. F., 'A Short-Run Aggregate-Demand Model of the Interdependence and Effects of Monetary and Fiscal Policies with Keynesian and Classical Interest Elasticities', *The American Economic Review (Papers and Proceedings)*, May 1967.

Christ, C. F., 'A Simple Macroeconomic Model with a Government Budget Restraint', *Journal of Political Economy*, January/February 1968.

Clower, R. L., 'The Keynesian Counter-revolution: A Theoretical Appraisal', in F. H. Halm and F. P. R. Brechling (eds) *The Theory of Interest Rates* (London: Macmillan, 1965).

Coghlan, R. T., 'Special Deposits and Bank Advances', *The Bankers' Magazine*, September 1973.

Coghlan, R. T., 'Bank Competition and Bank Size', *Manchester School*, June 1975.

Coghlan, R. T., 'The Partial Adjustment of Simultaneous Consumption and Saving Decisions', Mimeograph 1977(a).

Coghlan, R. T., 'Analysis Within the "New View"', *Journal of Money, Credit and Banking*, August 1977(b).

Coghlan, R. T., 'Alternative Portfolio Approaches to Balance of Payments Adjustment', *Scottish Journal of Political Economy*, February 1978(a).

Coghlan, R. T., 'A Transactions Demand for Money', *Bank of England Quarterly Bulletin*, March 1978(b).

Coghlan, R. T., 'A New View of Money', *Lloyds Bank Review*, July 1978(c).

Coghlan, R. T., 'A Small Monetary Model of the Economy', *Bank of England Discussion Paper No. 3*, May 1979(a).

Coghlan, R. T., 'Squeezing into "the corset"', *The Banker*, September 1979(b).

Coghlan, R. T., 'The Role of Domestic Credit Expansion in Money Supply', *The Banker*, January 1980(a).

Coghlan, R. T., *The Theory of Money and Finance* (London: Macmillan, 1980) (b).

Coghlan, R. T., 'Money Supply in an Open Economy', *Applied Economics*, forthcoming, 1980(c).

Coghlan, R. T. and Jackson, P. M., 'The U.K. Personal Savings Ratio: Past, Present and Future', *Scottish Journal of Political Economy*, November 1979.

Coghlan, R. T. and Sykes, C. J., 'Managing the Money Supply', *Lloyds Bank Review*, January 1980.

Cohen, J., 'Integrating the Real and Financial via the Linkage of Financial Flow', *Journal of Finance*, March 1968.

Cohen, J., 'Copeland's Money Flows after Twenty-five Years: A Survey', *Journal of Economic Literature*, March 1972.

Coppock, D. J. and Gibson, N. J., 'The Volume of Deposits and the Cash and Liquidity Assets Ratios', *Manchester School*, September 1963.

Cripps, T. F. and Fetherston, M., 'CEPG Methodology', paper presented at the LBS Conference on Economic Model Building, July 3–5, 1978.

Cripps, T. F. and Godley, W. A. H., 'A Formal Analysis of the Cambridge Economic Policy Group Model', *Economica*, November 1976.

Cripps, T. F., Godley, W. A. H. and Fetherston, M., 'Public Expenditure and the Management of the Economy', Memorandum submitted to the House of Commons Expenditure Committee, and published in the Ninth Report on *Public Expenditure, Inflation and the Balance of Payments* (London: HMSO, 13 August 1974).

Crouch, R. L., 'Special Deposits and the British Monetary Mechanism', *Economic Studies*, December 1970.

Crowther Report, *The Report of the Committee on Consumer Credit*, Cmnd 4596 (2 volumes) (London: HMSO, March 1971).

Culbertson, J. M., *Macroeconomic Theory and Stabilization Policy* (New York: McGraw-Hill, 1968).

Currie, D. A., 'Macroeconomic Policy and Government Financing', in M. J. Artis and A. R. Nobay (eds) *Contemporary Economic Analysis* (London: Croom Helm, 1978).

Dacey, W. M., *The British Banking Mechanism*, 5th edition (London: Hutchinson, 1967).

Davidson, J. E. H., 'An Econometric Model of the United Kingdom Balance of Payments', *London School of Economics Discussion Paper*, mimeograph, August 1978.

Davidson, J. E. H., Hendry, D. F., Srba, F. and Yeo, S., 'Econometric Modelling of the Aggregate Time-series Relationship between

Consumers' Expenditure and Income in the United Kingdom', *Economic Journal*, December 1978.

Davidson, P., *Money and the Real World*, 2nd edition (London: Macmillan, 1978).

Davis, K. T. and Lewis, M. K., 'Monetary Dynamics and the Monetary Sector of RBA 76', in Reserve Bank of Australia (1977).

Dicks-Mireaux, L. A., 'Discussion on Econometric Models', in G. A. Renton (ed.) *Modelling the Economy*: Proceedings of the SSRC Conference in Modelling the UK Economy, held at the London Graduate School of Business Studies in July 1972 (London: Heinemann, 1975).

Dow, J. C. R., *The Management of the British Economy 1945–60* (London: Cambridge University Press, 1964).

Duck, N. W. and Sheppard, D. K., 'A Proposal for the Control of the UK Money Supply', *Economic Journal*, March 1978.

Economic Report on 1965 (London: HMSO, 1966).

Fausten, D. K., *The Consistency of British Balance of Payments Policies* (London: Macmillan, 1975).

Financial Statement and Budget Report 1972–73 (London: HMSO, 1973).

Fisher, G. R., '"Discussion" of Knight and Wymer (1976)', in M. N. Artis and A. R. Nobay (eds) *Essays in Economic Analysis* (Cambridge: Cambridge University Press, 1976).

Fisher, G. and Sheppard, D., *Effects of Monetary Policy in the United States Economy: A Survey of Econometric Evidence*, OECD Economic Outlook Occasional Studies, Paris, December 1972.

Foot, M. D. K. W., Goodhart, C. A. E. and Hotson, A. C., 'Monetary Base Control', *Bank of England Quarterly Bulletin*, June 1979.

Frenkel, J. A. and Johnson, H. G. (eds), *The Monetary Approach to the Balance of Payments* (London: Allen & Unwin, 1976) (a).

Frenkel, J. A. and Johnson, H. G., 'The Monetary Approach to the Balance of Payments: Essential Concepts and Historical Origins', in J. A. Frenkel and H. G. Johnson (eds), *The Monetary Approach to the Balance of Payments* (London: Allen & Unwin, 1976) (b).

Friedman, B. M., 'The Inefficiency of Short-Run Monetary Targets for Monetary Policy', *Brookings Papers on Economic Activity*, No. 2, (1977(a).

Friedman, B. M., 'Financial Flow Variables and the Short-run Determination of Long-term Interest Rates', *Journal of Political Economy*, August 1977(b).

Friedman, M. (ed.), *Studies in the Quantity Theory of Money* (Chicago: University of Chicago Press, 1956).

Friedman, M., 'The Role of Monetary Policy', *American Economic Review*, March 1968.

Friedman, M., *The Optimum Quantity of Money* (London: Macmillan, 1969).

Friedman, M. and Meiselman, D., 'The Relative Stability of Monetary Velocity and the Investment Multiplier in the United States, 1897–1958', *Research Study Two in Stabilization Policies* prepared by

E. Cary Brown *et al.* for the Commission on Money and Credit (Englewood Cliffs, N.J.: Prentice-Hall, 1963).

Friedman, M. and Schwartz, A. J., *A Monetary History of the United States, 1867–1960*, National Bureau of Economic Research (Princeton, N.J.: Princeton University Press, 1963).

Gibson, N. J., 'Special Deposits as an Instrument of Monetary Policy', *Manchester School*, September 1964.

Gibson, N. J., 'Monetary, Credit and Fiscal Policies', in A. R. Prest (ed.) *The U.K. Economy: A Manual of Applied Economics*, 2nd edition (London: Weidenfeld and Nicolson, 1968).

Girton, L. and Roper, D., 'A Monetary Model of Exchange Market Pressure Applied to the Postwar Canadian Experience., *American Economic Review*, September 1977.

Godley, W. A. H. and Cripps, T. F., 'Demand Inflation and Economic Policy', *London and Cambridge Economic Bulletin*, No. 84, reprinted from *The Times*, 22 and 23 January 1974.

Goodhart, C. A. E., 'Monetary Relationships: A View from Threadneedle Street', in *Papers in Monetary Economics* Vol. I (Sydney: Reserve Bank of Australia, 1975) (a).

Goodhart, C. A. E., 'Problems of Monetary Management: The U.K. Experience', in *Papers in Monetary Economics* Vol. I (Sydney: Reserve Bank of Australia, 1975) (b).

Goodhart, C. A. E., *Money, Information and Uncertainty* (London: Macmillan, 1975) (c).

Goodhart, C. A. E., 'Monetary Policy', in M. Posner (ed.) *Demand Management: Proceedings of the National Institute of Economic and Social Research 1977 Conference on Economic Policy* (London: Heinemann, 1978) (a).

Goodhart, C. A. E., 'Money in an Open Economy', paper presented at the LBS Conference on Economic Model Building, July 3–5, 1978(b).

Goodhart, C. A. E. and Crockett, A., 'The Importance of Money', *Bank of England Quarterly Bulletin*, June 1970.

Gowland, D., *Monetary Policy and Credit Control* (London: Croom Helm, 1978).

Griffiths, B., 'Resource and Efficiency, Monetary Policy and the Reform of the UK Banking System', *Journal of Money, Credit and Banking* , February 1973.

Hahn, F. H., 'The Monetary Approach to the Balance of Payments', *Journal of International Economics*, August 1977.

Hansard (London: HMSO, 6 April 1976).

Hansard (London: HMSO, 22 July 1976).

Hansen, B., *The Economic Theory of Fiscal Policy* (Cambridge, Mass.: Harvard University Press, 1958).

Harrison, T. and Smith P., 'Hash, A Programme for Econometric Modelling: User's Guide', University of Southampton, May 1977.

Heathfield, D. F. and Pearce, I. F., 'A View of the Southampton Econometric Model of the UK and its Trading Partners', in G. A. Renton (ed.) *Modelling the Economy*: Proceedings of the SSRC

Conference in Modelling the UK Economy, held at the London Graduate School of Business Studies in July 1972 (London: Heinemann, 1975).

Helliwell, J. F., 'Monetary and Fiscal Policies for an Open Economy', *Oxford Economic Papers*, March 1969.

Hendry, D. F., 'Predictive Accuracy and Econometric Modelling in Macroeconomics: The Transactions Demand for Money Function', paper presented at the LBS Conference on Econometric Model Building, July 3–5, 1978.

Hewitt, M. E., 'Financial Forecasts in the United Kingdom', *Bank of England Quarterly Bulletin*, June 1977.

Hicks, J. R., 'A Suggestion for Simplifying the Theory of Money', *Economica*, February 1935; reprinted in J. R. Hicks *Critical Essays in Monetary Theory* (London: Oxford University Press, 1967).

Hicks, J. R., 'Mr Keynes and the "Classics"; A Suggested Interpretation', *Econometrica*, April 1937.

Hodjera, Z., 'Short-term Capital Movements in the United Kingdom, 1963–67', *Journal of Political Economy*, July/August 1971.

Johnson, H. G., 'Towards a General Theory of the Balance of Payments', in *International Trade and Economic Growth* by H. G. Johnson (London: Allen & Unwin, 1958), pp. 153–68; reprinted in J. A. Frenkel and H. G. Johnson (eds.) *The Monetary Approach to the Balance of Payments* (London: Allen & Unwin, 1976).

Johnson, H. G., 'The Report on Bank Charges', *The Bankers' Magazine*, August 1967.

Johnson, H. G., 'The Monetary Theory of Balance of Payments Policies', in J. A. Frenkel and H. G. Johnson (eds.) *The Monetary Approach to the Balance of Payments* (London: Allen & Unwin, 1976).

Jonson, P. D., 'Money, Prices and Output: An Integrative Essay', *Kredit und Kapital*, 1976(a).

Jonson, P. D., 'Money and Economic Activity in the Open Economy: The U.K. 1880–1970', *Journal of Political Economy*, 1976(b).

Jonson, P. D., Moses, E. R. and Wymer, C. R., 'A Minimal Model of the Australian Economy', *Reserve Bank of Australia Discussion Paper, 7601*, 1976.

Kaldor, N., 'The "New" Monetarism', *Lloyds Bank Review*, July 1970.

Keynes, J. M., *The General Theory of Employment, Interest and Money* (London: Macmillan, 1936).

Keynes, J. M., 'Alternative Theories of the Rate of Interest', *Economic Journal*, June 1937(a).

Keynes, J. M., 'The "Ex-Ante" Theory of the Rate of Interest', *Economic Journal*, December 1937(b).

Keynes, J. M., 'Professor Tinbergen's Method', *Economic Journal*, September 1939.

Keynes, J. M., *How to Pay for the War; A Radical Plan for the Chancellor of the Exchequer* (London: Macmillan, 1940); first published as three articles in *The Times* in November 1939.

Klein, L. R., 'A Post-War Quarterly Model: Description and Application', in *Models in Income Determination*, Studies in Income and Wealth, 28 (Princeton: Princeton University Press, 1964).

Klein, L. R., *The Keynesian Revolution*, 2nd edition (London: Macmillan, 1968).

Klein, L. R., 'The Supply Side', *American Economic Review*, March 1978.

Klein, L. R., Ball, R. J., Hazlewood, A. and Vandome, P., *An Econometric Model of the United Kingdom* (Oxford: Basil Blackwell, 1961).

Klein, L. R. and Goldberger, A. S., *An Econometric Model of the United States, 1929—52* (Amsterdam: North Holland, 1955).

Knight, M. D. and Wymer, C. R., 'A Monetary Model of an Open Economy With Particular Reference to the United Kingdom', in M. J. Artis and A. R. Nobay (eds) *Essays in Economic Analysis* (London: Cambridge University Press, 1976).

Kouri, P. and Porter, M., 'International Capital Flows and Portfolio Equilibrium', *Journal of Political Economy*, May/June 1974.

Kuh, E. and Schmalensee, R. L., *An Introduction to Applied Macroeconomics* (Amsterdam: North Holland, 1973).

Kuntsman, A. and Kloek, T., 'Solution of Econometric Equation Systems by Means of a Modified Gauss-Seidel Procedure', *University of Rotterdam Report 7606/E*, 1976.

Laidler, D. E. W., 'Information, Money and the Macroeconomics of Inflation', *Swedish Journal of Economics*, March 1974, reprinted in *Essays on Money and Inflation* by D. E. W. Laidler (Manchester: Manchester University Press, 1975).

Laidler, D. E. W., 'A Monetarist Viewpoint', in M. Posner (ed.) *Demand Management: Proceedings of Economic and Social Research 1977 Conference on Economic Policy* (London: Heinemann, 1978).

Laidler, D. E. W. and O'Shea, P., 'An Empirical Macro Model of an Open Economy Under Fixed Exchange Rates: The United Kingdom 1954—1970', Department of Economics, The University of Western Ontario, *Research Report 7810*, April 1978.

Latter, A. R., 'Some Issues in Economic Modelling at the Bank of England', paper presented at the LBS Conference on Economic Model Building, July 3—5, 1978.

Leijonhufvud, A. *On Keynesian Economics and the Economics of Keynes* (New York: Oxford University Press, 1968).

McKinnon, R. I., 'Portfolio Balance and International Payments Adjustment', in R. A. Mundell and A. K. Swoboda, (eds) *Monetary Problems of the International Economy* (Chicago: University of Chicago Press, 1969).

Melitz, J. and Sterdyniak, H., 'An Econometric Study of the British Monetary System', *Economic Journal*, December 1979.

Middleton, P. E., Mowl, C. J., Odling-Smee, J. C. and Riley, C. J., 'Monetary Targets and the Public Sector Borrowing Requirements', paper presented at The City University Conference on Monetary Targets 9—10 May 1979.

Minford, P., Brech, M. and Mathews, K., 'Speculation and Portfolio

Balance – A Model of the U.K. Under Floating Exchange Rates', paper prepared for the Konstanz Seminar on Monetary Theory and Policy, 1978.

Modigliani, F., 'The Channels of Monetary Policy in the Federal Reserve – MIT – University of Pennsylvania Econometric Model of the US', in G. A. Renton (ed.) *Modelling the Economy*: Proceedings of the SSRC Conference in Modelling the UK Economy held at the London Graduate School of Business Studies in July 1972 (London: Heinemann, 1975).

Modigliani, F., 'The Monetarist Controversy, or Should we Forsake Stabilization Policies', *American Economic Review*, March 1977.

Morris, W. (ed.), *The Heritage Illustrated Dictionary of the English Language* (New York: McGraw-Hill, 1973).

Mundell, R. A., 'Barter Theory and the Monetary Mechanism of Adjustment', in *International Economics* by R. A. Mundell (New York: Macmillan, 1968), Ch. 8; reprinted in J. A. Frenkel and H. G. Johnson (eds) *The Monetary Approach to the Balance of Payments* (London: Allen & Unwin, 1976).

National Board for Prices and Incomes, Report No. 34, *Bank Charges*, Cmnd 3292, (London: HMSO, 1967).

Norton, W. E., 'Debt Management and Monetary Policy in the United Kingdom', *Economic Journal*, September 1969.

O'Brien, L., 'Key Issues in Monetary and Credit Policy: text of an address by the Governor to the International Banking Conference in Munich on 28 May 1971', *Bank of England Quarterly Bulletin*, June 1971.

Oates, W.E., 'Budget Balance and Equilibrium Income: A Comment on the Efficacy of Fiscal and Monetary Policy in an Open Economy', *Journal of Finance*, September 1966.

Organisation for European Economic Co-operation, *Internal Financial Stability in Member Countries*, Paris, 1950.

Ormerod, P. A., 'The National Institute Model of the U.K. Economy: Some Current Problems', paper presented at the LBS Conference on Economic Model Building, July 3–5, 1978.

Ormerod, P. A., 'Theory, Policy and Macroeconomic Models', in S. T. Cook and P. M. Jackson (eds) *Current Issues in Fiscal Policy*, (Oxford: Martin Robinson, 1979).

Ott, D. J. and Ott, A. F., 'Budget Balance and Equilibrium Income', *Journal of Finance*, March 1965.

Parkin, J. M., Cooper, R. J., Henderson, J. F. and Danes, M. K., 'An Integrated Model of Consumption, Investment and Portfolio Decisions', in *Papers in Monetary Economics*, vol. II (Sydney: Reserve Bank of Australia, 1975).

Parkin, J. M., Gray, M. R. and Barrett, R. J., 'The Portfolio Behaviour of Commerical Banks', in K. Hilton and D. F. Heathfield (eds) *The Econometric Study of the United Kingdom*, (London: Macmillan, 1970).

Patinkin, D., 'Price Flexibility and Full Employment', *American Economic Review*, September 1948.

Patinkin, D., *Money, Interest and Prices: An Integration of Monetary and Value Theory* (London: Harper and Row, 1965).

Patinkin, D., 'Keynes and Econometrics: On the Interaction Between the Macroeconomic Revolutions of the Interwar Period', *Econometrica*, November 1976.

Peston, M. H., 'Comparisons of the Four Econometric Models', in M. Posner (ed.) *Demand Management: 1978 Proceedings of the National Institute of Economic and Social Research Conference on Economic Policy* (London: Heinemann, 1978).

Polak, J. J., 'Monetary Analysis of Income Formation and Payments Problems', *International Monetary Fund Staff Papers*, November 1957.

Posner, M. (ed.), *Demand Management: Proceedings of the National Institute of Economic and Social Research 1977 Conference on Economic Policy* (London: Heinemann, 1978).

Purvis, D. D., 'Portfolio and Consumption Decisions: Towards a Model of the Transmission Process', in *Papers in Monetary Economics*, vol. II (Sydney: Reserve Bank of Australia, 1975).

Radcliffe Report, *The Committee on the Working of the Monetary System, Report*, Cmnd 827 (London: HMSO, 1959).

Radcliffe Memoranda, *Committee on the Working of the Monetary System, Principal Memoranda of Evidence, Volume I* (London: HMSO, 1960).

Radice, E. A., 'A Dynamic Scheme for the British Trade Cycle, 1929–37', *Econometrica*, January 1939.

Renton, G. A. (ed.) *Modelling the Economy*: Proceedings of the SSRC Conference in Modelling the UK Economy held at the London Graduate School of Business Studies in July 1972 (London: Heinemann, 1975).

Reserve Bank of Australia, *Conference in Applied Economic Research*, December 1977.

Richardson, G., 'Reflections on the Conduct of Monetary Policy', *Bank of England Quarterly Bulletin*, March 1978.

Robinson, J., 'The Rate of Interest', *Econometrica*, January 1951.

Samuelson, P., 'Recession to Order', *Financial Times*, 31 December 1979.

Savage, D., 'The Channels of Monetary Influence: A Survey of the Empirical Evidence', *National Institute of Economic and Social Review*, February 1978(a).

Savage, D., 'The Monetary Sector of the NIESR Model: Preliminary Results', *National Institute of Economic and Social Research Discussion Paper No. 21*, 1978(b).

Sayers, R. S., *Financial Policy, 1939–45* (London: HMSO and Longmans, Green, 1956).

Shepherd, J. R., 'Some Problems in the Development of the Treasury Model', paper presented at the LBS Conference on Economic Model Building, July 3–5, 1978.

Shepherd, J. R., Evans, H. P. and Riley, C. J., 'The Treasury Short-term Forecasting Model' in G. A. Renton (ed.) *Modelling the Economy*:

Proceedings of the SSRC Conference in Modelling the UK Economy held at the London Graduate School of Business Studies in July 1972 (London: Heinemann, 1975).

Silber, W. L., 'Fiscal Policy in *IS−LM* Analysis: A Correction', *Journal of Money, Credit and Banking*, August 1970.

Smith, D., 'A Monetary Model of the British Economy 1880–1975', *National Westminster Bank Quarterly Review*, February, 1977.

Spencer, P. and Mowl, C., 'The Model of the Domestic Monetary System', part one of 'A Financial Sector for the Treasury Model', Government Economic Service Working Paper No. 17 (Treasury Working Paper No. 8), December 1978.

Spencer, R. and Yohe, W, 'The "Crowding Out" of Private Expenditures by Fiscal Policy Actions', *Federal Reserve Bank of St. Louis Review*, October 1970.

Tarling, R. and Wilkinson, F., 'Inflation and the Money Supply', Ch. 5 in *Economic Policy Review, No. 3* (University of Cambridge Department of Applied Economics, 1977).

Tavlas, G. S., 'Chicago Schools Old and New on the Efficacy of Monetary Policy', *Banca Nazionale del Lavoro Quarterly Review*, March 1977.

Taylor, C. T., '"Crowding Out": Its Meaning and Significance', in S. T. Cook and P. M. Jackson (eds) *Current Issues in Fiscal Policy*, (Oxford: Martin Robinson, 1979).

Theil, H., *Applied Economic Forecasting* (Amsterdam: North Holland, 1966).

Tinbergen, J., *An Econometric Approach to Business Cycle Problems* (Paris: Hermann, 1937).

Tinbergen, J., *Statistical Testing of Business Cycle Theories, II, Business Cycles in the United States of America, 1919–32* (Geneva: League of Nations, 1939).

Tinbergen, J., *Business Cycles in the United Kingdom, 1870–1914* (Amsterdam: North Holland, 1951).

Tobin, J., 'Money, Capital, and Other Stores of Value', *American Economic Review (Papers and Proceedings)*, May 1961.

Tobin, J., 'Monetary Policies and the Economy: The Transmission Mechanism', *Southern Economic Journal*, January 1978.

Tsiang, S. C., 'The Monetary Theoretic Foundations of the Modern Monetary Approach to the Balance of Payments', *Oxford Economic Papers*, November 1977.

Volker, P. A., 'The Role of Monetary Targets in an age of Inflation', *Journal of Monetary Economics*, March 1978.

Walters, A. A., 'The Radcliffe Report– Ten Years After: A Survey of Empirical Evidence', in D. R. Croome and H. G. Johnson (eds) *Money in Britain 1959–1969* (London: Oxford University Press, 1970).

White Paper, *Public Expenditure to 1975–76*, Cmnd 482 (London: HMSO, November 1971).

Whitman, M. V. N., 'Global Monetarism and the Monetary Approach to the Balance of Payments', *Brookings Papers on Economic Activity*, No. 3, 1975.

Williams, D., Goodhart, C. A. E. and Gowland, D. H., 'Money, Income and Causality: The U.K. Experience', *American Economic Review*, June 1976.

Wymer, C. R., 'Econometric Estimation of Stochastic Differential Equation Systems', *Econometrica*, May 1972.

Wymer, C. R., 'Computer Programs: RESIML Manual', Mimeograph, 1968.

Index